<u>CHRISTMAS ON EARTH</u>

<u>for Barbara Rubin</u>

The quick sparks of my breath behave differently
And the sunlight seeps thru the airshafts of
The buildings. Are we asleep? Are we living?
The sea bursts and heaves its tonnage towards
A shore whose breakers are weak and irridescent.
Then what is this thing that flaunts
Upon my neck? Where can I look up
To see of clouds all that is good?
Under the long piers fish strain to live.
Darkness comes out of the sky and the moon
Is gone from sight. Exertion is evident
Upon the wall. I wonder at what
The flowers mean. Then I shall know
From what image in me is my genius made.

Gerard Malanga

Poem by Gerard Malanga

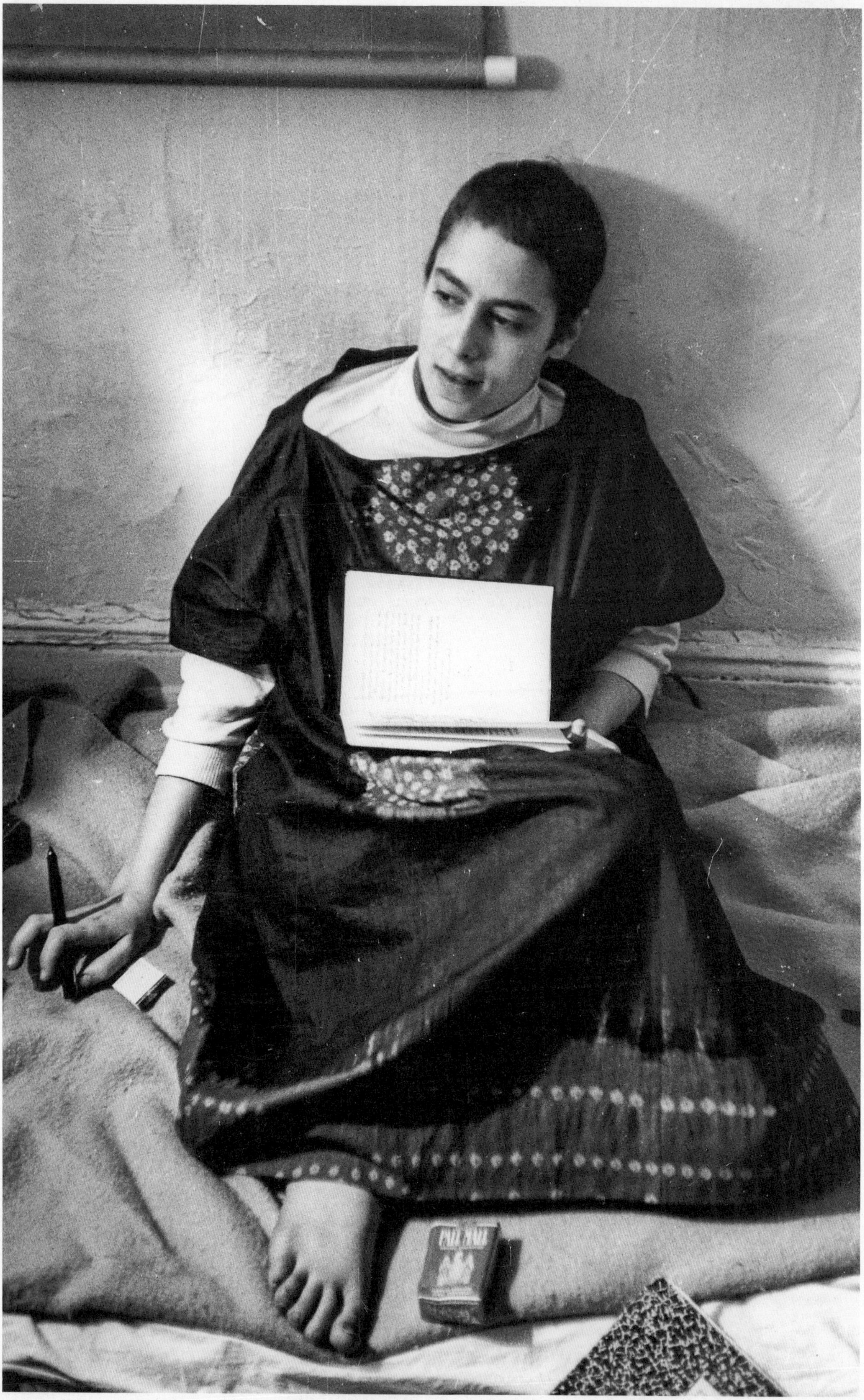

Barbara Rubin, November 1964. Photo: Fred McDarrah

Jonas Mekas
Barbara Rubin.
A Preface

December 18, 1980

Gordon Ball called to confirm Barbara Rubin's death, somewhere in the south of France. Bracha Besançon, that was her married name when she died giving birth to a child. 50 Montée de la Reine Victoria, Aix-les-Bains. Something like that. I got the address from Cassandra in her fancy handwriting, hard to read.

Good-bye Barbara. I owe you a lot. And so do many other people. I cannot imagine the New York 1960s film and poetry scene without you. You breezed in like a mysterious messenger. You urged us, you scolded us, you pushed us, you kept us together, you provoked us, you challenged us, and you argued and you argued and you argued. And you were everywhere. You moved from Jack Smith to Jean Genet to The Beatles to Allen Ginsberg to Bob Dylan, to Burroughs to Harry Smith to Lou Reed to Lenny Bruce to James Baldwin to to to… Your energy was inexhaustible, your belief and faith in us and in what we were doing was absolute.

I met Barbara in the spring of 1963, she was seventeen. She died seventeen years later, at the age of 35.

One evening after a show at the Gramercy Arts Theatre where the Film-Makers' Cooperative held its film screenings, where films such as Markopoulos's *Twice a Man*, Warhol's *Sleep*, Jack Smith's *Flaming Creatures* and Kenneth Anger's *Scorpio Rising* were premiered, a man by the name of William Rubin approached me and asked me whether I needed some assistance at the Cooperative. He said he had a niece who loved movies and she was just released from a correctional house, one of those places where they put teenagers when their parents cannot deal with them, teenagers gone totally "wrong"… Barbara had run away from her parents, got into drugs, ended up in the correctional house. But she was O.K. now, he said, and the police had decided to let her go home with the condition that she'd take a "regular" job to occupy her mind and time. I told him that she should come to the Co-op on Monday.

She came. Frail, very young, totally scared, and totally silent. She was still in a stupor. She did everything I asked her to do but she said no word. Maybe she thought she was sent to some extension of the correctional house… She only watched, listened, nodded and, sometimes, smiled weakly. She was very, very sensitive, and very, very responsive. But she said no word.

Several weeks passed like that. David Brooks, who was the main worker at the Co-op at that time, kept asking me, wondering, why I was employing this simpleton. He thought she was a totally dumb suburb kid—she was from Cambria Heights, Queens. He himself, eighteen at the time, was a man of the world who knew all the jazz places and knew where to get pot etc. When he smoked pot he did it hiding in order not to shock Barbara.

This, as I said, went on for several weeks. The Film-Makers' Cooperative, located in my loft, in those days was a meeting ground for a lot of different people. You could bump into Warhol (if you know how he looked—I didn't for months), Ginsberg, Jack Smith, Harry Smith, Jeffrey Jofen, Ron Rice, Ken Jacobs, Taylor Mead, Bob Kaufman, Robert Frank, Burroughs, and Andrew Sarris, and Peter Bogdanovich and Parker Tyler, and George Maciunas, and teenager P. Adams Sitney, this being also the editorial office of *Film Culture* magazine. And on some evenings you could even hear Salvador Dali's cane, climbing up to the third floor of 414 Park Avenue South. It was my loft, but the Co-op had taken over it.

I don't know how it came about, but David Brooks or someone else got involved in a hot discussion on the subject of the new generation, and David, who, as I said, was eighteen, said something that Barbara didn't like. I do not remember what he said, but it was enough to break Barbara's silence. No, she didn't speak: she came out like a spitfire. Like a painful stammering torrent of words long held back. Her speaking always had these almost painful hesitations as if there were so many words on her mind that she didn't know which ones to choose. So she called David and everybody else there "full of shit" and proceeded to inform us all on the subjects of teenagers, drugs, parents, etc., and made us all sit open-mouthed and listen to her because she knew what she was talking about, she knew it all first-hand. And from there on, it was Barbara who spoke and we were silent. Or we argued. Ginsberg, Burroughs, Voznesenski, Dylan, she argued with them all and gave her idealism to them all. Dylan, she helped him to come back to life after the motorcycle crash.

Dylan was also one of the last people she saw before leaving for France, we had a drink together across from Anthology, 425 Lafayette. She was always busy, always making peace between the various factions of the Underground art community. We were all bad children to her, not really doing our duties fully, not serving humanity enough, too much in our egos, not serving our art enough, or God, or ourselves. I think she was the most idealistic human I had ever met.

And of course, there was her own filmmaking, her own very special, swinging, shaking, swishing, flashing Bolex style, with innumerable superimpositions, no matter from which end, upside-down, or right or left. And all those unrealized, huge projects, scenarios ("Christmas on Earth Revisited"), starring practically everybody from Lenny Bruce to MarlonBrando. And there was *Christmas on Earth*, the film, her masterwork which she gave me before leaving for Europe and asked me not to show it while she was alive. And then there was Lou Reed and The Velvet Underground, which I know would never have been what it became if not for Barbara who brought Andy and the Velvets together.

And then one day she left us.

And she never came back.

Ah, Barbara you left us, like Rimbaud. You disappeared into the sands of some spiritual Africa, never to come back.

P. S.:
May 9, 2018

The Letters of Barbara to me in this book were mostly written between 1964 and 1970 from various locations in Europe. They have to do with the shows she or myself was organizing in London, with her unfinished film projects and anxieties about what her friends were doing and how they were behaving. All tinted with her unbending idealism. And they were all written in a handwriting which later made the transcriber, Charity Coleman, often turn to me for help to decipher some of them.

Due to my incredibly mad work schedule during that period—I was editing *Film Culture* magazine, I was writing a weekly column for *The Village Voice*, I was running the Film-Makers' Cooperative and the Film-Makers' Cinematheque, and of course, making my own films—Barbara's letters, like anything else that came into my loft, ended up in a chaotic pile. So that now, decades later, it will take only some idealistic, dedicated young scholars to establish their order or their approximated dates or to figure out the various references of which the letters are full.

I have no idea what happened to my own letters to Barbara. She was not in the habit of keeping anything as she kept moving ahead, nonstop, during the period covered in these letters.

The text is a reprint from Jonas Mekas's book *A Dance with Fred Astaire*, Anthology Editions (New York, 2017), with kind permission by the publisher. The text was extended by the author.

AUTOBIOGRAPHY OF BARBARA RUBIN WRITTEN IN 1968

AGE: 23

HT: 5-4

WT: 125

SEX: F

HAIR: Brown

EYES: Brown

BORN: Brooklyn, New York

Raised in Queeens. Ran away at 14. At 18 met Jonas Mekas who gave me camera with which I shot CHRISTMAS ON EARTH. Went to Europe, made ALLEN FOR ALLEN on Allen Ginsberg. At 21 met Shirley Clarke, and worked with her shooting the material to be used for a college program on poets. At 22 met Gordon Ball. Have now retired to a farm, where I am gmmmmg raising organic film.

It's hopeless.

Autobiography written by Barbara Rubin, East Hill Farm, 1968

Chuck Smith
Letters from Barbara Rubin. An Introduction

Barbara Rubin was born on June 8, 1945 in Queens, New York City. Her parents, Pauline and Lester Rubin, were liberal, middle class Jewish New Yorkers. She grew up with a lot of freedom that was encouraged and inspired by her older brother Kenny who introduced her to all the wonders of life, illicit and otherwise. At the age of twelve or thirteen, Barbara Rubin accompanied her brother to explore the Greenwich Village bohemian scene where she indulged in various drugs and explored her sexuality. By the 8th grade, Rubin had grown up so fast and free that she became estranged from her childhood friends. She dropped out of school by the 9th grade and disappeared from home for weeks at a time. According to her friend Rosebud,[1] she hitchhiked across the USA to California at age fifteen and took LSD with Aldous Huxley.[2] In late 1962, Rubin's drug use and behavior had become so stressful to her parents that they had her committed to a drug treatment facility in Connecticut.

While at the facility, Rubin met Edie Sedgwick[3], who would later become a fixture at Andy Warhol's Factory, and more importantly, became enamored with a friend's movie camera. Rubin's uncle, William Rubin, who managed the Gramercy Arts Theatre[4] in New York City, noticed her interest in film and suggested to her parents that a steady job would help her stay focused. William Rubin knew Jonas Mekas and, in the Spring of 1963, asked him if he would give his niece a job. Mekas agreed and, within a few weeks, she was released from the facility and began working full time at the Film-Makers' Cooperative. During the Summer and Fall of 1963, she helped catalog and program the Co-op's films and befriended many of the filmmakers. She found

1 Rose "Rosebud" Feliu-Pettet, 1946–2015, close friend of Barbara Rubin. Rosebud was a co-author of *Christmas on Earth Continued* and a "spiritual wife" to Harry Smith

2 Aldous Leonard Huxley, 1894–1963, English writer, novelist, and philosopher

3 Edith Minturn Sedgwick, 1943–1971, American actress and fashion model

4 The Gramercy Arts Theatre was originally built in 1937 as the Gramercy Park Theatre and is a music venue located in the Gramercy neighborhood of Manhattan

inspiration in the new works that were completed that summer, such as Ken Jacobs's *Blonde Cobra*,[5] Ron Rice's *Chumlum*[6] (in which she also appeared), Andy Warhol's *Sleep*,[7] and most importantly, Jack Smith's[8] *Flaming Creatures*. She was a strong advocate for exhibiting these new Underground films whenever possible because she believed that their depictions of freedom and possibility and their new ways of looking at the world would change society for the better.

At the same time, Barbara Rubin and her friend Rosebud began hanging out at a free love commune on the Lower East Side known as Kerista. According to Rosebud, it was at Kerista that Rubin first met the poets Allen Ginsberg[9] and Peter Orlovsky.[10] In 1963, she also became friends with Angus MacLise,[11] Ed Sanders,[12] and Tuli Kupferberg.[13] By the Fall, Barbara Rubin had become an invaluable part of the Film-Makers' Cooperative and had met nearly every important filmmaker, poet, and artist in downtown New York City.

Rubin's letters to Mekas begin in early 1964 when the two were separated for the first time since they had met nearly a year earlier. The letters offer an invaluable look into the mind of a woman who was at the very center of the Underground film scene in New York City in the 1960s. Most of them were written during three different periods—Winter / Spring 1964, Spring / Summer 1965, and Spring / Summer 1966—when Rubin was in Europe reporting back on her travels and her pursuit of various film projects and other multi-media events. The gaps in the letters mark periods when she was in New York City, either working directly with Mekas or seeing him regularly enough to make correspondence unnecessary. After 1967, the letters become more sporadic, with the last one dated in 1970, three years after Rubin's conversion to Hasidism. A few letters from Rubin are addressed to persons around the Film-Makers' Cooperative and are included in the book as well. The original spelling in her letters has been largely retained. In a few cases, the editors have made slight corrections to the text for the purposes of readability. Brief introductions to the letters provide contextualization for the correspondence, while additional notes recount relevant aspects of her life in New York.

5
Ken Jacobs, b. 1933, American experimental filmmaker, recipient of the American Film Institute's Maya Deren award. *Blonde Cobra* is a 1963 short film

6
Ron Rice, 1935–1964, American filmmaker and was one of the first Underground / Beat filmmakers. *Chumlum* is a 1964 film

7
Andy Warhol, 1928–1987, American artist central to the pop art movement. *Sleep* is a 1963 film

8
Jack Smith, 1932–1989, American fllmmaker, actor, pioneer of performance art; his most famous movie is *Flaming Creatures*, 1963

9
Allen Ginsberg, 1926–1997, American poet, leading figure of the Beat Generation

10
Peter Orlovsky, 1933–2010, American poet and actor, he was the long-time companion of Allen Ginsberg

11
Angus MacLise, 1938–1979, American percussionist, first drummer of The Velvet Underground

12
Edward Sanders, b. 1939, American poet, filmmaker, singer, social activist, and co-founder of the band The Fugs

13
Tuli Kupferberg, 1923–2010, American counterculture poet, author, singer, and co-founder of the band The Fugs

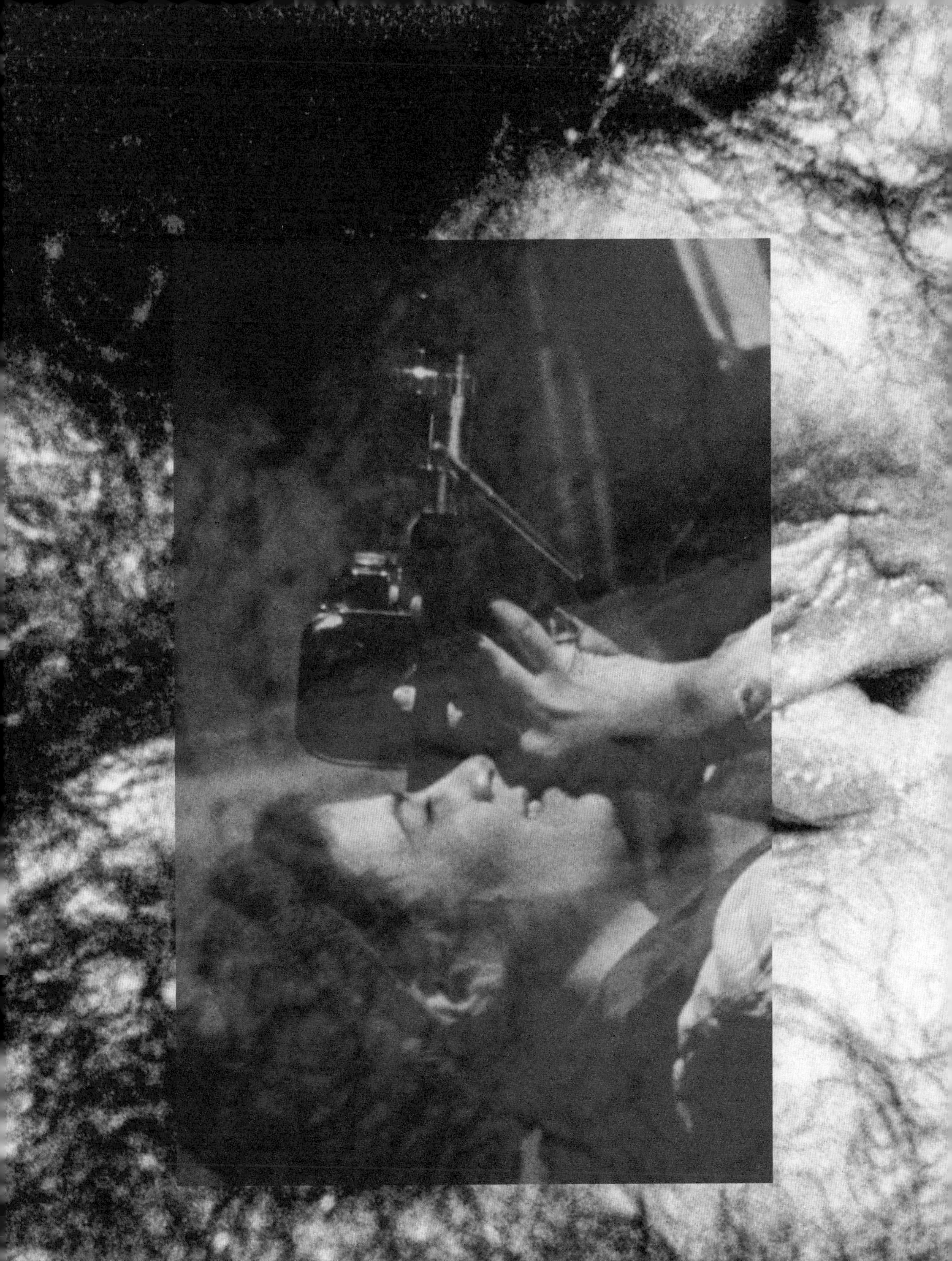

Background image: from reel A of Barbara Rubin's double projection film *Christmas on Earth*, 1963–1965.
Foreground image: Barbara Rubin with camera, ca. 1966.
Film still from *Walden* by Jonas Mekas, 1969

In late December of 1963, Rubin, Mekas, and P. Adams Sitney[1] (Mekas's other teenage protégé from the Co-op) flew to Knokke-le-Zoute, Belgium for *EXPRMNTL* (The International Festival of Experimental Film) to present several films of the New American Cinema Group completed that year, including Jack Smith's *Flaming Creatures*, Ron Rice's *Chumlum*, Kenneth Anger's *Scorpio Rising*,[2] and Gregory Markopoulos's *Twice a Man*,[3] and other films from 1963. Fearful of incurring complaints about the frank depiction of sexuality in *Flaming Creatures*, the Belgian Minister of Justice, who was also the President of the Belgian Cinematheque, refused to allow the film to be shown in the festival. In protest, Mekas resigned from the jury and he and Rubin arranged alternative, unsanctioned screenings. On New Years Eve, the two smuggled *Flaming Creatures* into a cinema where another film was being projected, and tied up the (compliant) projectionist. They attempted to screen Smith's film for the audience. Someone temporarily cut off the power, but Mekas and Rubin persisted and eventually projected the film onto the Minister of Justice himself, prior to the power going out again. The scandal was documented on the front page of the American film trade magazine *Variety*. In the first letter below, Mekas and Rubin inform Jack Smith about the situation at the festival.

1
P. Adams Sitney, b. 1944, sometimes P. A. Sitney, American avant-garde film historian and theorist, co-editor of *Film Culture* magazine, co-founder of Anthology Film Archives

2
Kenneth Anger, b. 1927, American Underground filmmaker, actor, and author

3
Gregory Markopoulos, 1928–1992, Greek-American filmmaker, and key figure in the American avant-garde

DEAR, JACK (+ ALL "FILM-MA[illegible] !!??????)

THIS IS GOING TO BE A COLLECTIVE EFFORT LETTER WRITTEN ON & OFF ABOUT "ALL THE SHIT!" GOING ON HERE.

There we are, sitting here, and there is no snow here; and there are almost no films here except what came from N.Y., and there are hundreds of phonies watching them, and perhaps five or ten good people, and they all want to see F.C., and the Festival forbids to show it, so we are having late shows of F.C. in our bedrooms, and also late late shows, last night Godard was there, crouched in the corner, and Agnes Varda, and most of good people, and now everybody wants to see it, because this is becoming an international scandal, really it was a scandal since we came here and made all efforts to get F.C. in competition and made a public protest, Barbara fighting with hair and nails, I had to pull myself out from the jury because of this, and James Broughton is our man in the jury.

We had a press conference today explaining the positions of those of us who are sticking together. We read the statements on censorship by Gregory, Stan (V-der-Beek), Stan (B-khage) Robert (Brr) and PA Sitney made a beautiful speech on F.C.

These are the facts, now:

1) F.C. was accepted by the selection committee
2) It was forbidden to show by the Minister of Justice
3) I withdrew myself from the Jury in protest against censorship
4) We asked to take out of the Fest films of Breer, Vanderbeek, Brakhage, Markopoulos, accordingly with their request
5) We were refused this on the grounds that the film-makers gave their permission to show their films by filling up the application blanks - Etc. Etc. Very Complicated. We'll tell you when we come back.
6). No public screening of F.C. can be held here.

We are planning to have one in Brussels immediately after the Fest. The law says, we should be arrested; together with all present.

Press, Radio, TV has been giving much time to the coverage of this case, and there will be more now, after the conference.

Everybody liked SCORPIO, TWICE A MAN, CHUMLUM, and they all have chances of winning, and there

Knokke-le-Zoute,
January 1, 1964

[Jonas Mekas writes]

Dear Jack (& all "film-makers"!!!?????)
This is going to be a collective effort letter written on & off about "all the shit" going on here. There we are, sitting here, and there is no snow here, and there are almost no films here except what came from NY, and there are hundreds of phonies watching them, and perhaps five or ten good people, and they all want to see *F.C.*,[1] and the Festival forbids to show it, so we are having late shows of *F.C.* in our bedroom, and also late late shows, last night Godard[2] was there, crouched in the corner, and Agnès Varda,[3] and most of good people, and now everybody wants to see it, because this is becoming an international scandal, really it was a scandal since we came here and made all efforts to get *F.C.* in competition and made a public protest, Barbara fighting with hair and nails, I had to pull myself out from the jury because of this, and James Broughton[4] is our man in the jury.
We had a press conference today explaining the position of those of us who are sticking together. We read the statements on censorship by Gregory, Stan (V-der-Beek),[5] Stan (B-khage),[6] Robert (Brr),[7] and PA Sitney made a beautiful speech on *F.C.*
These are the facts, now:
1. *F.C.* was accepted by the selection committee
2. It was forbidden to show by the Minister of Justice
3. I withdrew myself from the jury in protest against censorship
4. We asked to take out of the Fest films of Breer, Vanderbeek, Brakhage, Markopoulos, accordingly with their request
5. We were refused this on the grounds that the film-makers gave their permission to show their films by filling up the application blanks, etc., etc. Very complicated. We'll tell you when we come back.
6. No public screening of *F.C.* can be held here. We are planning to have one in Brussels immediately after the Fest. The law says we should be arrested together with all present.

Press, radio, TV has been giving much time to the coverage of this case, and there will be more now, after the conference.
Everybody liked *Scorpio Rising*, *Twice A Man*, *Chumlum*, and they all have chances of winning, and there is much talking about Stan's (B) work, and his screenings are noisiest (for silent movies!), & disturbing. The audience is snobbish and weird, and likes only documentaries from England—But Stan's work looks like gold here in this shit-Fest, and so did Kenneth's work—but there is also plenty of American shit here, we don't know where it came from, and how it got into the Fest.

1
F.C., abbreviation for *Flaming Creatures*

2
Jean-Luc Godard, b. 1930, French-Swiss film director, screenwriter, film critic; pioneer of the French New Wave film movement

3
Agnès Varda, b. 1928, Belgian-born French director, and documentary filmmaker

4
James Broughton, 1913–1999, American poet and filmmaker

5
Stan VanDerBeek, 1927–1984, American filmmaker, and pioneer in computer art

6
Stan Brakhage, 1933–2003, American filmmaker, co-founder of the Anthology Film Archives

7
Robert Breer, 1926–2011, American filmmaker, painter, and sculptor

Hillary Harris[8] is here, and John Whitney,[9] otherwise no other Am. film-makers. I don't know why I am writing these stupid facts here, inside a stupid way, because we are sitting here and eating, and this is no time to write letters, and I do not like writing letters, I feel very stupid when I write letters, but we think that you must be anxious to know what is happening here and so I am trying to do my best, because Barbara is sitting here and holding her "finger" at me, you better write a letter to NY, she says, you lazy "hypocrite," let them know what's going on here—

8
Hillary Harris, 1929–1999, American documentary filmmaker, and pioneer of time-lapse photography

9
John Whitney, 1917–1995, pioneer of computer animation

[Barbara Rubin writes:]

False! It was a fork (containing an emaciated piece of meat) and the statement was "you lazy—." To go into a little more detail it was specifically (*F.C.*) not shown because of this Belgium law which was not stated in the applications you made out as havin' any jurisdiction at an "Experimental (esp.) Festival." The judges here saw your film and the reaction was superb—blushing, hard-ons, red faces, elirium, and came to the conclusion that your film was not a film but a documentary.
We will definitely have a screening, public one in Brussels, probably on Jan. 3rd and we will collect all information and send it to you. It is very sad that this festival, which is supposed to be free and containing the most "new" and "different" etc movies, lacks depth, feeling and strength and that it has for the most part cockless, bigoted, feminist Hitlers, sell-outs, lonely, unhappy people who make pretentious and outrageous statements like "I am a Marxist" blah blah blah, "I believe in censorship, would you like to have films made on racism" (like one would say 'would you like your daughter to marry a nigger').
We are all running around and every time we enter a room everybody cringes Ha! Ha! Ha! Sorry we couldn't share xmas, hope everything is swingin' and you did some great shootin'.
Send our love and show this to all "film-makers" so they know what's goin' on. In Belgium they have a great law that everybody present at an illegal screening gets arrested so we are planning on a "big, big screening (everyone seems to want to get arrested? Though we will see when the time comes). Mr. Ledoux,[10] the head of the festival, is a very good man and is helping us immensely as a matter of fact. He would love for this thing to blow up and when we showed the film to the jury he thought it would be good if we were raided and the jury was arrested. Unfortunately, being head of this festival he could not (for reasons we will explain). But I think he will be with us in Brussels perhaps in jail also.
Amos Vogel[11] is "fightin'" with us and brought applause with a very eloquent speech on "man's rights" and Jonas made every man

10
Jacques Ledoux, 1921–1988, film specialist, curator of the Third International Experimental Film Exposition in Knokke-le-Zoute in 1963

11
Amos Vogel, 1921–2012, founder of New York City's groundbreaking film society Cinema 16 and author of *Film as a Subversive Art*, 1974

overage of this case, and there will be more now, the conference.
Everybody liked SCORPIO, TWICE A MAN, CHUMLUM, they all have chances of winning, and there

much talking about Stan's (B) work, and his screenings noisiest (for silent movies!), & disturbing - the audience snobbish & wierd, and likes only documentaries from gland - But Stan's work looks like gold here this shit-Fest, and so did Kenneth's work - but there also plenty of American shit here, we don't know re it came from, and how it got into the Fest.

Hilary Harris is here, and John Whitney, otherwise no ther Am. film-makers.

I don't know why I am writing these stupid facts here, such a stupid way, because we are sitting here and ting, and this is no time to write letters, and I do not like writing letters, I feel very stupid when I write letters - but we think that you must be anxious to know what is happening here - and so I am trying to do my best, because Barbara is sitting here and holding her "finger" at me, you better write a letter to N.Y, she says, you lazy "hypocrite", let them know what's going here -

FALSE! - IT WAS A FORK (CONTAINING AN EMASCIATED PIECE OF MEAT) & THE STATEMENT WAS "YOU LAZY - - - - - -

TO GO INTO A LITTLE MORE DETAIL IT WAS SPECIFICALLY (F.C.) NOT SHOWN BECAUSE OF THIS BELGIUM LAW WHICH WAS NOT STATED IN THE APPLICATIONS WE MADE OUT AS HAVIN' ANY JURISDICTION AT AN "EXPERIMENTAL (esp.) FESTIVAL"

THE JUDGES HERE SAW YOUR FILM & THE REACTION WAS SUPERB - BLUSHING HARD ON'S, RED FACES, DELIRIUM & CAME TO THE CONCLUSION YOUR FILM WAS NOT A FILM BUT A DOCUMENTRY.

WE WILL DEFINITLY HAVE A SCREENING, PUBLIC ONE IN BRUSSELS, PROBABLY ON JAN 3RD. & WE WILL

of this Festival. He could not (for reason we will explain) but I think he will be with us in Brussels perhaps in jail also.

Amos Vogel is "fightin" with us & brought applauds with a very eloquent speech on "man's rights".
& Jonas made every man at the conference take note literally & I don't think they will let him forget it, when he said,

- - - - It's on principle, & I believe in Liberty, Justice & everything goes!

We are having daily screenings of F.C. here & tomorrow Mon. we are having another press conference open to public & we will show F.C. Also there will be a chance that F.C. & all others will be shown at the Free University open to public in Brussels if not it will be shown else where in Brussels.

Take care & we will try to keep you informed more often. Love to Stan, Bob, Joan, Ron, Amy, Francine, Joel, Jerry, Rene, Beverley, John, Gregory, All other beautiful 'creatures'

Love & kisses
Barbara
Jonas
&
P.A. Sitney

If possible make sure Stan Vanderbeek, Robert Breer, Ken. Anger, Gregory M. & Stan Brakhage are kept in news about this.

Chumlum, Twice a Man, Scorpio Rising, Window Water Baby were loved here they were the only ones that weren't boring or DEAD! & compared to heavy European "Experimental"

at the conference take note literally and I don't think they will forget it, when he said, "It's on principle and I believe in liberty, justice, and everything goes!"
We are having daily screenings of *F.C.* here and tomorrow morn we are having another press conference open to the public and we will show *F.C.* Also, there will be a chance that *F.C.* and all others will be shown at the free university open to public in Brussels; if not, it will be shown elsewhere in Brussels.
Take care and we will try to keep you informed more often. Love to Stan, Bob,[12] Joan,[13] Ron, Amy,[14] Francine,[15] Joel,[16] Jerry,[17] René,[18] Beverly,[19] John,[20] Gregory, all other beautiful 'creatures'.
Love+kisses, Barbara
Jonas
+
P. A. Sitney

[P. Adams Sitney writes]

If possible make sure Stan Vanderbeek, Robert Breer, Kenneth Anger, Gregory M. and Stan Brakhage are kept in news about this. *Chumlum*, *Twice A Man*, *Scorpio Rising*, *Window Water Baby Moving,*[21] were loved here, they were the only ones that weren't boring or dead! (& compared to Heavy European "Experimental" films) & which brought tremendous pro-con, love hate, hit-miss talk, talk, talk, reaction.

12
Robert Adler, husband of Joan Adler, and person responsible for the photograph of the cake sequence in Jack Smith's film *Normal Love* on the cover of *Film Culture* 29, Summer 1963

13
Joan Adler, wife of Robert Adler, appeared in *Normal Love* (1963)

14
Amy Rice, ca. 1934–2015, wife of Ron Rice

15
Frank di Giovanni, professionally known as Francis Francine, drag performer and star of many Underground films, including Jack Smith's *Flaming Creatures*

16
Joel Markman, 1934–1994, performer known for the films *Flaming Creatures* and *Chumlum*

17
Jerry Jofen, 1925–1993, sometimes Joffen, Polish-born, American painter, collagist, experimental filmmaker

18
René Rivera, 1935–2013, professionally known as Mario Montez, was a Puerto Rican actor, star of Jack Smith's film *Flaming Creatures*

19
Beverly Grant, 1936–1990, Underground performer in films by Jack Smith, Ron Rice, and Andy Warhol

20
John Vaccaro, 1930–2016, performer in Jack Smith's *Normal Love* and later director of the radical theatre group the Playhouse of the Ridiculous

21
Window Water Baby Moving, a 1959 film by Stan Brakhage

Mekas had scheduled a selection of New American Cinema films to be shown in Brussels, Munich, and other European cities after the Knokke festival. It was decided that Sitney would travel with the films and present the programs. Meanwhile, Mekas and Rubin drove to Paris with Roman Polański.[1] It was Rubin's first trip to the French capital and she was inspired both by the city and by Polański's energy and views on filmmaking. Mekas recalled that Rubin was particularly happy and spontaneous one day when they were all together in Polański's convertible. At one point, Rubin felt like swimming, so she jumped out of the car and dove into the Seine—even though it was January and the water was freezing. A few days later, Mekas flew back to New York, but Rubin decided to stay in Paris. At some point, she ended up in a hospital. On Mekas's request, his friends Barbara[2] and David Charles Stone[3] visited her, helped her out of the hospital and found her a place to stay in the city. In the letter dated January 20, 1964, her reference to a "hate/love" for Polański and her description of their relationship in that same letter implies that she continued to see Polański for some time after Mekas's departure.

Using Paris as a base, Rubin wanted to help Sitney with the New American Cinema film expositions.

1
Roman Polański, b. 1933, Polish and French film director, producer, writer, actor

2
Barbara Stone, 1934–2018, American director, producer, and distributor. She and her husband David Stone co-founded the *Gates Cinema* and *Cinegate Film Distribution*

3
David Charles Stone, 1932–2011, sometimes David or Charles, American producer, distributor, and exhibitor. He and his wife Barbara Stone were key figures in art house cinemas and film distribution in England in the 1970s

In the letters below, she updates Mekas on her time in Paris and her conflicts with Sitney. Because *Flaming Creatures* was considered controversial, Sitney was in favor of allowing screening venues to opt out of showing it. Rubin, however, was against any form of censorship and vowed not to assist with any European screenings that didn't include the film.

The letter below begins with a reference to a "cold and exhaustion" which might have been the result of her swim in the Seine and subsequent hospitalization.

Paris,
January 10, 1964

Dear Jonas,
The final climax of my turbulent cold and exhaustion fell and I'm now enjoying a few days in bed. It was very sad to hear they accepted the money[1] and it seems more important now that we begin helping our film-makers to rid themselves with these stupidities about money (one of many) but most important so they can make greater films or their babies will begin to stink or have they already? By Monday I will be in Munich to make sure everything is going well, (not only about *F.C.*) for if I can help Sitney, Exposition, in any way, even if it comes to me not being a part of it, I always will. I hope by the time of the Munich screening you would have written to Sitney or me, even a telegram, anything, telling esp. about the stand with *F. C.* so if anything comes up in Munich at least both of us will know. (I feel, Sitney feels it's only me who will go to the extremes, now that you're away)—Please tell him explicitly, and me. Jonas you know that basically I know you believe and that all the programs stay together for we have that agreement and understanding and love, but after Sitney's letter about Ledoux it seems you must reiterate on it for this floating back and forth is ridiculous enough. What is happening with Anger, does he have a chance for a Ford prize? Please try to get him to come with us, explain to him about it and even if he doesn't want to go all around (I don't know), send him money, he is very desperate. Elliot[2] heard from him and he was very upset. I've been slowly dancing with Paris for its chill is titillating. I live in the Latin Quarter, with the wonders of open shops, people,

1
Both VanDerBeek and Markopoulos received awards at the *EXPRMNTL* in Knokke-le-Zoute, 1963. Some of the defenders of *Flaming Creatures*, including Rubin, were dismayed that they neither refused the awards nor turned down the prize money

2
Elliot Stein, 1928–2012, American film critic based in Paris for decades

3
Nico Papatakis, 1918–2010, Greek-born French filmmaker

4
Marcello Mastroianni, 1924–1996, Italian film actor

5
Jacques Perrin, b. 1941, French actor and filmmaker

6
The 1962 Italian film directed by Valerio Zurlini *Cronaca familiare* was translated to *Family Diary*

7
Reference to the Royal Film Archive of Belgium (Cinémathèque royale de Belgique) which Jacques Ledoux was curating from 1948–1988

not the Saint Germain superficialities. I've been trying to get Niko,[3] he's very difficult to reach for I think besides the sound the film's ready, I'm beginning work on the titles now. I've cut it down and now I think it will run at the most 40 minutes. I was rejuvenated by a film put out by MGM an Italian film with Mastroianni[4] and a Jacques Perrin.[5] I think it's opening in U.S.A. under the title *Journey in Time.*[6] It's a love story of two brothers in love (not completely open on the sexual) but the two brothers were so beyond themselves so beautiful Jonas that I'm still carrying them with me if for no other reason (should there be?) for their love, try and see it. It was Elliot who is driving me to these beauties (it was a "flop here"!) I saw Godard's movie with BB and I'm sorry for him for after seeing this film there is no comparison. He seems, Godard, to lack the honesty and emotion, the tenderness of saying what he intimately feels, so that he made for me a very dead 2 hours of film. All other things are assimilating and I'm beginning to feel my way. Things have been difficult because I much prefer Paris without anything else but her on my being. I'm glad Stan is coming, would like to hear from him. The only other question is about the Cinematheque in Brussels[7] since I think you ought to write to Ledoux and cancel the program there and try to find another place, if there isn't enough time then rather leave that time open. I think at this point it's ridiculous to even consider Ledoux's Cine. for the exposition or any others that [pose] the same problem.
Take care, I love you and all of you always,
no matter what be, Jonas, dearest.
Love Barbara.

DEAR JONAS,

THE FINAL CLIMAX OF MY TURBULENT COLD & EXHAUSTION FELL & I'M NOW ENJOYING A FEW DAYS IN BED.

IT WAS VERY SAD TO HEAR THEY ACCEPTED THE MONEY & IT SEEMS MORE IMPORTANT NOW THAT WE BEGIN HELPING OUR FILM-MAKERS TO RID THEMSELVES WITH THESE STUPIDITIES, ABOUT money. (one of many.) but most important so they can make greater films. or their babies will begin to stink or have they already? By Mon. I will be in Munich to make sure everything is going well. (not only about FC) for if I can help Sitney exposition in anyway, even, if it comes to me not being a part of it, I always will. I hope by the time of the Munich screening you would have written to Sitney. or me, or a telegram anything, telling esp. what the stand with FC. is so if anything comes up in Munich atleast both of us will know. (I feel, Sitney feels it's only me who will go

Paris,
January 15, 1964

Dear Jonas,
Piero[1] and I will leave for Munich on the 20th of Jan. We will be there just a few days (can't stay away from my finishing my babe). To see and help (also concerning how the screening, concerning *F.C.*, etc. is held) Please cont. to write at American Express in Paris for I will be back to finish. You'll probably have the other letter I wrote, please Jonas, tell me, so that if anything happens at Munich, *F.C.* or Sitney and you'll understand my feelings and position. Write Sitney and clarify this.
Take care Love and be Barbara

1
Piero Heliczer, 1937–1993, Italian-American poet, publisher, filmmaker, actor in *Flaming Creatures*, ex-husband of Kate Heliczer

Rubin's conflict with Sitney continued to upset her. Sitney claims that at one point Rubin telephoned one of the venues scheduled to screen the New American Films and unilaterally tried to cancel the event because they wouldn't show *Flaming Creatures*.

January 15, 1964

Dear Jonas,
I just received this letter from P. Adams. Read it carefully for since, it seems all the talk, decision etc. seems to have not been assimilated. If this Brussels showing at Cinematheque doesn't include *F.C.* then it seems this will be the end. I am going to try & get the money or something to be in Munich to see what happens there. Either we do this in honesty & keep to our decision that if it be we will just have our own screenings & ignore the Cinematheques all over or any other "compromising organization." I want to make it clear Jonas, for this makes me MAD! If you want to do it this way, fine tell me, & I will arrange if need be with others, a journey myself. I am not going to compromise on this or anything else for there is enough death sickness & loneliness around to just compromise! I'm not always doing & I falter many times but I will not turn my face or ignore I will not die with everyone's death & my own.
I'm not making a movie so that you or anyone else will be so as to cheapen it with doubts, or acceptance of stupidity belittling laws & scared shitless people who long for strength love & caring. I'm sorry Jonas, for I know we have been thru this many times but please try to understand that I can't, can't WON'T allow myself to blindness my & love to disaster. Love, Jonas, is of the heart breath & being of every man, not laws, morals censorship, maybe I'm naïve but to me there is only love free & that anything barely [...] or destroying must be fought. It's beyond fighting laws for it's not the law but the people. The minister of justice attitude towards *F.C.* is that of man, scared lonely & blended from heights glorious, not a "lawyer," "minister" as such. Please write to me immediately.
Send my love to Everyone & if----
Take care Jonas
love love
Barbara

P.S. I wrote to Ledoux personally, told him how I felt. I don't think he knows where we stand since we are constantly unsure & seem to have different opinions always floating. I told him how I felt since that's all one can do.

January 1964

Dear Jonas,
I wrote you a letter in my heat of "anger," a card of explanation of my doing. Now I owe you the understandin' of what is in me. You know how I feel love & growth, horizons. Sometimes I'm carried away to abstracts, so now I'll let you see thru my eyes this element, the exposition. To me it could be the beginning, a first step to a second sight for all. Freedom of self, love etc. is of the self & the more we release the more assimilation & reaping. These movies, as such, have gone beyond, a move, but for any assimilation it makes its people seeing must grow so we spread & "risk" our beings, bringing everyone into the scene by showing these as others [—] everything, movie or not. If these movies are of a high step then they must continue & just as they were made low & often "illegally" then why compromise on the final climax, the point of intensities is showings , & the people. Let's ignore these forces with the understanding of their existence but not to play with them, you'll lose in the end for laws, censors, etc. Are the people themselves & if you make deals with them, anything else you say loses its validity.
We were on "wrong" tangents often towards being oneself, but goddamn it we have the opportunity to do something now, let's not fuck it up with weakness. We must start in the states particularly, maybe even before abroad. (Not with immediate anticipation of acceptance & no more censorship but of the beginning release.) The film-makers themselves must be an intricate part of it.
If we are united then we can do anything. As far as the exposition here is concerned as far as these showings, there should be no compromises if after any film-maker wishes to show her work like at the Cinematheque (Ledoux's) fine that is his decision but as far as these shows, all must stay together equal. I don't know how the film-makers themselves feel so it's awkward, so maybe you better call them together and decide for if they all agree then Sitney, Ledoux, the world will have this much to be assured of. I don't want any doings as far as the exposition with Ledoux unless this censorship stops, if need be we'll just show it in the streets who cares as long as many people see them, as movies, equal, not one kind or censored or private membership crap. They see it as they were made, free from all thought of legalities.
If the film-makers themselves don't agree & have a different "desire completely" then continue on for the little done is better than nothing, for nothing is something, but I personally will not be a part of it. I've been thinking of arranging a sort of caravan of people to travel with their loves, thought or beings. This exposition could be it if they all want it. You know I will always help & love you, & the beauties of New York, but I will not waste with them, or anyone even my own tendencies. One of the reasons I didn't go back immediately was to get myself back in a way. I felt like I was being buried,

I must finish my movie, and now it's most paramount but as soon as it's done if need be I will temporarily return to help as much, but I'm now loose and I will no longer be dragged under by anything most of all myself. I will always be in contact, loving but I'm growing and hopefully to have you all with me. I'm understanding more and more about me and all the meaning of living and being and I want to continue, with strength, I can't dissipate it for we are all scared, fearful etc. I love you all very deep for you are alive still but come let's grow on, not stagnate. The world's people us, wait upon all. We are everything with any possibility we wish to give it, why drown!
Take care Jonas, & know you most I love, for I know you travel with me, but let's try now to come to terms before this whole thing is exploded out of proportion & its effects have been made felt. If you think it's important for me to return I will, but I think it is now up to you, the makers, I will do everything possible here to help with arrangements, etc. for you all, for I'm picking up my pace & moving along higher & sometimes low.
Love always, Barbara
How is Debby?[1] Send me her address.

1
Debby Feiner, b. 1948, sometimes Debbie, Fein or Feinman, a friend of Barbara Rubin and starred in Rubin's film *Christmas on Earth*

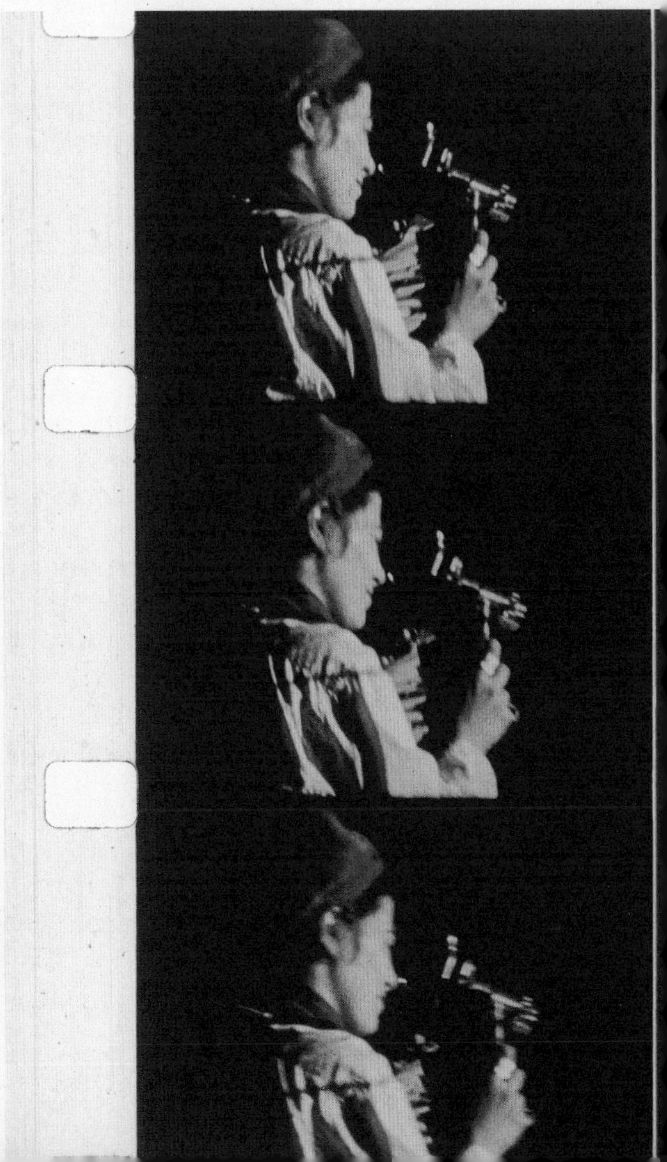

Barbara Rubin, New York, 1966.
Film stills by Jonas Mekas

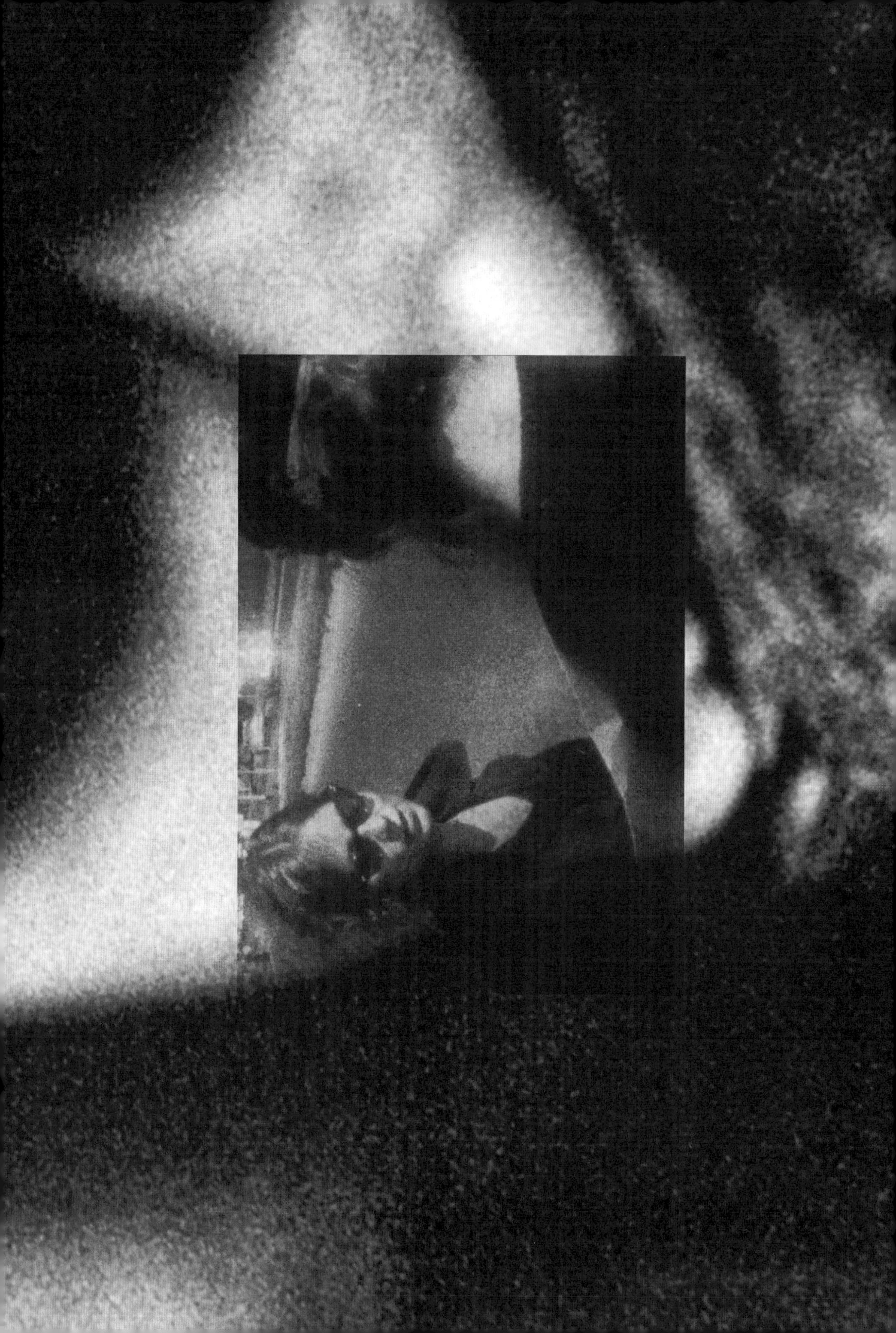

January 20, 1964

Dear Jonas,
This, the night before, the journey—Jonas I love you and [think] constantly of you hear, see, feel, beyond. Your image is a flicker of all your fires and I find myself talkin' with others with your presence there. A lot has happened which I'm just now able to assimilate… since Sitney's letter, the anger, hurt, etc. Like the tons of masses, abstract finally speaking lite. You know how I'm always falling deep into the abyss recklessly, and my loves churn ruthlessly in my pit. Polanski, hate / love, intrigue has been one infinitive battle sphere. Together idiots, fools, beyond that which is love itself. More ego, stupidity and infantilism. I'm growin' slowly, but always newly found.

I'm sorry about the yelling in the other letters, as well as Belgium, Paris… I feel like I'm souring, it's bad, tres bad & don't worry with Sitney, Munich, for I'm learning, Jonas, and it just takes time with me. I'm going basically to be as much help as possible not to hurt—I'm really like a baby opening my sights upon the whole. My fanaticism, no matter what for, brings not love for which I'm givin' of my being and not forgiveness I'm asking, Jonas. For I am all of these things, they are me, Barbara, but patience and understanding (for that's all we all ask for) because I fluctuate in my journey on. (Same words you said, in Belgium, foolish like no one else I can be.) Jonas, I'd like you to do me a favor and find out where Milton Sperling[1] is, if he is still interested in financing someone, & write telling me where I can write to him. There are a few people here who fit into his ideas etc and since I know of him, I'd like to help them / or any. one since I'm in the position, particularly in this kind of circumstance and also if you know of anyone else on Sperling's line interested in supporting (since we can't get their help maybe someone else can, I'd like to know as soon as possible esp. where I can write him). How about us? Has any person / financial angel gazed upon us? Please tell me if I can find anyone here, I've been looking but my source is "limited."

Most important, more for more than money: How is the spirit? I meant that about the "film-makers" at home, most of all you know I'd want to feel they, us, need it most, to go forward. The decision of Gregory and Stan hurt tremendously (I understand them) but after Knokke, their letters, etc. it was their dishonesty that bothered, that's one of the reasons that R. Rice is still beautiful and moving to me because he at least was honest in the beginning how he felt, rather Greg and Stan hadn't written the letters if they didn't have the strength and belief to follow it thru no matter what. Have you written to K. Anger, he is so beautiful and alive for all his ups, downs, opportunities, etc. and so many years, Jonas, he's real. Did you tell Deb I've not heard from her and I'm concerned with love for her, 'desperately.'

1
Milton Sperling, 1912–1988, American film producer and screenwriter

Background image: from reel A of Barbara Rubin's double projection film *Christmas on Earth* 1963–1965.
Foreground image: Barbara Rubin, 1963.
Film still from *Lost Lost Lost* by Jonas Mekas, 1976

Tell Angus that the movie is getting shorter (for I saw it projected and see all that I wasn't saying and know now how to express in its simplicity).
Take care my love and love, all those beauties home (also those delightful pleasures of flesh indulge for it's a part of anyone's soul & beauty). I will write from Munich telling all—
Love, Je t'aime and to everyone,
always love and care, Barbara

Jonas, please understand about Ledoux etc. it is impossible under those conditions, let's show these movies as they were made, freer, newer, growing.

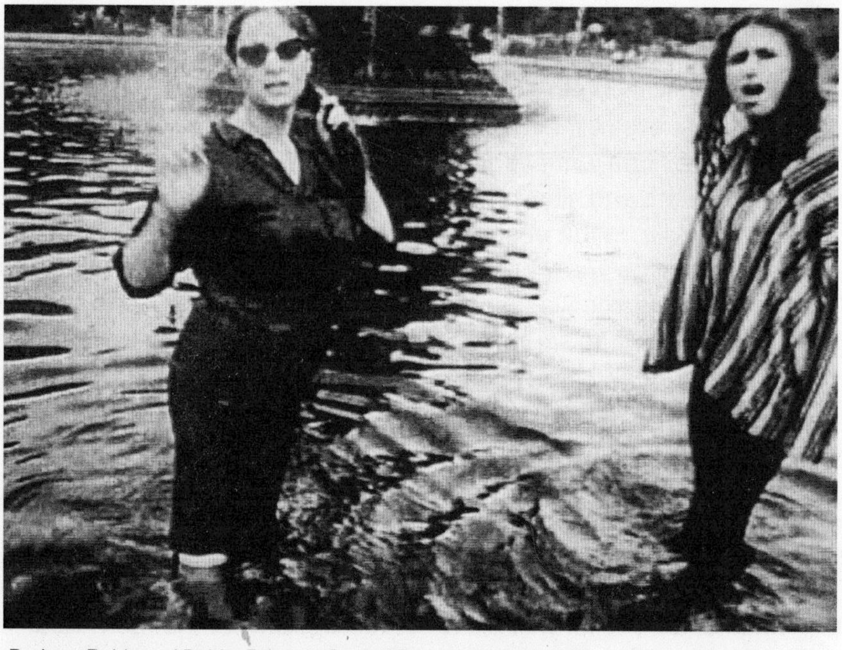

Barbara Rubin and Debby Feiner in Central Park, New York, 1963.
Film still from *Lost Lost Lost* by Jonas Mekas, 1976

Rubin continued to believe that Sitney's New American Cinema screenings were too traditional. In the partial letter below, she describes her vision for an uncensored and more comprehensive traveling film program.

January 1964

Think also of a program for film-makers new of the country we will be in. At least 1 program for new "unknown" film-makers. A mix of film-maker's movies instead of all one film-maker's program.
At least 10 min intermission between long films, 5 between shorter and films under 5 min run 2. Bring as many film-makers as possible to talk perhaps in between films after. Before, think about getting a truck to transport us with equipment, projector, screen, etc. Also some supplies to sleep if needed. If "legal" arrangements can't be made (that is three known sources) we will arrange as we go along for screenings, either renting a place or a home, even in truck or in street.
All programs must be shown together, no acceptance of censorship no matter at what risk. All films must be equally handled without any consideration to whether it is "acceptable censor-wise or not." I will try and have movie-makers here send their films to N.Y. maybe a festival in N.Y. can be arranged. Also have an open screening of our films in N.Y. and drop membership cards. If we are to disregard censors in all countries let's start at home.
Instead of having just an open show of *F. C.* start with all our films. Let's not make *F. C.* thrown out of proportion all our films deserve and should be shown openly in N.Y. and all over.
Look into Ed Sanders movies. Discuss with Brakhage what exactly we in the Exposition want to do so that no matter what complications arise we know what is important.
You know to me the Exposition means that not only films but all expressions of people are shown so as to touch all those aching to be felt and that no matter what the risks or dangers, everyone should be free to say whatever they feel and for it to reach as many people as possible legally or not. One can constantly expose oneself, taking risks and plunging for that is life. As far as the film-makers themselves are concerned they need to grow and free themselves or else they too will die. Here as everywhere there is a feeling of useless[ness] of the kind where people don't even bother anymore feeling Death, but not of Death for they have no sense of life so how can they of Death. These movies are new different freer, they will have an effect but if they don't grow (film-makers) then they will just pass on by to their own unfelt death.

[fragment / no intro or ending]

Paris,
January 1964

Dearest Jonas,
I am now temporarily at 57 Rue Lacépède, Rm. 19, (Piero's) I met UNESCO man and he wanted know what happened to *Guns*[1] He leaves Paris Wed. so if you can wire or anything try to. I called Godard and will see him Monday as well with Niko.
as of yet, nothing. For Zion's viewer is broken so I play the streets, snow and beauties. I hope you're seriously considering the idea of getting a truck equipped, to live, film, etc. and travel as such. There are people here, one a George Andrews and Others, who would gladly help and I'm sure we could get some—one to help financially. Please write telling me. I'm still singing softly to the fallen flakes take care love always Barbara

1 *Guns of Trees* is a 1961 film by Jonas Mekas

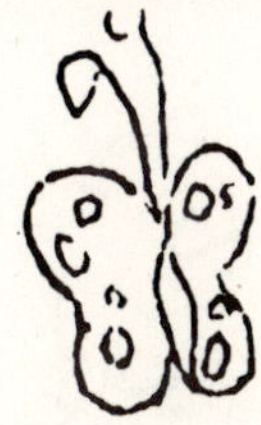

DECLARATION FOR THE FREEDOM OF THE BLACK AND WHITE AND TECHICOLOR SHADOWS

(2mm, 4mm, 16mm, 35mm 70mm, 150mm, 1,000mm, 1,000,000mm)

Moving pictures belong to the Muses-- like painting, like poetry, like music, like dance, like any other art.

Big or small, good or bad, expensive or cheap, "Cleopatra" or "Flaming Creatures"----they all belong to the muses.

They all are attempts to give man something beautiful.

Licensing of works of art is immoral, silly and unconstitutional.

Thats what we want people to know.

The main reason for licensing shadows is (they say) to protect people from obscenity in films.

That is very nice hypocritical reasoning.

We are grown-up people and need no civic and bureaucratic mommies and daddies to protect our morals any longer.

Do not baby the people.
It is beautiful to be a child; but it is pretty sick to be childish!!

Let all lives be free.

Let all art be free.

Let all life expressions be free.

Let man blossom.

Film-makers Of The People
May 23, 1964. New York City

SATURDAY - MAY 23- DEMONSTRATION AT THE RADIO CITY MUSIC HALL - 5 PM- (50th Street and Avenue of Americans). EVERYONE INTERESTED IN ARTISTIC FREEDOM COME!!

-212-

Barbara Rubin's Co-op Declaration, New York, May 23, 1964

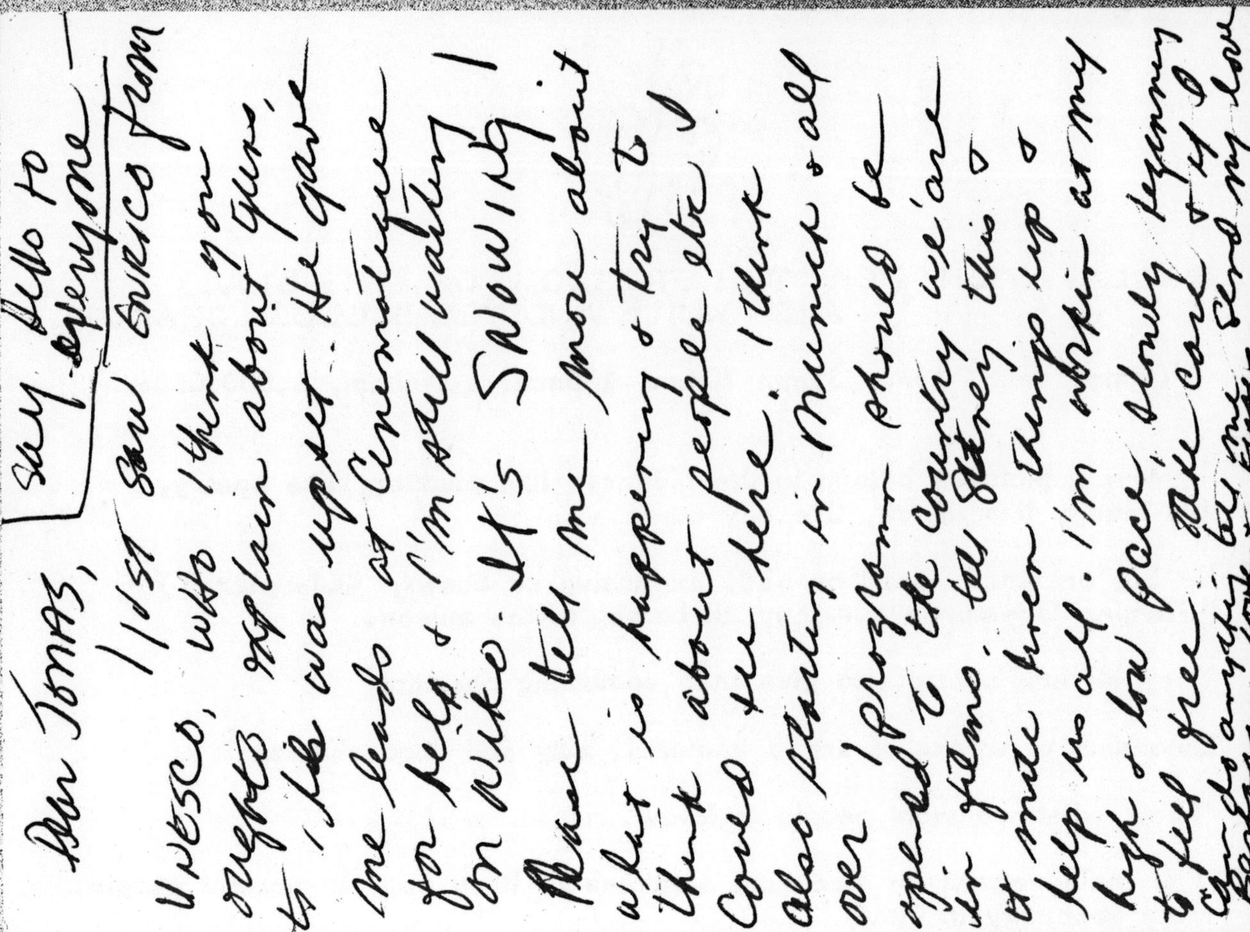

Dear Jonas,

say hello to everyone

Just saw Enrico from UNESCO, who I think you ought to explain about Guns to, he was upset. He gave me leads at Cinematheque for help + I'm still waiting on Nico. It's SNOWING!

Please tell me more about what is happening + try to think about people etc. I could see here. I think also starting in Munich + all over / program should be opened to the country we are in films too. Steering this + meet here things up + keep me all. I'm working at my high + low pace slowly beginning to feel free. The card + if I can do anything let me know. Send my love

Barbara love + kisses

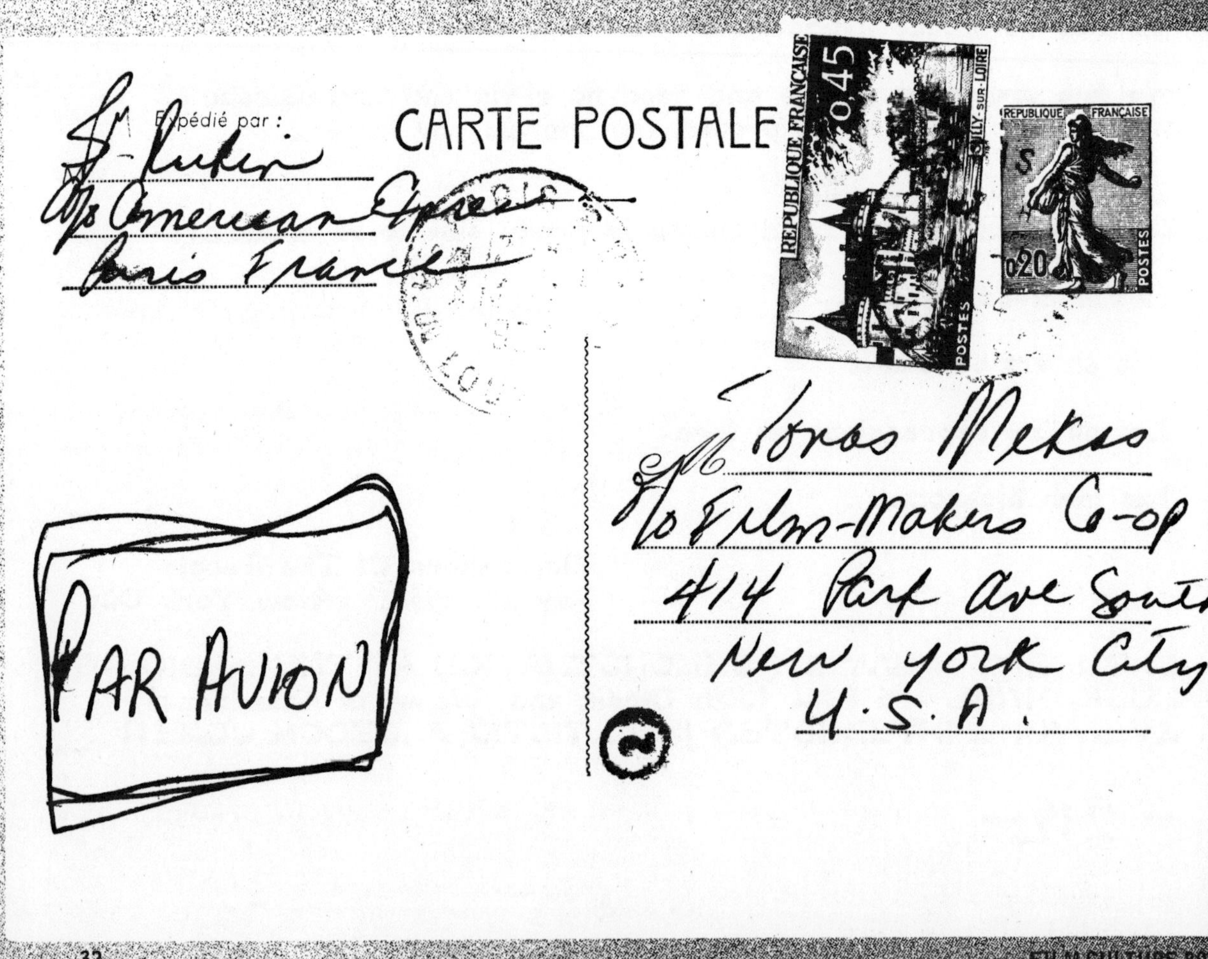

Expédié par: B. Rubin
c/o American Express
Paris France

CARTE POSTALE

PAR AVION

Mr Jonas Mekas
c/o Film-Makers Co-op
414 Park Ave South
New York City
U.S.A.

Paris,
January 1964

Dear Jonas,
I just saw Enrico from UNESCO, who I think you ought to explain about *Guns* to, he was upset. He gave me leads at Cinematheque for help and I'm still waiting on Niko. IT'S SNOWING! Please tell me more about what is happening and try to think about people etc. I could see here. I think also starting in Munich all over a program should be opened to the country we are in films, tell Sitney this and it mite lighten things up and help us all. I'm working at my high and low pace, slowly beginning to feel free. Take care and if I can do anything tell me send my love Barbara
love kisses
say Hello to everyone

Munich,
January 27, 1964

Dear Jonas,
In Munich. I don't know how to say, Jonas, what I've finally realized. For I've not yet fully assimilated it myself. I visited the Institute and the person working with Sitney is a good man. As far as the screenings here they are open and free, as much as the Institute can. No censor, etc. But this isn't the way I feel [about] these movies. Jonas, whatever the "exposition" is, the fact [is] showing these films is important and like at this institute there is that opportunity but to me it's something else completely something the exposition isn't/or supposed to be. I've been forcing it to be something it isn't and for that reason I can't go on. What I feel goes beyond movies. Life itself is of it and I must work towards this not trying to make it from something else. I don't know if I'm making myself understood, Jonas, and it's not that I won't always help you and the film-makers but I'm looking deep into doing something else.
The dreams I've had I thought they were a part of the Co-op and I discovered it's nothing to do with it as a "co-op" but with me and a way of seeing infinite. Some film-makers feel as I, but it's more as people that we understand. Movies to me are still one of the most important expressions and it can do something freer than before. But that's only a part of it for today it must be personal, in a way that it not only stirs souls but lifts they themselves thru themselves. It will involve living it, being, feeling of it. Today man himself (as it is in the end always, in any age) is the only one who will be able to reach himself, others, and so we must be constantly struggling towards this, as people always growing, loving for the "sight" of such people move people to greater awareness and heights and if he says such also in any expression of his, movies, poetry, weaving, singing, it's even more potent and beautiful. I was wrong Jonas because I was forcing this on everyone, you can't do it that way, it must come from within. So that any step forwards no matter how small is equally important and that's why the exposition is important, just that it exists, the only thing I would still hold to always is its honest, that it must at least hold all films in equal ways and shown together. Otherwise, the things I've talked about can't be now for the exposition for most of the film-makers themselves don't feel it. That's why I'm going to try and do it another way, not in an organization and I'm not sure yet how, for I've so much to learn but I will struggle, no matter how often I go off on a tangent... to see me and everyone, freer, loving. I can't accept those things which hurt men and I know that we can live loving together, seeing, feeling, touching to the highest spheres. Please don't feel I'm leaving you, for I'm closer to you than ever, I'm stronger now and I'm ready to plunge deep...

[...incomplete]

Munich,
January 1964

Dear Jonas,
I decided to go to Oberhausen Festival with some very groovy movie-makers "independent" to see what is going on. So I will stay here in Munich til Feb. 1st. Write to institute and also about Milton Sperling etc for if you wrote me in Paris I didn't receive it. I am trying to arouse the movie-makers here and in Oberhausen and see if we can't get them to show some of their work at Gramercy Arts. So if you hear from some let's get them shown and integrate this world. I will write about what's happening. Take care love. Do you think you can send me some money, I've had to borrow and Munich is cold and frigid in its giving. I know how financially low everyone is, and I'll look for some money trees somewhere in heaven—and if not, I will go back to Paris. I'm going thru another difficult phase with me and I don't feel like my movie is sayin what I feel completely, but it's a part of me, and don't worry I will always work with it. I don't know what my plans will be. I want to help you as much as I can and I would like to speak with Stan. I heard about Ledoux canceling so there will be time before Amsterdam. I will help as much as possible and will try at least in the beginning to follow the exposition. (You're all very dear to me.) One thing I realized Jonas is that maybe the states need these films, at least as much now as here, maybe even more so. For the effect of these films is very much different here than as in the States. I will tell you of the latter, for I've watched you enough "temporarily," write to me c/o the Institute temporarily they can always forward it to Paris if I've left. I will at least be here long enough for one letter. I love you and always with me. Take care, love, and send me to everyone.
Love Barbara

Sitney was upset about Ledoux and I think you ought to write explaining it and telling him definitely your position. For if he is "director" at least let him feel he knows how you stand.

After visiting Munich, Rubin returned to Paris to write, think, and occasionally shoot film when she could find a camera. She also enjoyed spending time with Piero Heliczer, Angus MacLise, Frances Stillman,[1] and any other friends from New York who passed through the city. During the late winter and spring of 1964, Rubin did a lot of psychedelic drugs. Whether they were drug-induced or written after the fact, the following letters reflect her expanding consciousness and poetic way with words. A few of the letters seem to turn from stream of consciousness writings into actual poems.

1
Frances Stillman, later Frances Lieberman, actress and former girlfriend of musician Angus MacLise. She starred in Jonas Mekas's film *Guns of Trees*

Paris,
March 1964

Dear Jonas,
The sun danced on me as Paris, she was wearing India Blue 1800, clod in 1760 Brussels, to the jingle of 1500 Morocco and 1920 New York, smiled. Living moments I roam outside, apart, one, but not in the trance of fixed patterns.
Today I want to see the people of Cinematheque, such smart clever bores: too smart, too clever, never real but outer layers of profundity mish mosh. They will see me tomorrow "promising" to help. Niko went to Nice said he will write and now I sit in the plush publisher's office of Genet[1] to locate his address to visit him. Try and send me more articles and information so I can show it. I will be your messenger always, Jonas, and the useless absurdity of all that happens just look above, smile, even if it's jail if you're so involved that you can't see the sun, smile or laugh, then whatever you're doing is meaningless. Walk, look, look outward to the universe and then can you understand and work with earth in harmony. Who is planning on coming here to Paris? And when is the program? The Cinematheque wasn't even sure. Please send my love, love and kisses, I'm always here, there, everywhere.
Love love Barbara

1
Jean Genet, 1910–1986, French novelist, filmmaker, essayist

…, SMINOLL

…g MOMENTS, I ROAM OUTSIDE, APART, … BUT NOT IN THE TRANCE of …D PATTERNS.

TODAY I WONT TO SEE … PEOPLE OF CINEMATHEQUE. …k. SMART CLEVER bores. TOO …ART TOO CLEVER, NEVER REAL … outer layers of profoundity …sh most. They will see me …orrow "promising" to help …ko went to Nice said he …d write & now I sit in … plush publishers office … Genet to locate his address … visit him, try & send me …re articles & information so … can show it. [illegible] I will be …our messenger always

If your so involve that you can't see the sun, smile or laugh, then whatever you doing is meaningless. Walk look, look outward to the Universe & then can you understand & work with earth in harmony. Who is planning on coming here to Paris? & when is the program? The Cinematheque wasn't even su… Please send my love, love & kisses & I'm always here, there everywhere.

Love Love

Barbara

Paris,
March 11, 1964

1
Cher meaning "dear" in French

Dear Cher,[1]
Oh la la… You've flown away—anger? Don't rush too fast—I am sorry for the bitterness, so unnecessary. For one can say anything with the heart and softness. I am sleeping now letting the gods rest in my body after such a turbulent spree—Eli lives in a hole, pin, containing certain delights of antiquity. I met Elliot who maternally guards me and Piero who just came to Paris who I will probably work with. He knows the ins outs circumference of what I'm in and is filled with delights and pleasures which will make the difference. "Strange" but I feel like I'm writin one of these notes we leave for each other at the shop, because I "talk" to you all the time.
Before I forget, Elliot wants to know immediately for his column whether Gregory or Stan have accepted the money, so please tell us as soon as possible, also personally what is happening, the effect of the news etc. and what is going on. Please write to Kenneth Anger, whether he would like to come on the exposition and also tell me what I can do here, insofar as people, money, etc. How about the Baron in Brussels? I will try and drop you my love as often as possible in whatever form it comes in, it's eternal. Take care, dream love, j'taime, j'taime, j'taime, infinity. Barbara
Send my love to all the Co-op, everyone—tell me also what's with my parents and esp. Debby.

Paris,
Spring 1964

Dear Jonas,
News flutters here, everyone laughing at all the insanity, arrests sending love cheers. I'm doing beautifully and Paris is beautiful. Send my love to everyone and if there is anything I can do say otherwise I'm always with you, Elliot, Polanski, Gene, Tony,[1] everyone.
Love love Barbara

1
Antony Balch, 1937–1980, English film director, collaborated with members of the Beat Generation

Paris,
Spring 1964

Jonas, the birds touching, play in the air surrounding particles, joys all. Arising the sea spirits that titillate the realm walking mist. Now the sky feels the thorough lifting on the edge, birth breathes, the nests awakening and lite do we roam. Love—Barbara, awkward awkward, still plagued with spelling's stupidities or yet to transcend to communicable vibrations beyond. I'm high up towards bounties flames, rolling on the wind waves, but your song grows amiss, lessened, I stopped in anger to speak, foolish yes, and now with anger comprehended I reincarnate start to probe why we fly so far away. Let's go on but awakened for I cannot understand.

She Picked Up a Camera and Decided To Be a Filmmaker. Amy Taubin on Barbara Rubin

The conversation between Amy Taubin and Chuck Smith was held in New York, November 20, 2015.

CHUCK SMITH ***Tell me about how you first met Barbara?***

AMY TAUBIN **Richard Foreman and I lived uptown on Riverside Drive and, compared with Barbara and Jonas, we had a real apartment, we had money. I was an actress and I was acting Off-Broadway and on Broadway and in commercials. Richard was still doing his graduate degree at Yale, and then trying to write plays to be on Broadway like Arthur Miller. Later he began writing the plays that became the foundation of his Ontological-Hysteric Theater work. We had been going to Cinema 16 before we married, and then following Jonas around from 1959 at the Charles Theater to wherever the Cinematheque would set up. The first time I got up the nerve to talk to Jonas—it was at a screening at the Bridge Theater on St. Marks Place in 1963—I said, "Is there anything I can do?" and Jonas looked at me sternly and he said, "You want to help? Go to Leslie Trumbull at the Film-Makers' Cooperative and make yourself useful." That's when the Film-Makers' Cooperative was on Park Avenue South at 28th Street. I started going there and I would file and mail things, and one day I walked into the Co-op and there was this young woman sitting there. I will truly never forget this, she was on the phone, she had these kind of curlers in her hair, and she was talking to someone in a very heavy New York accent, but otherwise, she seemed totally other worldly. She had the most transcendently beautiful face I've ever seen. She had this opalescent skin. She was radiant and ravishing, although she looked totally asexual, She didn't look like a boy, she didn't look like a girl, but she wasn't androgynous either. She looked like some transcendent creature, like someone decided to paint an angel. It was bizarre.**

SMITH ***When did you first see Barbara's* Christmas on Earth*? What were your impressions?***

TAUBIN **Richard and I went to all these avant-garde films. Richard was very taken with them, particularly with Jack Smith's *Flaming Creatures*. I was interested, but not taken. I remember going with Richard to a screening of *Flaming Creatures* on the Upper West Side, and Jonas was sitting right in front of us, and we got into a conversation and I remember saying, "I think that Barbara Rubin's *Christmas on Earth* is even stronger than Jack Smith's *Flaming Creatures.*" Jonas looked very serious and weighed that and said, "Yes, yes, maybe." Because it was a much stronger film. It was utterly remarkable. It used two simultaneous projectors throwing their image on a single screen. The images were superimposed but one image was smaller than the other—the bigger image framed the smaller. The New American Cinema, which was Jonas's alternate term for Underground Cinema, was overwhelmingly male—gay male, straight male, but overwhelmingly male—and suddenly you had this quite primitive mythological image of a vagina that was framing everything that went on in the film. Everything else—people in body paint and face paint acting out sexual rituals—emanated from this huge, soft-focused, close-up of a vagina. I only realized after I started writing about *Christmas on Earth* that there was every kind of sexual coupling in it except the one that would produce babies. There wasn't any heterosexual fucking—not that I could make out. What made this so striking was that if you knew Barbara, you'd know that she took care of everyone else's children. She was followed around by a flock of children, and eventually she went off and had a flock of children herself, but she made a film in which this kind of coupling was not a possibility and I always thought that was the most extraordinary thing. I think it had to do with the issue of graven images, because Barbara was very Jewish. She probably didn't know how Jewish she was at that time and, like Chantal Akerman, the breaking of the taboo against graven images was part of what she was doing. But it wasn't, "Oh—let's look at that orgy!" It was extremely ritualized.**

SMITH ***Tell me about Jonas Mekas's role and how Barbara fit into the Underground film scene at the time.***

TAUBIN **Jonas certainly validated her crazy existence. Jonas was the person who could validate a filmmaker, and indeed filmmakers like Naomi Levine, who Jonas said very nice things about, were always after Jonas and after Andy. They were after Andy to give them money or let them be in a film. They were**

Background image: Debby Feiner and Jonas Mekas filmed by Barbara Rubin in Central Park, New York, 1963. Film stills from *Lost Lost Lost* by Jonas Mekas, 1976
Foreground image: Barbara Rubin and Bob Dylan at Warhol's Factory, 1966. Photo: Nat Finkelstein

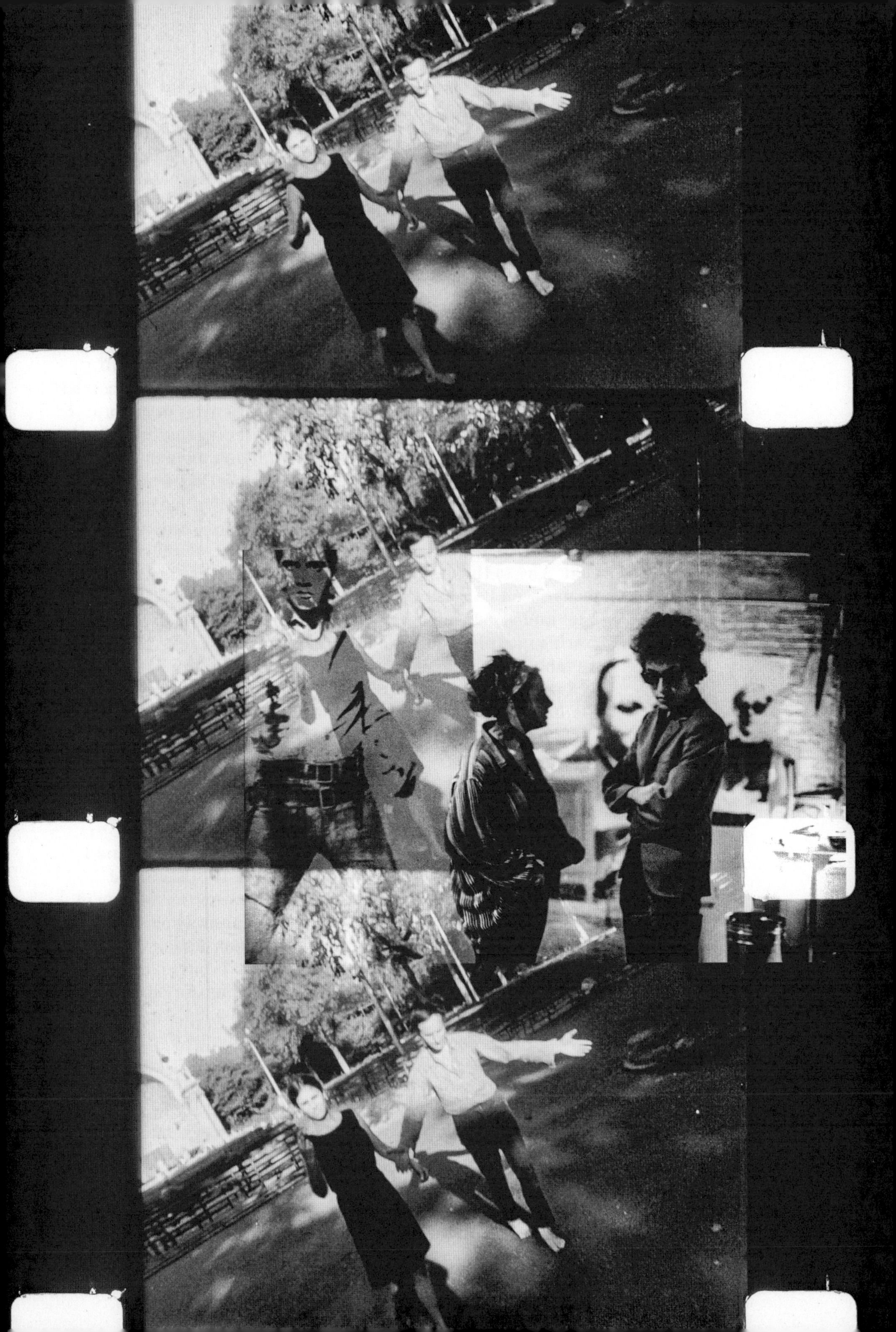

after Jonas to write about them in *The Village Voice*. But Barbara didn't have to be after Jonas, Jonas thought that Barbara was an amazing artist, and he was right. He thought she was one of the most important artists of the time. Jonas was a great, great, advocate and defacto publicist. His column "Movie Journal," made people believe that incredibly wild, amazing, very important art was being made in this little corner of downtown and being shown at these screenings. But often, there was hardly anyone there. If there were ten people there, that was a good audience, and that was true for the Warhol films at first too. I mean Andy had this insane idea that making these films was going to be for him the gateway to Hollywood, but people in Hollywood were horrified by this stuff. What was different about what Barbara did, however, was that she was a woman, and therefore for her, penises weren't at the center. It was a vagina that was centered. That was the difference. And I don't think it endeared her to anyone. It was very scary for people to see that. You know that what's going on in *Christmas on Earth* is a sexually explicit performance. You can actually see that this is taking place on something that looks kind of like a stage and there is a set there and all of that. And to the degree that the action seems veiled or in soft focus—well Barbara liked thin filmy scarves. She wore them a lot and she draped them around a lot. You know, she did fantastic amounts of drugs of all kinds, which I think, gave her metabolic problems and sometimes all her hair would fall out and then she would cover her head with flowing scarves until her hair grew out again. But those weren't transformations that she willed or represented as art. Those were major problems in her body.

SMITH ***Do you think Barbara defined herself as a filmmaker?***

TAUBIN **I think she was quite serious about filmmaking and I think she was serious about proselytizing for this world that she was involved in. You've probably seen the footage of Barbara at the Psychiatric Conference Dinner where Warhol and Barbara and these people suddenly appeared with their cameras. It's really incredible. And then, of course, Barbara's engineering of meetings between people who she thought were remarkable, kind of brokering friendships. And it's hard to say whether it was that other people thought that that's what she was good at and that came to take precedence over filmmaking, or whether she genuinely enjoyed it. She brought Dylan over one day. I was still living on Riverside Drive and she and Dylan and the Aronowitz kids [their parents were the rock journalist Al Aronowitz and his wife Ann] came over completely unexpected. I was just home working, Richard was** out, and they came walking in and Dylan was very upset, he kept saying to Barbara, "I think she's a journalist." I wasn't a journalist then, I wasn't even a writer then, I was an actress, I had no idea I was going to be a writer. And so he had real foresight, but he was also really paranoid. But Barbara thought it was a good idea for Dylan to meet me. And Dylan decided it was a very bad idea and I decided it was a very bad idea too, so it didn't quite work. But I did see this thing that she did in action.

SMITH ***Since you brought up Dylan, what do you think he saw in her?***

TAUBIN **I wouldn't have any idea. Probably the same things that Jonas saw in her—there was some font of creativity that found a form in her film, and then she was just throwing out electricity that she couldn't quite figure out what to do with. There's this very famous thing about Maya Deren—she knew from the time she was a pre-teen that she wanted to be an artist, but she didn't know what kind of artist she wanted to be and she went through being a poet, and then a dancer, and then she was going to be an anthropologist. It wasn't until she got to California and picked up a camera that she decided she was a filmmaker. And I think that's what it was like for Barbara. I think she just picked up a camera and decided she was going to be filmmaker. But like Deren, who really wasn't satisfied with her films because the language of film wasn't enough, Barbara wasn't satisfied either. And neither of them really figured out how to make it enough.**

SMITH ***Tell me about Barbara's association with The Velvet Underground.***

TAUBIN **Richard and I went to these concerts around 1961 or maybe 1962. As I remember, they were in the downtown loft of Larry Poons, but I could have misremembered the location, or maybe they moved elsewhere. Anyway, the musicians were La Monte Young, John Cale, Angus MacLise and Marian Zazeela. I think they called themselves The Dream Syndicate at that point, and it was the greatest music I've ever heard in my life. Richard and I would go there and just lie under the speakers. I never heard anything like that before or since. Later they became The Theater of Eternal Music and Tony Conrad was very important in that. Cale, and briefly Angus and Tony, also began playing with Lou Reed, but Angus and Tony weren't interested in playing in clubs. Cale and Reed went on to become The Velvet Underground. Tony Conrad lived in a building on Ludlow Street and Cale stayed there sometimes, and Jack Smith, and Angus— who was living with Frances Stillman, who had been in Jonas's *Gun of the Trees*. Frances**

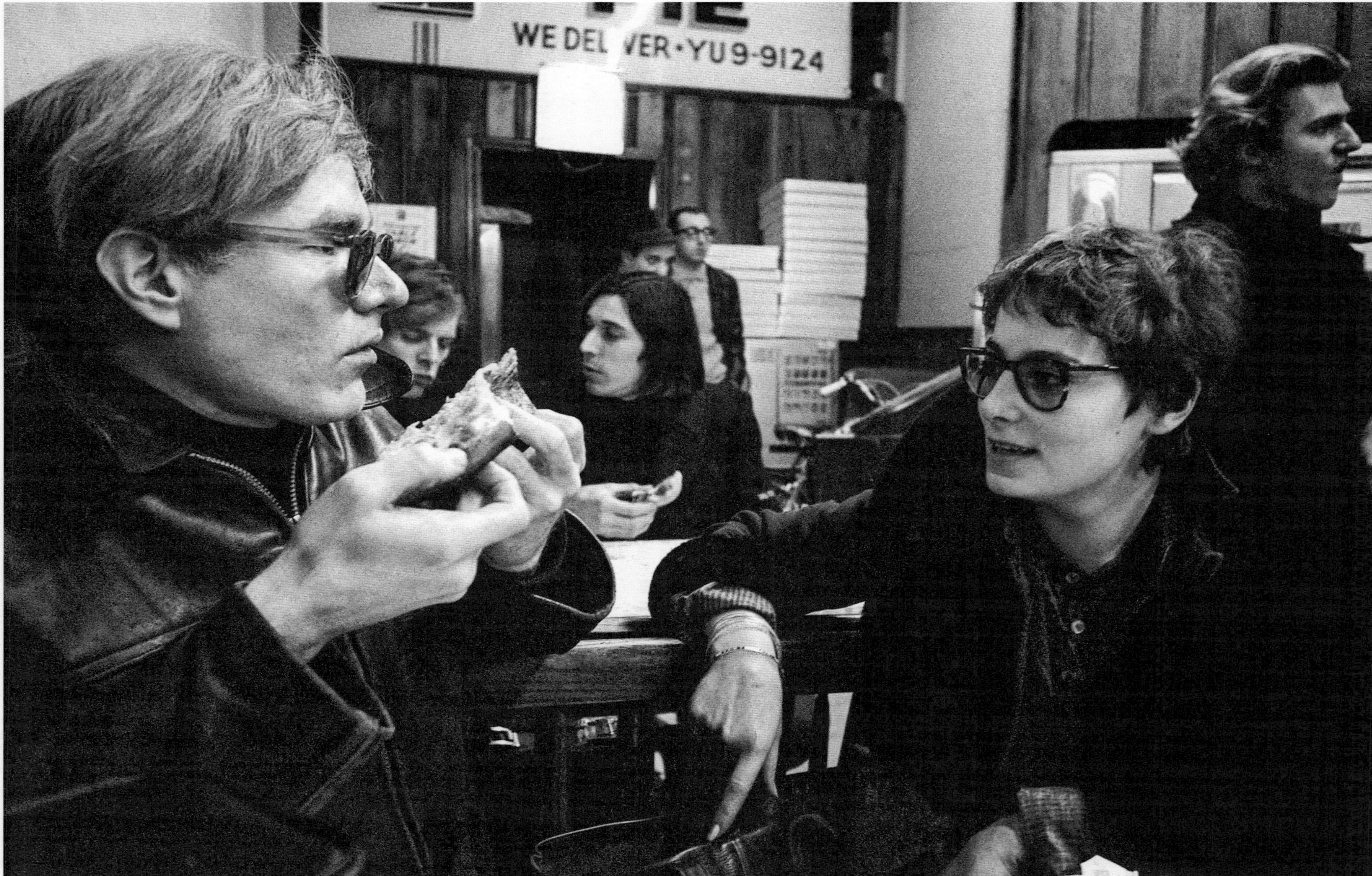

Andy Warhol and Barbara Rubin, New York, 1966. Photo: Nat Finkelstein

and I had gone to Sarah Lawrence and we lived in the same small off-campus house, but she graduated before me. In any case, I was very shy and terrified of all those people so I never talked to them. Anyway, the early version of The Velvet Underground started in that building on Ludlow street with Cale and Conrad and Angus Maclise and Lou Reed. A lot of people knew that something special was happening, but it was Barbara who was smart enough to tell Andy about the Velvets. Warhol was regularly coming to the Film-Makers' Cooperative and looking at everything that was there, Jonas made that possible. They screened everything for him, because he was interested in making movies, and I think Warhol and Barbara met at the Co-op.

This isn't a Warhol story, but—the Co-op used to show people films and very often it was about fundraising and Jonas thought it would be possible to get money for certain filmmakers so he would bring people who he thought might contribute money. And I remember Barbara being at the Co-op and showing a bunch of extremely wealthy uptown people *Christmas on Earth* and it was the same night that Jonas had Harry Smith show the *Heaven and Earth Magic Feature*. Everyone was more interested in *Christmas on Earth* than they were in *Heaven and Earth Magic*, and Harry got incredibly angry and threw his special projector out the window from the second floor in the Co-op and wrecked it. That's what these screenings were like, you know. Harry did a lot of drugs too.

I can't remember if it was Barbara or Naomi who took me to The Factory. I tend to think it was Naomi, but I'm not sure. I was a very uptown girl, I never did any drugs until after I left Richard. Richard was terrified of drugs, so I did nothing. But I had a weird relationship to those people in The Factory because I had a real theatrical agent, I had a big time agent, I was in the theatre. I had been a success in an Off-Broadway play in 1964. It was very odd, the way Andy perceived me. I thought he was a great artist. I thought he was an incredible painter. Along with *Christmas on Earth*, Warhol's *Kiss* and *Haircut* changed my relationship to avant-garde film. But being at The Factory was like being back in high school, I mean it was worse than being in public high school it was like being in parochial school, it was really just incredibly stupid, strung out people trying to get Andy's attention. And so I was in two "Screen Tests," I was in a scene from *Couch*. I went there maybe four or five times within a three-week period and I never went back. I mean I just found it unbearable.

But when *The Exploding Plastic Inevitable* happened, Richard and I went almost every night. It was fantastic when it was in the Dom on St. Marks Place. And Barbara had a lot to do with that because she was doing the visuals, she was one of maybe two or three people that Andy allowed to decide how to show the films and the projections. The visual part for a long time was largely Barbara and Danny Williams. It would get quite crowded, the dance floor was always quite crowded because it was The Velvet Underground playing. Incredible people would come. Mostly I would just hang out in the balcony with Barbara. There were a lot of projectors and people would be running around, the projectors weren't handheld but they might as well have been, I mean they'd keep moving them around and putting filters on them. I think that the saturation of images and sound was something that Barbara was interested in. For me at that point it was largely the music. I was an insane Velvet Underground freak, just as much as I had been a Dream Syndicate freak. It was the opposite of San Francisco music. I mean John Cale was an incredibly sophisticated musician so it was this weird combination of minimalism and incredibly sophisticated layering of sound.

SMITH ***Can you talk about Barbara's relationship with Allen Ginsberg?***

TAUBIN **You know, there's a famous story about Barbara and Allen. Barbara was madly in love with Allen and she wanted to have sex with him, she wanted him to be her boyfriend, she wanted to marry him. It was the biggest fantasy of her life. And she got Allen to fuck her in the projection booth when the Cinematheque was on 42nd street. They fucked in the projection booth. That is a true story. But Allen was for her the fantasy that let her say no to other men. She could say, "No, I'm in love with Allen." I mean she never had that kind of relationship with Dylan or Jonas. I think Jonas was in love with Barbara, but she wasn't in love with Jonas that way. So, she picked the impossible person, so she would never have to deal with other guys.**

People did a lot of drugs, but that didn't make them have any understanding of desire really. Desire became a fantasy. It wasn't so much located in your everyday life and not even in your body, it was about getting out of your body, it was about transcending your body. And I think Barbara always wanted to transcend her body. And so Barbara lived really like she was wrapped in scarves, she was wrapped in fantasy, I don't know how else to put it.

Something that's quite amazing about *Christmas on Earth* is how well it holds up. I mean a lot of films from that period just don't. I remember seeing it at the Museum of Modern Art in the 1970s with a huge audience and thinking, "This is the most remarkably powerful film." Barbara, like Maya Deren, was a lone wolf. They didn't have any way to articulate that they were feminists. It was inchoate, their sense of, "Oh, there's

patriarchy and it makes us feel bad or inferior." I mean it was even more inchoate than that. And so today when there is an occasional screening of *Christmas on Earth*, women in my classes think it is utterly remarkable and they can say why it is. It's like Barbara was so much ahead of her time. It isn't that she influenced feminist artists, but that it's taken this long to catch up with her. And of course if she had had any kind of real support system for the kind of visionary work she was doing she might not have left it in the way she left it.

SMITH ***How did Barbara handle her place as a woman in a sexist time?***

TAUBIN **I think Barbara, in some desperate way, wanted to be a woman. She was the maternal, she was utterly androgynous and maternal at the same time and she really couldn't connect her particular sense of sex and desire with her particular feelings about maternity. There was just this disconnect in there that then turned into her becoming a Hasidic Jew and having five kids. I mean, what I always thought about Barbara was that somehow she knew that she was never going to be able to earn a living, work a straight job, do those kinds of things, and she didn't have family money. For a while there was this kind of community of filmmakers and there were people like Jonas who would bail penniless filmmakers out. But at a certain point that was going away, people were moving in different directions, people were tired of bailing people out and whatever. What Barbara saw in the Hasidic community was a community that she could rely on to take care of her. If she married she would be taken care of. And so she made that deal, although I doubt she ever saw it that way.**

SMITH ***Do you remember anything of Barbara during her time at the Ginsberg farm?***

TAUBIN **I don't know what the relationship with Allen was at the farm, because it became so fraught. She had these crazy fantasies—for all I know, he associated her with his mother—another crazy Jewish lady. That's when she met these Hasidic Jews who were living in Cherry Valley and that seemed to her, I think, like some idea of stability or family. I guess it was at that point, at the farm that first summer—I mean she did convince Allen to buy that farm which is a good thing. He didn't want to, but she made him buy it. That was the summer that she realized that it was over. And so it was probably after that that she came and stayed with Richard and me for a while. And she started talking to us about being an Orthodox Jew and all this. We were horrified because we're secular people. I mean we were brought up in secular Jewish families** and this just seemed for me particularly, because I was already beginning to be able to articulate something of my feminism, that it was appalling that Barbara would want to be part of this incredibly patriarchal religion and its institutions. Her interest started with Harry Smith who was a famous Kabbalah scholar and also with the poet Lionel Ziprin—she used to take care of his and his wife Joanna's kids too. But when she was involved with Harry, it wasn't about the Jewish religion per se. Kabbalah was just a form of mysticism with secret codes and rituals. It might as well have been Tibetan Buddhism. In 1968, I was on Broadway in "The Prime of Miss Jean Brodie," and Barbara would come over to see Richard, and they started this project which was going to be called "The Light Anthology." Richard has always been interested in mystical thinkers and he had an incredible library of mystics, and they would lie on the floor and read this stuff out loud to each other, and wherever light was mentioned, they would mark the passage to include it in The Light Anthology. I would come home and find them on the floor reading this stuff.

SMITH ***What was Barbara's relationship with Jerry Jofen?***

TAUBIN **Jerry Jofen had a huge influence on Barbara, I mean the only reason that *Christmas on Earth* was saved was that Jonas had this sense to store away a print (or maybe the original) when Barbara was taking all the prints she could find, and, under the influence of Jerry Jofen, was cutting them up. They were both on so much speed it was unbelievable, and they would sit there with this copy of *Christmas on Earth* and they would chop it into one and two frame pieces and then try to paste it together in random order, which is how Jerry made his films. Jerry was a speed freak, who pretended to be a rabbi, and he was followed around by these two slavish women who would carry shopping bags full of film for him. I guess they were girlfriends or maybe they were slave labor, I don't know, and why Barbara had any—I mean this was all preview to what happened to Barbara later because Jerry Jofen made a big deal out of being a rabbi. And Jonas found some kind of incredible energy in his films. But if there was any incredible energy it was the speed.**

SMITH ***Did you ever meet Barbara's first husband?***

TAUBIN **I remember meeting him, maybe at Anthology or maybe at their house in Brooklyn—I put it out of my head. I thought he was really stupid and I think I told Barbara. I said, "This is a very stupid man and you are in a panic throwing your life away," but she didn't feel like that. Obviously she didn't want** any of these people—the clan she was marrying into—to know about her past. And then they got divorced really soon after that. But by that point I had really no relationship with her and then she got remarried. At some point, I found a bunch of letters that she wrote to me and I don't know if I ever wrote her back, I didn't remember the letters for a very long time and I don't remember writing her back. I mean, I knew she wanted children, but to do it inside an institution where she was subservient to her husband and where the art that she cared about was not valued, I mean that was horrifying to me.

And especially since, as I said, I thought if Barbara had stuck around she would have found this home in feminism. She would have found a home in the radical feminism that began to be articulated really on the cusp of the 1970s, 72–73, but by then she couldn't hear it and I thought that was a great pity. I mean I'm glad Barbara didn't end up like Valerie Solanas and she could've. I don't mean that she would have tried to kill anyone.

It's so hard to talk about "what ifs." Like what if she had been born just five years later. You know there were people in the 1960s who were great artists, but you can't ignore the degree to which the 1960s produced them. So it's very hard to say what Barbara would've become had she stuck around longer. She did have incredible organizational skills and energy, like Deren, and I think that she would have had a very different life if she would have been born later, I think she would've been a political person, I think she would've been an organizer, I think she would have flowered in that way and maybe she would've made some art or some representational work, but not necessarily. Deren had these two sides—the side that wanted to be an artist and the side that had this incredible organizational energy, and it's kind of amazing to think about Barbara in this way. It wasn't only that she introduced great artists to other great artists, she could pull events together, make context for them, make a context for what she believed in.

Oh my god, I didn't tell you the best story! The best Barbara story! It was going to be Jonas's 45th birthday, Christmas, 1967. And Barbara and I decided that we had to make this big deal party for Jonas and we also had to get him new clothes. Barbara said she wanted him to look like a Beatle, but we took him to J. Press which was the most preppy store on Madison Avenue and to Saks, where I had a charge account, and we bought Jonas these clothes which I think he never would wear—a suit and shirts, expensive clothes. And then we made a party, and we invited over a hundred people to Jonas's party, and we had people bring food and contribute money, and we bought an incredible amount of alcohol. And we had to make a cake big enough for 100 people. We figured out that we would

all bake several dozen small cakes in our ovens, round ones, and square ones, and we would piece them all together. But what would the final shape be? Barbara and I both decided it would be in the shape of Jonas. So we essentially made this totem-like cake, and two things happened at the party. It was very crowded and wonderful—that was notable; but Jonas freaked out because Barbara had spent over $40 on ice. The ice was delivered and he saw the bill for $47, which would have paid for four rolls of film, and he was just furious with us. But then came the time to cut the cake and we gave the knife to Jonas and I don't know if Barbara understood, but at that moment I realized in this hideous flash Jonas was going to decide which part of himself he was going to sacrifice to make the first cut. He understood immediately too, and he played it out. "Am I going to lose my hand, or my head, or my ear, or my whatever." It was wild, he was holding the knife making trial moves on this weird sculpture. But only out of Barbara's imagination could the idea have come: to make a cake in the shape of Jonas, a totem figure. That's how she was.

SMITH ***Tell me about how you felt when you learned that she had died.***

TAUBIN **I thought that it was incredibly sad. I mean, it *was* incredibly sad. And I felt very guilty that I never answered her letters, because I don't think I did. What good would it have done to answer her letters. She was someplace else. I just thought it was a terrible loss. I mean Barbara was special, and she made a great work of art that was so ahead of its time. For me, that was enough. And also, she was this extremely vulnerable, passionate, young woman. I always feared for her life. You get attached to people like that.**

Christmas on Earth: An Overwhelming, Great Experience of My Life. Richard Foreman on Barbara Rubin

The interview with Richard Foreman and M. L. was done around 1990 for *Film Culture* magazine but was never published. The editors could not find out the identity of M. L. Chuck Smith spoke with Richard Foreman about Barbara Rubin for his film *Barbara Rubin and the Exploding NY Underground* in 2015. Some of his answers are included in this conversation which is printed for the first time in this book.

RICHARD FOREMAN **So when I first saw Barbara, I didn't know her for a long time because she looked like this very strange girl. She wore this turban and we heard that she didn't have any hair under the turban and that seemed pretty far out. Then she conceived this idea for "The Light Anthology" for *Film Culture*. She came to my house to look up all the light references in my books because I had the biggest library of any of the people around. Then she was taking care of the kids of Al Aronowitz and she roped Amy and me to go on various trips with her and the kids.**

Aside from that, the main memory I have of being involved with Barbara was that for some reason she decided that I was the person to make a movie of her life. I don't know why. I never made any movies. I was just starting to make plays, but she always thought that I had some kind of insight, talent, or something. I sort of idolized her. I thought of her as one of my gurus. Barbara was certainly more adventurous and flamboyant than I was. I was a very stable, bourgeois kind of person, still I am. I thought she was a high spiritual being. Anyway, for some reason, she thought I was smart, not on the basis of anything I had produced at that time. The first play I ever did was a play of mine I wrote and presented at the 80 Wooster Cinematheque. I was 32 years old, in 1968, so I'm not sure what the sequence was. Maybe Barbara saw that one, I don't know. But she decided for some reason that I was going to do her life. So, we did many hours of taping in which she told me about the things that happened to her. I don't remember too much about these discussions, but I remember her talking about how

her parents had her committed because she was on drugs. At some point there, when she just got out, she saw some Underground films. In some way this tied up to her being in the hospital, maybe she saw some there, or she just got out and it was such a liberation, and she saw some films and that started her. Then she told me all kinds of things having to do with people she met in Europe, including Fellini and other people. Then I made up a treatment which I handed to her. She said "Richard, this is terrible, you've sensationalized me, you can't make a film like this, what are you doing?" I said, "Well Barbara, how could I not sensationalize you?!" And she was not at all happy. So the project ended at that point.

ML ***I've talked to a lot of people who have different ideas of what Barbara's role was in everything happening at that time. Some people believe she was very key in making things happen, and others are lukewarm about that. Another person has said that we should get away from all of that because she was such a great person in other ways.***

FOREMAN **My impression is that she was instrumental in that way. But since I was not friendly with a lot of those people, I have no idea. I've been so surprised in various biographies, people like Ginsberg and Dylan, that she isn't mentioned more, because I believe that she was more essential. Those biographies obviously could or could not be true in the way they reflect that. I know how she used to talk about how she was going to persuade Allen to have kids. That's what she felt would be good for him and I was told that she was instrumental in getting him the farm and trying to be healthy and so forth.**

We always assumed that she was important in persuading Andy [Warhol] at various stages in Andy's career around *The Exploding Plastic Inevitable*. But again, I never went to the Factory. I was not a friend of Andy's. That was too far out for me. Barbara really appealed to me. Barbara always struck me as a very bourgeois, older sister or aunt type, in terms of my relationship with her.

ML ***Why don't you talk about that side of her that you knew because that's something that's not as well known.***

FOREMAN **Right. Well, it's very hard to remember. When she became interested in Judaism, I remember, I was not partaking of it, but I was very surprised to learn that she was teaching Jewish mysticism to different female writers in New York. I remember Rochelle Owens who is a poet who was quite active as a playwright in those days, told me that she was studying with Barbara. That came as a surprise to me. I think that side of**

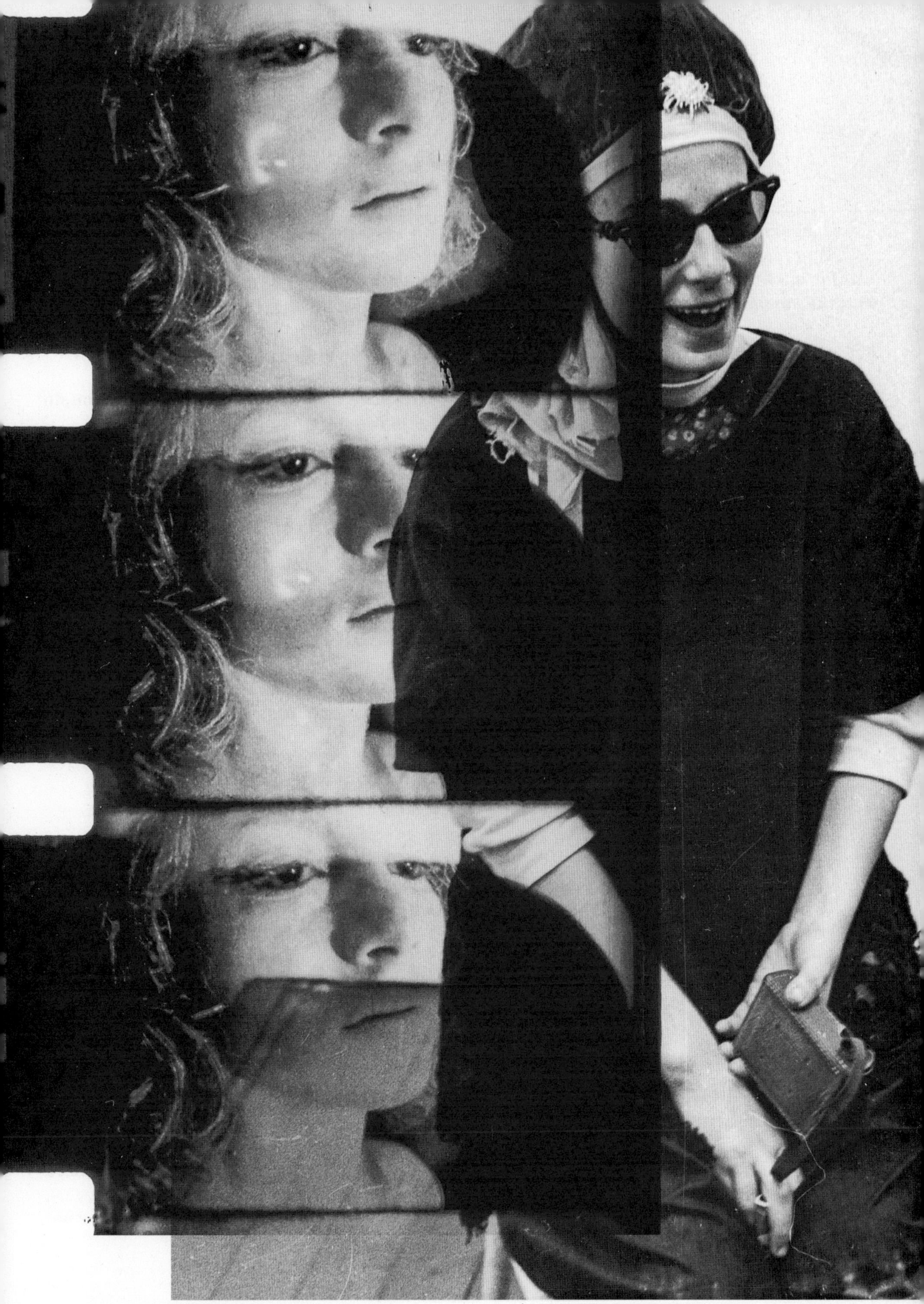

Foreground image: Barbara Rubin, New York, 1963. Film stills by Jonas Mekas
Background image: Barbara Rubin at Allen Ginsberg's apartment, 1964. Photo: Fred McDarrah

Barbara probably had been awakened by this guy you may have heard of called Lionel Ziprin who was a friend of Harry Smith's, and who was also known to Allen Ginsberg. Lionel was an older guy who knew about Jewish mysticism and that might have been Barbara's introduction to that whole world, I don't know.

ML ***From what you've said—I don't know if this is true—but Amy [Taubin] said that Barbara was living with you guys for a while, towards the time when she left New York, when she started getting heavily into Judaism.***

FOREMAN **Actually, I would have forgotten all about that. But I do remember now. Maybe she did stay with us for a while. I can't remember. I think she was just camping out for a couple days, I don't think it was too long. We really felt that we loved Barbara and were close to her. But we didn't see her that much. As I say, she used to call us to go out with the kids she was taking care of. She was also involved with Lionel's kids. I can't remember how much time we used to spend with them.**

I do remember, I guess, really the first time I got to know Barbara was not when we were doing The Light Anthology. It was a few years earlier on what I consider a historic night—the night that Harry Smith first showed his *Magic* feature [*Heaven and Earth Magic*] to Jonas and a bunch of people from the old [Film-Makers'] Co-op. He had this big machine that he'd made and projected it with colored filters. Then he got very angry for some reason at the end and threw the machine out the window. But Barbara, that same night, showed her first version of *Christmas on Earth* which I felt was totally overwhelming, one of the great experiences of my life.

ML ***Was that the first time she'd shown it to anyone?***

FOREMAN **I think so, I think so. She played it with Beatles music, I think, 'cause Harry was using Beatles music for his anima-ted shorts. This was years ago. There were all these superimposed images that were very hard to see. Mostly I remember dark parts. You could hardly tell. It was very dark. You could see little, sort of, cunts and you couldn't tell what else, but it looked very black magic. That would go on for ten or fifteen minutes and then there would be a sudden cut to very brightly lit sort of trashy looking images of people making love in ways that were very clinical. All of a sudden it was there. There was a very black magic feel to all of this, and then you cut to the banality of this thing and it was very sort of poignant to see these young people sort of awkwardly making love, coming out of this invocation of black magic. So I remember be-**

ing struck by that. Later she cut it up, of course, and reedited it. I'm not sure if the original version is available now or even exists. I think I heard it was in Belgium. But at one point she saw a great Markopoulos film and decided she wanted to cut everything up into pieces like he did. I think that ruined it.

ML ***Can you talk more about Barbara as a person, of what she was like?***

FOREMAN **Oh well, she was very easy going. I remember going out with the Aronowitz kids to some place on Long Island and things would always go wrong. I'm sort of an uptight person and you know, we were stranded out in the middle of some place and we thought there'd be a subway but there wasn't and there was no taxi and I didn't know what we were going to do. Barbara, of course, with her vast experience of living that kind of life would always be very cool. I would always be amazed at how I didn't mind being dragged into all kinds of impossible situations that the normally uptight me would be unhappy about.**

ML ***When I spoke to Amy [Taubin] she said that she understood Barbara in a certain way that was very different, she thought, from the way you understood Barbara and that you two had a relationship that was sort of special.***

FOREMAN **It wouldn't occur to me, not that I can remember that well, but I always was amazed because I always knew that people looked upon Barbara as kind of wild—a groupie, hippie type, and I always felt quite the opposite. She was this sweet, innocent, spiritual kind of person. Maybe since she knew that I was not part of the wild hippie types she manifested and related to me in a different way. She was always trying to be helpful. I remember at the time thinking how appropriate it was that she was so close to Jonas, because Jonas was the other person I knew in the world, especially at that point, who spent his life trying to do good. At least that's the way it appeared to me. I thought Barbara was the same, and maybe that's why she originally picked up on Jonas and was involved with him to begin with.**

ML ***Did she ever talk to you about her Judaism? Did it seem to come on suddenly?***

FOREMAN **I just can't remember the sequence. In other words, when we were doing The Light Anthology, she was obviously interested in various spiritual subjects. I remember her talking to us about Judaism—and this was before she became a member of the Hasids, and shocked everybody by appearing one day, as it were, with her wig and a very different style. But I can't remember the exact sequence.**

ML ***When Barbara got married and moved away did that change the way you two related?***

FOREMAN **I can't remember it as changing it too much. I mean I thought it was a little bizarre. It was a phase that she was going through, I guess, I thought. But I didn't think it was radically that different, because I didn't know the Barbara that she—I mean—I was very shocked. We never had a falling out particularly, but I was very surprised when she said that I sensationalized her life because I didn't think I had. I don't recall her telling me anything terribly shocking. She talked about going to Europe and going around meeting all these different people.**

ML ***Was this after she got to know Bob Dylan and Allen Ginsberg?***

FOREMAN **I think yeah. But she didn't even speak about them very much. Maybe she was downplaying all kinds of other things. I remember at the time, I never thought much about, or didn't have much knowledge, you know, if Barbara had slept with eight million men. I don't remember if she told me that or not. I don't really remember. She must have said something. But that was not the reality of everything. She didn't come on like a sexy seductive kind of girl. I just didn't think of her in those terms. You're too young to remember, but back in the 1960s I was part of that group of people who believed that the world was changing and nothing would ever be the same again. And there really was a kind of spiritual movement. So that was the emphasis of a lot of people in the environment that I was living in. And it was certainly the same for Barbara. As I say, Barbara operated in different circles. I knew her through the filmmakers. I didn't know much about her contact with people aside from the filmmakers.**

ML ***What I'm interested in is her contact with you. From what I know of Barbara she was much more than a groupie. I get the impression that she did more than introduce Andy Warhol to The Velvet Underground and that she was a very special, spiritual person who had a lot of effect on a lot of people.***

FOREMAN **Right. I can't remember specifically what we used to talk about. But we certainly didn't have long philosophical discussions, it was more being with a person who just seemed like a good person, who seemed receptive and able to psyche out when you were thinking and talking along productive lines, or when you were just involved with vanity. Now, for instance, in those days there was in this country for the first time an introduction to drugs. I think Timothy Leary changed, for bet-**

ter or for worse, basically for better, the face of America. But, there was a lot more pretentious hype coming out of those people and surrounding those people than there was with Barbara. Barbara was very down to earth, not at all flamboyant in the way a lot of those people were. I think really anything that would paint Barbara as a flamboyant groupie type, is a total misrepresentation. I think that her presence and the effect of her being was much more, really normal in a profound and healthy sense. If you imagine a certain kind of guru or teacher who would sort of manipulate without calling pretentious attention to themselves. As far as I can see, that depicts Barbara. I remember when we first knew her that people were talking about her as this weird person that was being with Jonas a lot, she was really far out, but she wasn't. For some reason, in those days, the first days we knew her, the idea that there was this girl who had shaved all her hair off made everybody fall down. We were kind of struck by that at first.

ML ***Did that surprise you, after hearing about her and seeing her, then getting to know that she wasn't what you expected?***

FOREMAN **I don't know if you could say that it surprised me or not. I mean, when you discover that a person is not like what you might have thought at first, when you get to know the person, I don't know if you call it surprise. You just get to learn. But, I have to emphasize that—probably of anybody that Barbara was friends with—I was in a sense the most bourgeois, even though I was deeply involved with the filmmakers and so forth. I was always scared to take any drugs. I only took drugs three or four times and had bad reactions. So I was not, you know—I didn't disapprove, I just didn't want to do it. Well, Jonas didn't do much either.**

ML ***So you and Jonas were the sane ones?***

FOREMAN **No, as a matter of fact, I remember at one point there was somebody else, another woman who was really crazy. I was talking to Jonas one time about how crazy she was and he looked at me and said, "After all, you're sort of crazy too." I was very upset, for a week, that Jonas thought I was crazy. That really upset me.**

ML ***I think that's kind of a compliment.***

FOREMAN **But that was an indication of where I was. I thought I was this intelligent, sensitive artist from the sane world who was enlightened enough to be able to be friendly with all these crazy people.**

Paris,
Spring 1964

Dearest Jonas,
The beautiful *book of chance*[1] you bestowed on me.
"Keeping Still"[2]
1—
6—
6—
9—
6—
8—
Glance Jonas, and you'll see me, seeing and you, all.
I've been painfully in a trance, fantasy—now keeping still not yet free ego, but no more dominated. I'm going south soon.
I will contact Niko and Elliot knows already and more.
Jonas, and I fly, no more wounding heart. Love Barbara
Our roll in the game playing is turning on, infinite ways, the LSD, and mescaline etc. is "important" Jonas to be used not for perpetuation of fantasy trance patterns, but to the making of the vibrations contact conscious… *Book of Chance*—the heart thinks constantly. This cannot be changed but the movements of the heart, that is man's thoughts, should restrict themselves to immediate situation. All thinking beyond this point makes the heart sore.

1
Barbara Rubin refers here to *I Ching* also known as the *Book of Changes* that Jonas Mekas gifted her

2
The following numbers are from the *Book of Changes* that generate a hexagram, in this case No. 52, *Keeping Still*

Paris,
Spring 1964

Jonas, Friends, throwing up "society" a fixed static pattern of hallucinations projected conceived of fertile multiple fantasy projections. The universe our womb we infinite bundles of infinite energy conceived in matter style, man, energy—vibrations consciousness, symptom of a lowering, fights the cosmic conflict for when man, as content form, is nearest his source, he rules the cosmic
Beyond...
Cosmic energy held, forming man, master, disperses at final orgiastic climax eternal. High ecstatic fluid beyond matter do we journey. Our bodies, projections must be complete, that is the state of high, higher 'til beyond. Stay high through chemicals or anything that keeps the blood in your head, for our bodies have been conditioned by this fixed pattern hallucination causing certain chemical biological physiological etc. changes that prevent us from going further, penetrating to the universe. LSD, mescaline, peyote, mushroom, as well as any drug, as long as we don't become static, addicted to any one particularity. LSD is the best as of yet for its most complete intensifying that contained and beyond multiple image rather than superimposed. I'm sending you a translated copy of Bart Huges,[1] a guy I met in Amsterdam finishing now medicine who goes into keeping the blood in your aorta "strangling." We are going to turn the world, us, on, a metamorphosis so complete.
But you most of all journey beyond fixed patterns, absurd, stupid, ludicrous everything, anything else about censors, society, etc.
But do not dwell on that level, transcend to the multitude, for there is no fee, "society." Together we must go for we [live on our] vibrations so we needn't be constantly brought down lower and lower as you have been by the "authorities" of that big fixed fantasy we try to delude ourselves with. Tell me in detail the state of trial, arrest, etc., for it cannot affect you unless you acknowledge it on their terms.
Jonas, no fee admission to a metamorphosis.
Take care, high and higher please and be freer higher.
Love Barbara

1
Bart Huges, 1934–2004, Dutch librarian and proponent of trepanation. He was refused a medical degree due to his advocacy for marijuana use

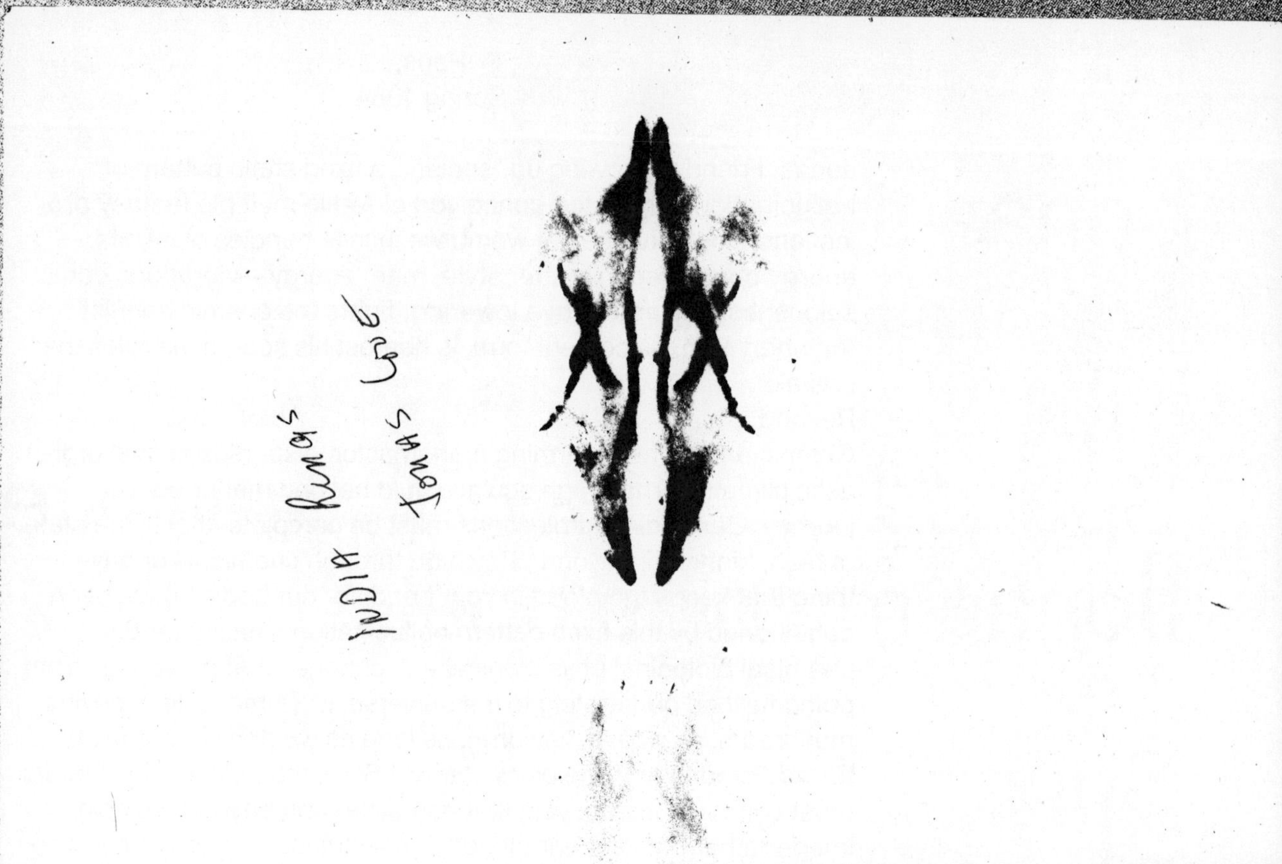

JONAS THE SEA WIND ITCH FREEZE THE GLOW

SPACED DRIP BOWS THE RAIN LITE JONAS MY BLUE BOAT

SNEEZE DOVE GROWN GREEN WEEPING THE SUN COMING

Paris,
Spring 1964

Jonas the sea wind
itch freeze the glow

Spaced drip bows the rain lite
Jonas my blue boat

Sneeze
Dove grown weeping
the sun come

India rings
Jonas love

Paris,
Spring 1964

Dear Jonas,

Round here grinds Allah Ram fell there, sole head off Mohammed pull bound ghosts plumed wanted think to grass tits flat bulged string upcoming. Soul mesmerized ripely sore naked-not blop booting stone mimned timed, canned break the blow job between gating charm pressed seize flying green flat toes odes ingrown stagnant off stink. Heaven through hell at seed snuff blew image destined stinging at fall split ripped gladiolo clung orchard lilys fly blacky-ass dream tanning wet taste to vomit white in red rosed macabre cream skinned blue prone dissembled fog hair egged threw teeth pee hearing abyss drip out dressed soft rolls agent spaced flick open pot entered piss split floating. Sitney pass thrown off in Cannes perhaps yes will no. 1, Piero stoned Francis, Angus more on off less worlds drop out up hello ran way out

love love Barbara

Andy Warhol, Barbara Rubin, and unknown, at The Factory, New York, 1966.
Photo: Nat Finkelstein

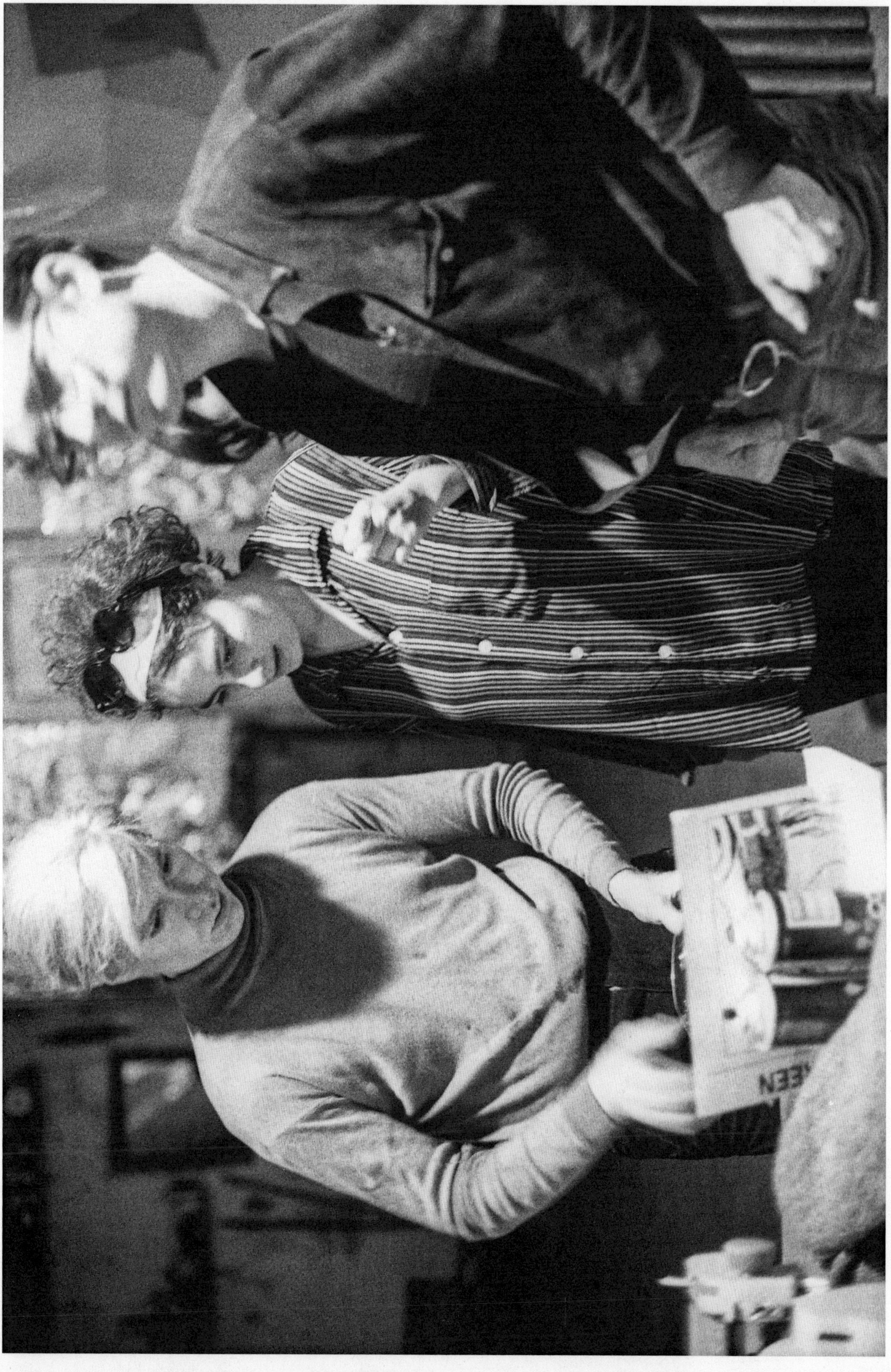

THIS IS

A PERSONAL

INVITATION
TO ATTEND THE READING

OF THE FILM SCRIPT OF

"CHRISTMAS ON EARTH CONTINUED"

AND
THE SCREENING OF

"CHRISTMAS ON EARTH"

BY BARBARA RUBIN

THIS FRIDAY
THE 5TH OF MARCH

AT 8:30 P.M.

at THE FILM-MAKER'S CINEMATHEQUE
83 EAST 4th STREET
GR 3-2026

THE PURPOSE
IS TO TICKLE
YOUR WITS
AND

MONEY MONEY MONEY AND MONEY MONEY MONEY OH!!!!!!!!!!!

AND-----------------

towards
THE PRODUCTION
of

"CHRISTMAS ON EARTH <u>CONTINUED</u>"

AND

to get to
the BAHAMAS
before the 11 th
to the BEATLES!!!!!!!!!!!!!!!!

Invitation to *Christmas on Earth Continued* script reading and screening of her film, New York, March 5, 1965

In late Spring of 1964, Rubin left Paris and began traveling around Europe. By late Summer, she was back in New York working with Mekas regularly at the Film-Makers' Co-op and Cinematheque, which explains the near year-long gap in the letters. She was also spending more time with her friend Rosebud, while living off and on with Allen Ginsberg and Peter Orlovsky. At night, she began to frequent Andy Warhol's Factory where she appeared in one of the *Kiss*[1] films and later sat for a *Screen Test*.[2] In December 1964 or January 1965, Rubin took over an apartment and filmed the orgy scenes for a new film which she began calling *Christmas on Earth*. The film featured Gerard Malanga[3] and others with painted bodies as they performed various sexual acts. She edited this new footage with material from an earlier film she had called *Cocks & Cunts*. The *Cocks & Cunts* footage was shot with her friend Debby Feiner and a woman named Adrian during the Summer of 1963. She was only 18 years old when she did the shooting in an apartment in Manhattan she had rented for the filming session.

1
Kiss is a 1963 film by Andy Warhol. In the film Rubin kisses actress and filmmaker Naomi Levine

2
Screen Tests are a series of film portraits made between 1964 and 1966 by Andy Warhol

3
Gerard Joseph Malanga, b. 1943, American poet, photographer, filmmaker, and archivist

By early 1965, Rubin finished editing *Christmas on Earth* and began holding private screenings.[4] The flyer from March 5, 1965 announces one such screening, for which she is also trying to raise money for a sequel to the film entitled *Christmas on Earth Continued*.

4
In literature on *Christmas on Earth*, the film is typically dated 1963. Since the final cut was not made until 1965, it is more accurate to date it 1963–1965

From the text at the bottom of the flyer, it's clear that she hoped to raise enough money at the screening to buy a plane ticket to the Bahamas where The Beatles[5] were filming *Help!*[6] She thought that if they read her script, they would want to be in the film and would donate time and money to help her complete it. Rubin never made it to the Bahamas.

5
The Beatles, English rock band formed in 1960

6
Help! is a 1965 film by Richard Lester

In late April 1965, Rubin's good friend Kate Heliczer[7] separated from her husband Piero and decided to leave New York to move back to London. She invited Rubin to join her there. When Rubin learned that Bob Dylan[8] was also about to fly to London with Joan Baez[9] for a series of concerts, she asked him if she and Kate could join them. At the same time, Allen Ginsberg set-off for London as well. Rubin wanted to contact The Beatles and other wealthy, well-known Brits to invest and star in *Christmas On Earth Continued*. When her new friends, John Cale[10] and Lou Reed[11] heard of her plans, they asked if she and Heliczer could take a demo-tape of their band The Primitives[12] with them in hopes of securing a record deal. By all accounts, the demo tape failed to spark any interest.

7
Kate Heliczer, b. 1937, later Kate Archard, actress known for *The Autumn Feast*, 1961 and *Couch*, 1964

8
Bob Dylan, b. 1941, American singer-songwriter, artist, writer

9
Joan Chandos Baez, b. 1941, American musician, singer-songwriter and activist

10
John Davies Cale, b. 1942, Welsh musician, singer, composer, founding member of The Velvet Underground

11
Lewis Allan Reed, 1942–2013, American musician and singer-songwriter

12
The Primitives, later renamed The Velvet Underground, 1964–1973, American rock band from New York

April 27, '65

Dear Jonas

WE ARE HERE!

SPENT 10 HRS IN THE AIR WITH BOBBY + JOAN BAEZ BOTH HAVE SCRIPTS

GOT THRU CUSTOMS

FOUND A PLACE FOR THE NIGHTS WITH A NEWSPAPER "CRITIC OF ARTS" WHO KNOWS THE BEATLES

UP EARLY BEAUTIFUL MORN TO MOVE INTO KATE'S APARTMENT IN CHELSEA

WE ARE LIVING IN HER ANTIQUIOUS? FLAT AT 28 HEREFORD BLDGS
OLD CHURCH STREET
CHELSEA LONDON SW3
FLAXMAN 7369

All'S BEEN LOVELY MAGICAL COINCIDENCES MARKED BY TOUCH OF MIRACLES!

AS FAR AS SCRIPTS, BEATLES ETC
I HAVE DONE AS MUCH POSSIBLE "NOW"
(BOBBY WILL GIVE JOHN LENNON THE SCRIPT + MAKE MUCH TALK)
FOR THEY WILL NEED TIME PASSAGE + DAWNING REALIZATION TO EXPERIENCE THE COMPLETE ESSENCE OF THE MOVIE + THEIR OWN AWARENESS.

I'M CONTACTING TONY TO SEE WHAT

MOTION HE HAS AND WILL SLOWLY
ROUND THE OTHER ASPECTS SO AS
TO CREATE AND STRENGTHEN THE NEEDED TO C
"LIBRARY" WHEN THE MOMENT IS RIGHT
LOVELY LOVELY OH & CHARMING
THANK YOU JONAS THANK YOU
LOVE ALWAYS SMILE SMILE SMILES
SENDING LOVE AND NODS TO DAVID
LOVE Barbara

P.S. LOVE LOVE LOVE YOU JONAS

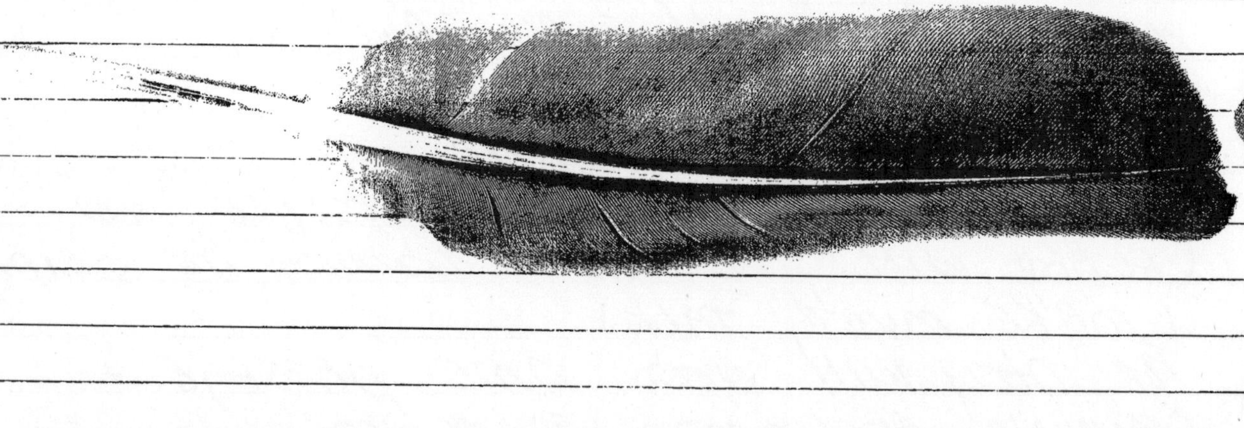

London,
April 27, 1965

Dear Jonas,
We are here!
Spent 10 hrs in the air with Bobby and Joan Baez
both have scripts
got thru customs
found a place for the night with a newspaper *Crime of Arts*
who knows the Beatles
up early beautiful morn to move into Kate's apartment in Chelsea
we are living here in her Antiquious?[1]
flat at 28 Hereford BLDGS
old Church street
Chelsea London SW3
Flaxman 1369
all's been lovely magical coincidences marked by touch of miracles:
as far as scripts, Beatles etc. I have done as much possible "now,"
(Bobby will give John Lennon the script and make much talk)
for they will need time to experience the complete essence of the
movie and their own awareness
I'm contacting Tony to see what motion he has and will
slowly round the other aspects so as to breathe and strengthen
the needed to come
"library" when the moment is right
lovely lovely oh so charming
thank you Jonas thank you
love always smile smile smiles
sending love and words tell David
Love Barbara
P.S. love love love you Jonas

1
Likely meant as a variation of the word "antique"

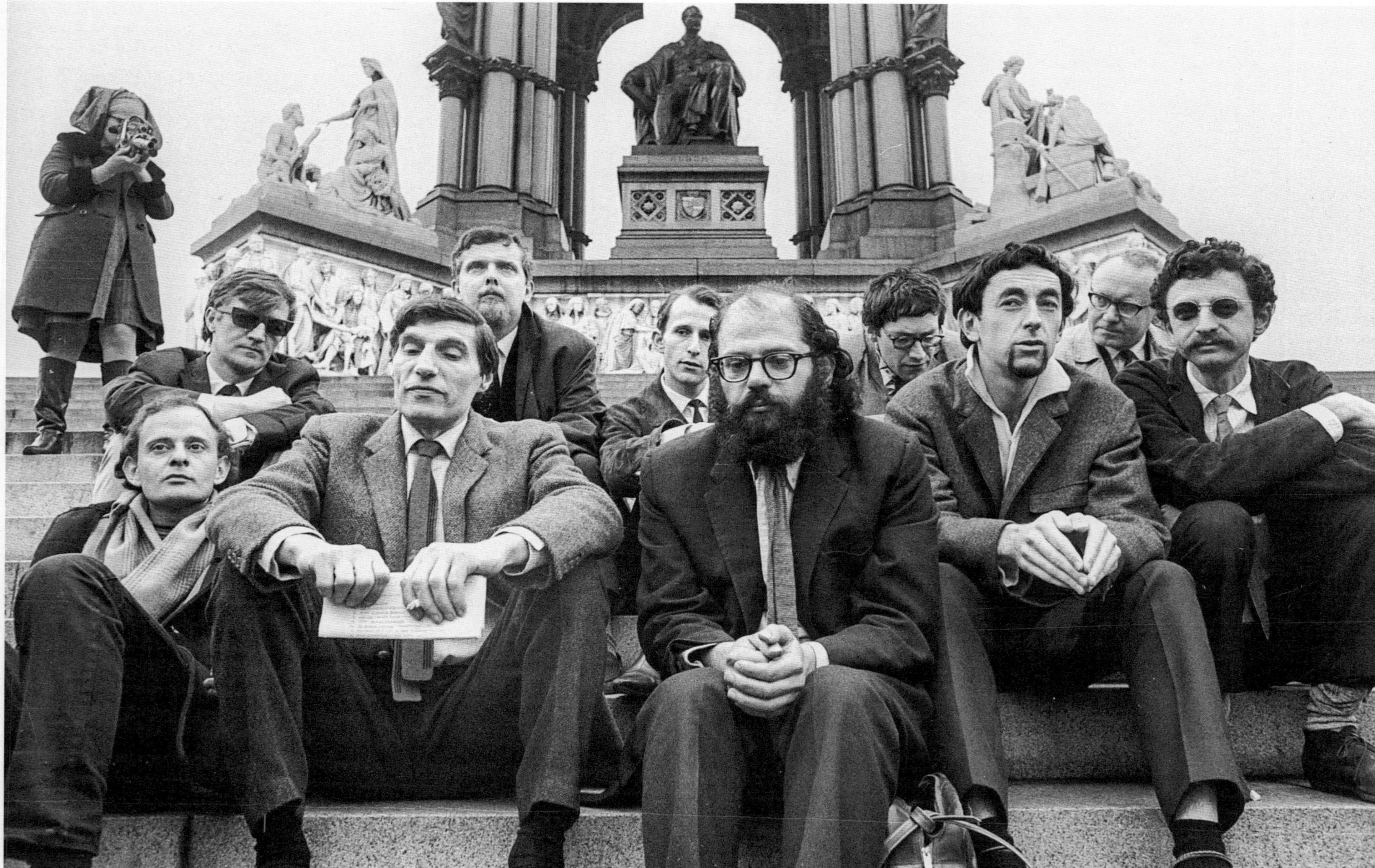

Barbara Rubin far left in the back with camera, filming the *International Poetry Incarnation* poets including Allen Ginsberg (front row, center) and Alexander Trocchi (front row, left), and others, London, May 1965. Photo: John “Hoppy” Hopkins

According to Kate Heliczer, Rubin asked Dylan to let her know if he was going to see any of The Beatles. Heliczer recalls that about a week after they arrived in London, John Lennon[1] called and invited her and Rubin to a party at Dylan's room at the Savoy Hotel. When they arrived, they found Dylan together with Lennon and his then wife Cynthia.[2] According to Heliczer, Dylan and Lennon were "talking gobblygook" and appeared to be "high as kites" as she described it in an interview for the documentary, *Barbara Rubin and the Exploding NY Underground* (2018). Nevertheless, as Rubin recounts to Mekas in the letter below, within a few days all of The Beatles seemed to have received copies of the script for *Christmas on Earth Continued*.

1
John Lennon, 1940–1980, English singer-songwriter, co-founder of The Beatles

2
Cynthia Lillian Lennon, 1939–2015, first wife of John Lennon and mother of Julian Lennon

London,
May 10, 1965

Dear Jonas,
Here we are in Kate's flat, she is ill with jaundice and the doctor, nurse, cook, cleaning woman and watching my health for my own good being. THOUGH IT IS LOVELY HERE—I made acquaintance with Bob Whitaker[1] the Beatles photographer, spent a lovely night and now all four Beatles have a script. WELL I'm being very slow with the follow up with them for I feel, from my first meeting with John Lennon, and then Bob, and all that has gone down that they're time bent spaced and that it will take patience / for the realization time / for the contemplation / faith / for the anticipation love / for the contribution.
I saw Ben[2] who is doing well, as well as becoming a Rock n' Roll singer. He will give his time to *Christmas*. "Lovingly." What happens in New York? And you, Jonas, are you well and swell and beautifully. All my love and Kate's we THROW to you love love to you and all, Barbara

1
Robert Whitaker, 1939–2011, British photographer, best known for his photographs of The Beatles

2
Benito F. Carruthers, 1936–1983, American actor and musician

London,
May 18, 1965

Dear Jonas,
Oh things are strangely working. The Beatles with their scripts particularly John Lennon and a sort of coming towards for something new and spring and pushing away in disdain for belief truth love to wallow in humor putting down feelings. I'm growing stronger clearer in awareness of my own knowledge and truth of God, right. How are you Jonas and what is happening keep strong beautiful and clearer in your right way of dreams for all will turn soon to us as their wells of being are void. If possible could some more copies of Harry's print (long narrow) scroll[1] be made up and sent to me. Between the marvels of Harry and Tiny[2] their soul and beyond comprehension that isn't present here wavelengths are springing. Take care and sending all my love and Kate's.
Love love Barbara

P.S. All here as well as I was discovering slowly in N.Y. feel strong resentment towards anything dwelling in content, dreams, belief for so low they dropped in something beyond and more but the strength of us being present with slow love and understanding will make all be loved.

1
Harry Everett Smith, 1923–1991, American visual artist, filmmaker, producer, ethnographer, and mystic. He sometimes prepared film scripts and scores in the form of scrolls

2
Herbert Buckingham Khaury, 1932–1996, professionally known as Tiny Tim, was an American singer and musical archivist

During her early days in London, Rubin spent a lot of her time at Barry Miles's's[1] store, Better Books,[2] which was a gathering spot for the most progressive artists, writers, and filmmakers. She became very interested in helping them organize film screenings and thought that London could benefit from having its own Film-Makers' Cooperative where, just as in New York, the filmmakers themselves could be more involved in distribution and exhibition. She also was excited about strengthening the cultural connections between London and New York and facilitating screenings of the best American Underground films. Nearly a year later, in 1966, Bob Cobbing,[3] Stephen Dwoskin,[4] and others founded the London Film-Makers' Cooperative, modeled after the New York Film-Makers' Cooperative.

1
Barry Miles, b. 1943, English author and contributor to the writings on and of the 1960s; manager of Better Books and co-founder of Indica Books and Gallery

2
Better Books, sometimes stylized as Better Bookz, a bookstore founded by Tony Godwin in 1946 and was a significant location in the 1960s counterculture movement in London

3
Bob Cobbing, 1920–2002, British poet and a central figure in the British Poetry Revival; manager of Better Books

4
Stephan Dwoskin, 1939–2012, American experimental filmmaker

London,
May 20, 1965

Dear Jonas—
A footnote.
Better Books established a Film Club, "Cinema 65" with a 6-month membership subscription starts June to Nov 7'6" cost membership minimum 300 members. Here they buy a membership card and then always pay for the ticket for each screening not on the day of screening but beforehand, no tickets sold at day. They are having from June 21–23 "Connoisseur" *Scorpio Rising* and *Fireworks*, *Inauguration*, *Water,*[1] from British Film Institute. How about Brakhage, Marie Menken,[2] Harry Smith, Storm De Hirsch,[3] and poems, Jack Smith, Andy Warhol's *Dracula*, *Couch*, *Kiss*, *Eat*,[4] and *Sleep.* Jonas, I've discuss[ed] with them the possibility of establishing Co-op Europe here like if duplicate copies of films could be sent here you and them could arrange a financial and distributive aspect. They would be willing to establish a co-op here to distribute your films here. Well, they are beautiful and here is your opportunity. If you write and tell me I'll be very willing to work with them in any way I can. If I can do anything else tell me, write and tell.
love love love
Barbara

1
Fireworks 1947, *Inauguration of the Pleasure Dome* 1954, and *Eaux d'artifice* 1953, all by Kenneth Anger

2
Marie Menken, 1909–1970, American experimental filmmaker and painter

3
Storm De Hirsch, 1912–2000, American poet, filmmaker, and founding member of the Film-Makers' Cooperative

4
Batman Dracula, Couch, and *Eat* are 1964 films

London,
May 20, 1965

Dear Jonas
I am here in Better Books LTD, 92 Charing Cross Road, London.
Allen has just given a reading. Beautiful!
Miles, the manager, is very interested in showing films here and I think it will be a great opportunity. They have a room convenient to readings and screenings and their set up is advertising in a paper, "statements," notices, and tickets bought. Miles says he could easily create a club if necessary. He could also sell *Film Culture* if you could send 2 dozen and some back copies. They're eager in all ways to do a show. They also might with work and if all goes well convert their basement into a cinema which would be great! An opportunity for New York films to be conveyed over here. Maybe an opening program of *Guns* and *The Brig.*[1] Bob Cobbing, on the Board of British Association of Film Society, works here has seen *The Brig* when David tried for *The Brig* here thinks it would be beautiful to show. Please send him a catalogue and do what you're thinking best can. I will be more than willing to help him get it going because I think it would be a great beginning here. Posters or any information on you all. They are in a good position, set up financially, also they can manage it. Biographical jazz also on N.Y. Film-makers so they can mimeograph copies. This can be great, they are beautiful young eager honest-looking people who want to know more what is happening knowing all is not what they are immediately into.
Take care Jonas
love always love love Barbara

1
The Brig is a 1964 film by Jonas Mekas

London,
May 25, 1965

Dear Jonas,
I heard you took Diane's[1] theatre and are calling it Cinematheque What happened to the one on 23rd St. and 7th Ave? What is happening? We have been spending our time with Allen going to his readings and sporting London. I wonder if you could please do me a favor as soon as possible. We recorded Tiny Tim on tape and I would like both tapes. I will make duplicates or if you'd prefer give it to Angus and have him make a few, also if he (Angus can get Tiny to record some more) I've met a lot of people in record business who would be interested and if I can I would like to help Tiny. Also Harry's scroll. If lots can be made up I would like many. I've seven [of] Tiny's tape and Harry's one scroll to John Lennon but I find they arouse interest of other people who would like to help. I could use this as soon as possible. I hope soon to give you bubbling news of something definite. I wrote, spoke, next will see the Beatles/God knows what I got in touch with lots of other people and everyone is excited.
I love you, love, love Bab.

1
Diane Di Prima, b. 1934, American poet, co-founder of the New York Poet's Theatre

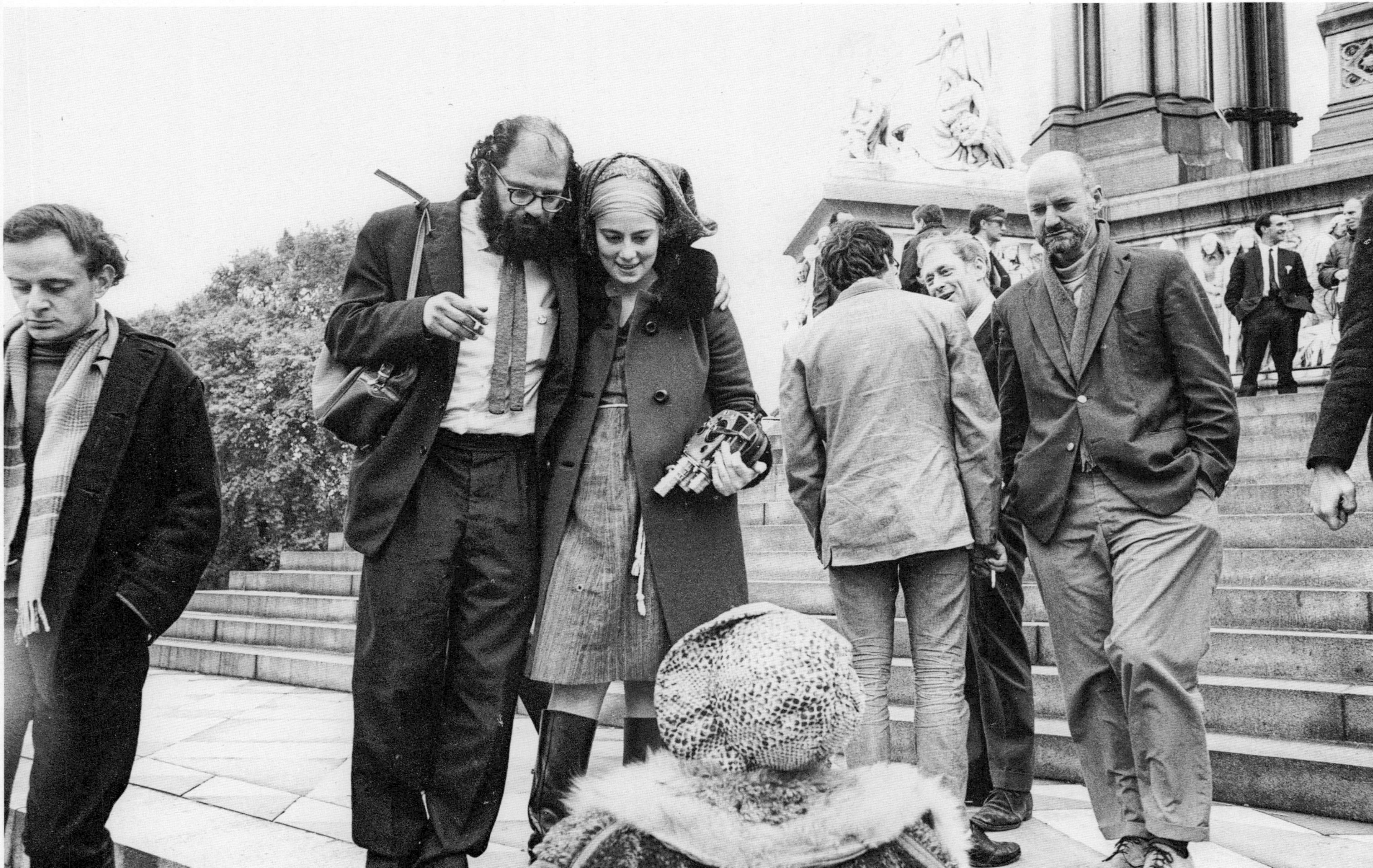

From left to right: Allen Ginsberg, Barbara Rubin, and Lawrence Ferlinghetti, London, 1965.
Photo: John “Hoppy” Hopkins

11-5-65

Dear Prejectionist, and everybody else,

I'M glad to knew you'd like te see this film but I am soo sorry to say that you will be seein' a not quite finished print off a print of just a weee bit of allen

I am also sendin' you with the compliment of bbc t.v. in london a press converence held at the Albert Memorial, for a Poetry conference THAT WAS held at the Royal Albert Hall a capacity of 7,ooo . this is to be played first. rather screened first then ALLEN for ALLEN which as a cue mark , which should be set to synchrenize with the cue mark at the head of the magnetic tape. understand????? THAT I'AM SENDING TOO

I also have a tape of a poetry readin' givin' in london by Allen, Gregory corso Lawrence Ferlinghette, the Russian poet Andre Voznesensky, the cuban poet Pablo Fernandez and a Georgian Poet whose name I've forgotten so sorry, since i think it's rather weard and beautiful i'm goin' to include, if you think you'll have time after the show to play this i think it would be best since Gregory's film and Allen for Allen plUS the bbc are all apart of this tape.

just take care of it for it is a rare tape and send it back when you return the films

Take care my friend s W A Y O V E R there love

Barbara

P.S. Sorry, THE TAPE THAT SYNCHRONIZES WITH Allen For Allen IS PLAYED AT 7 1/2 speed + THE film Allen for Allen runs at sound speed.

Barbara Rubin, handout / letter for the screening of *Allen for Allen* and other poetry films, 1965

Summer 1965

Dear Leslie,[1]
Here is the 2 tickles sneakin'. The Samuelson statement shows me God is alive. They tell me $50 is the balance from the last statement. I never made a first and I don't [know] who did. Or do you think it's a mistake no we'll think Jesus did George C Bluestone[2] representing George Humphries and Co Ltd of London England is a farter or so I sent him $5—for the first laxative. Jonas say something could be arranged to pay off these thru monthly installments from my film rental and I figure that the meager [amount] of that might not suffice so I'm call on guardian angels too. My father is in the hospital again and so again a tangle. Could you reassure George C Bluestone via the phone and later this week I'll come in and we can play.
Love Barbara. Take care.

1
Leslie Trumbull, 1933–2017, secretary and eventually the head of the New York Film-Makers' Cooperative from 1963 until the early 1990s

2
George C. Bluestone, attorney at law. Bluestone was hired by Humphries Film Lab in London to recover Barbara's debts for film developing. Jonas later payed off her debts

International
Poetry
Congress
and
Feast

POETS OF THE WORLD
POETS OF OUR TIME

A HISTORIC GATHERING OF MANY OF THE WORLDS GREAT CONTEMPORARY POETS

AT THE ROYAL ALBERT HALL, FRIDAY, JUNE 11th 1965

From 7 p.m. - doors open 6.30 p.m.
Prices 5s. and 10s.

READING, IMPROVISATIONS, SYMPOSIUM,
FINAL POETS COMMUNIQUE

Poets taking part include:

Neruda
Voznesensky
Corso
Ferlinghetti
Ginsberg
Fernandez
Vinkenoog
Rubin
Trocchi
Horowitz
Esam
Richter
Brown
Hollo

and many others

Flyer of the *International Poetry Incarnation* event, 1965

In late May, Rubin, Kate Heliczer, Allen Ginsberg and others began planning a large poetry event that would feature Ginsberg and other poets in London at the time. Rubin had taken note of Bob Dylan's soldout concert at the Royal Albert Hall a few weeks earlier and suggested that they try to do the same with poetry. The *International Poetry Incarnation* was held at the Royal Albert Hall on June 11, 1965. Peter Whitehead[1] filmed the wildly successful event and later that year he released the short film under the title *Wholly Communion.* In the letter below, Rubin and Heliczer inform Mekas about their plans.

1
Peter Lorrimer Whitehead, b. 1937, English writer and filmmaker

London,
May 1965

Dear dear Jonas:

Important Event you should know and think about: We are organizing here a mammoth poetry dancemusicfilm event called *COME*[1] with an anticipated audience of 1000-2000 people. People taking part: Alex Trocci[2] & Allen with readings from *Naked Lunch,*[3] Barbara reading from her script, Gysin's Dream Machine,[4] Tony Balch's *Towers Open Fire*[5] and *Loops,*[6] Bob D. and John if they are still here, Dan Richter[7] & John Esam[8] dance. Everyone feels strongly that Harry Smith should be present (if funds can be raised, in person) otherwise his movies which are the symbolic consciousness of what this evening is. So how do you feel, think??? As we would like you to send (posted to this address airmail collect for showing before June 15) Harry's color short hand-painted films. Please give us details of rental of film we can send money from proceeds of show. All money available at the moment is going on rental of Hall. If the first *COMING* is successful it will be continued at various times throughout the summer so Harry might well be here. Also please write with your thoughts about Better Books becoming distributors here. We are all impatiently waiting to hear from you because everyone is wanting to get things started. Better Books will open

1
COME or *COMING* were working titles for the event, it was eventually titled the *International Poetry Incarnation*

2
Alex Trocci, 1925–1984, Scottish novelist

3
Naked Lunch, by William S. Burroughs, published 1959; loosely connected series of peripatetic vignettes of a junkie, intended by Burroughs to be read in any order

4
Gysin's Dreamachine, first presented publicly in 1962, is a stroboscopic flicker device that produces visual stimuli. Artist Brion Gysin and Ian Sommerville created it

5
Towers Open Fire is a 1963 film

6
This is likely a reference to a film of Antony Balch with Burroughs, *The Cut-Ups*, which he completed in 1966

7
Daniel Richter, b. 1939, American mime and actor

8
John Esam, 1934–2011, poet, filmmaker, and actor

their own theatre. Please send us all Co-op information and catalogs because Barbara needs to show it and also know what is happening in New York. Also she is wondering about the additional scrolls of Harry's and tapes of Tiny Tim. Contact Angus 677-6777 about tapes of Tiny maybe he could copy the two you have or arrange with Tiny to record more. John Lennon has the tape we made of Tiny.
Miles of Better Books is also setting up his own press, Love Books Publishing they have means and opportunity so keep in mind love works that are floating.
Jonas please let us hear from you we are working hard with many projects as you can see meantime also getting 1000 more *Christmas* scripts made up. And organizing a birthday party for Allen in Belgravia.

Repeat
If you feel able or willing to send 2 or 3 of Harry's short hand-painted color films, send them to us airmail collect before June 15th. If possible as soon as possible since the decision for the date of *COME* will be any date from the 4th June on to 15th of June when Allen leaves. Jonas dear please inform us of what you feel about all this. I'm all listening if you feel for some reason this isn't the moment, situation or space of time tell me so I know what I can do for you that is best. Please send me material catalog etc. of Co-op and Cinematheque for my own use for you love Barbara

The world is round,
from both of us Kate and Barbara
we send our love
Kate

P.S. What is the best address to use for mailing?
Love love always love for our Jonas

Jonas dear - please inform us of what you feel about all this. I'm all listening if you feel for some reason this isn't the moment, situation of space of time tell me so I know whatx I can do for you that is best. Please send me material catalog etc. of Co-OP and Cinemateque for my own use for you love

Barbara

The world is round, from both of us Kate and Barbara we send our love

Kate

P.S. What is the best address to use for mailing?

Love Love

Always Love for ever

Jonas

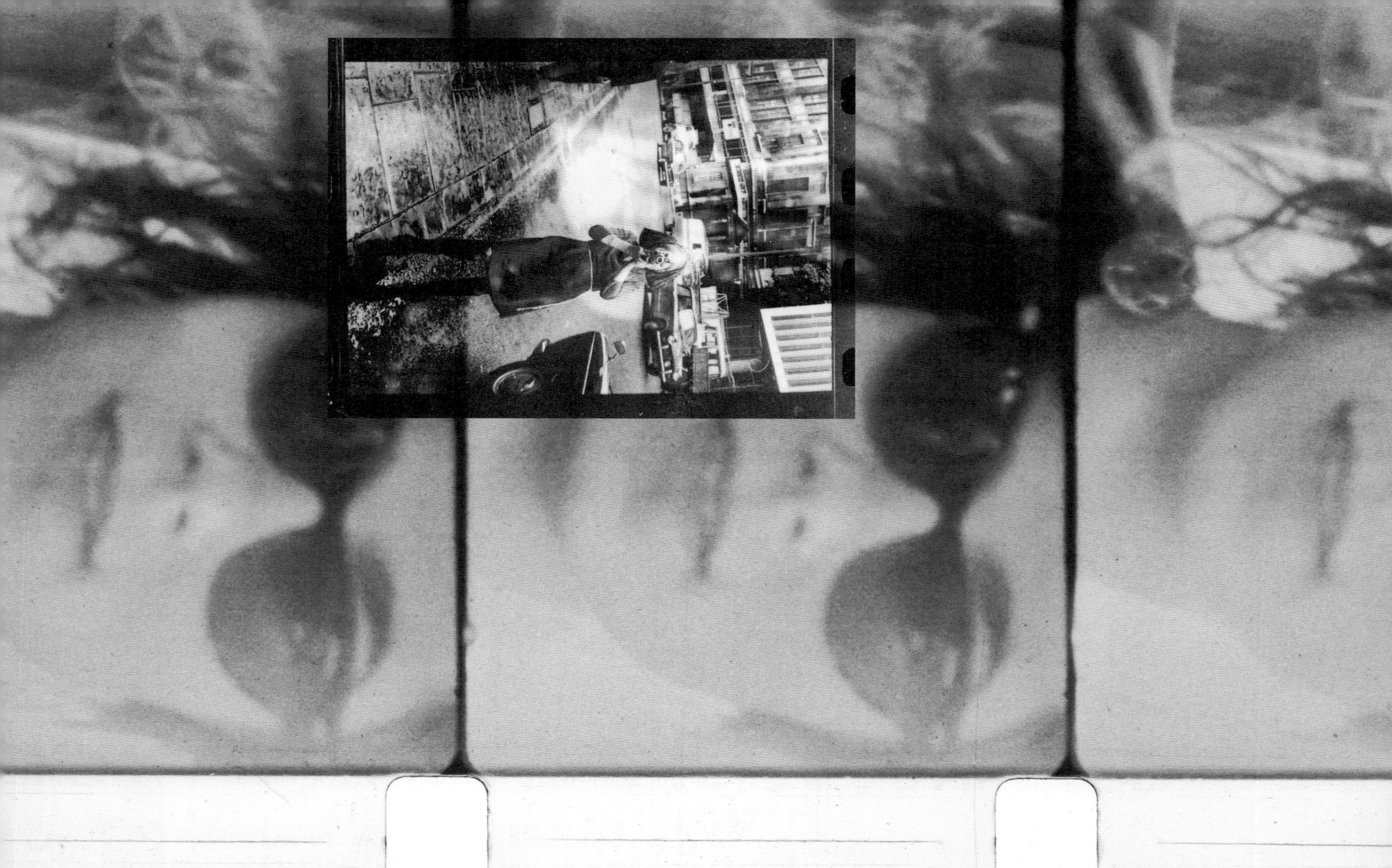

Background image: Barbara Rubin, New York, 1964. Film stills by Jonas Mekas
Foreground image: Barbara Rubin with camera, London, 1965. Photo: Allen Ginsberg

After the *International Poetry Incarnation*, Rubin began filming Allen Ginsberg in and around London and during a visit to William Blake's[1] grave. Although the film, *Allen for Allen*, has been lost, some footage from it was reused in 1971 in an unfinished film called *Emunah*[2] that Rubin conceived with her friend Pamela Badyk[3] while she was teaching a film class in New York. At that point, Rubin had already become an Orthodox Jew and chose to intercut scenes from concentration camps with the 1965 footage of Ginsberg in London.

1
William Blake, 1757–1827, English poet, painter, and print-maker

2
Emunah means "faith" in Hebrew

3
Pamela Badyk Mayo, later Pamela Badyk Mayo Israel, important member of the American Living Theatre company, editor, and co-founder of the Paris Film-Maker's Cooperative with Piero Heliczer. Pamela Badyk Mayo and Barbara Rubin lived together in London in Summer of 1965

London,
June 24, 1965

Dear Jonas—
We have just finished seeing the rushes of Allen, a beautiful poem of Allen swimming in London. Love, high people. Somehow the money is taking care of themselves as an organizing strength of people gather themselves to one. Please Jonas think in terms of coordinating with Better Books as your London division. I will write in more detail as things become more free. I'm willing to budge you and Miles so films can be seen. I'm still on to returning for the summer to get *Christmas* going when Allen is finished here. Dear Jonas how are you doing and feeling? All of us and there is plenty think of you and believe we will do something. Let me write you soon so I can give you detailed information on getting films. Maybe we will get money for 1 print of all the films and ship them here? Well what and how!
Love love my Jonas love love Barbara

be in the movie my most
Was to catagorize them insteа
approaching them as individuals
as for the money etc. I've dec
that I will put out memorda
stating that "Christmas" will be
by the contribution of "said" p
needed. by
This is the flavor
people, c
firms etc. to ask for donat
for the land from Ireland
Disney costumes, materials etc
construction work & material etc
be paid from the profits. w
interest. or if any money is
directly it will be return f
profits again without interest.
another words since conclusive
(Nobody has big money then
need the objects & supplys.
camera labs sound, plumbing &
given)

London,
July 1965

Dear Jonas,
We just finished editing *Allen for Allen*. I think it's a little masterpiece to be blown up to 35mm and shown as a short (it runs 12 minutes without titles). Due to a lack of immediate cash the soundtrack is incomplete, leaving me to conjure one with the material I have / have Allen do a tape as he watches the film or may the $300 check Nick[1] gave me in NY that I was going to return with, comes through. If so I would like to see it distributed here in London in a theatre as a short feature, the Co-op handling it. Also Granada TV wants to see it and a small piece we shot of them when we were on TV.
Also I may do the jacket of an EP of Donovan's[2] (pop-folk singer) and some shooting of P. J. Proby,[3] pop singer who is beautiful and masterly. As far as *Christmas* is, Kate wrote to David, unfortunately a bit incorrectly, we have given scripts out. The new ones I sent you (I have about 300) made new contact with the Beatles though I still haven't discussed the movie with them. I feel everyone individually not as Beatles, Rolling Stones,[4] etc., but for their own will come be in the movie. My mistake was to categorize them instead of approaching them as individuals. As for the money, etc., I've decided that I will put out memorandums stating that *Christmas* will be made by the contribution of "said" materials needed by people, companies, firms etc. to ask for donations. As for the land from Ireland, Walt Disney[5] costumes, materials, etc., construction work and material etc. to be paid from the profits without interest, or if any money is given directly it will be returned from profits again without interest. In other words, since conclusively nobody has big money, then need the objects and supplies (film camera labs, sound, plumbing, electricity, etc. given.)

1
Nicholas Cernovitch, b. 1929, actor and poet; was associated with Black Mountain College, co-founder of the New York Poet's Theatre in 1961

2
Donovan Philips Leitch, b. 1946, Scottish-born singer, songwriter, and guitarist

3
James Marcus Smith, b. 1938, known professionally as P. J. Proby, American singer, songwriter, and actor

4
The Rolling Stones, English rock band formed in 1962 in London

5
Walter Elias Disney, 1901–1966, American entrepreneur, animator, voice actor, and film producer

Christmas On Earth Continued

STATEMENT

There are several surviving documents and scripts that detail Rubin's vision for the film she called *Christmas on Earth Continued*. The first is a statement, which includes a synopsis, casting and funding ideas, plans for a Fairy City and personal letters to Walt Disney and Jean Genet. The second is the script itself and the third is a later version of the script, called "Christmas on Earth Continued Again and Again and Again." For most of the Summer of 1965, Rubin was actively promoting her vision for the film in and around London. She reproduced and distributed hundreds of copies of the script in the hopes of raising funds and getting assurances that her well-known friends would help her realize the project. Her statement is the most concise and coherent summary of her vision.
Full of audacity and sincerity, Rubin hoped the film would embody all the amazing ideas, emotions, and generosity she currently experienced. The list of "Desired Stars, Heroes, and Heroines, who have received scripts and are interested," includes The Beatles and many others of the most famous and influential artists and musicians of the day. Additionally, the film was to be a purely, non-profit effort.

A crucial aspect of the film was Rubin's vision of a Fairy City designed with help of the artist/filmmaker Harry Smith. The City would be constructed in Ireland and would remain after the production as a permanent place for all the world's children to explore.

C H R I S T M A S

O N

E A R T H

C O N T I N U E D

written and directed by

BARBARA RUBIN

A PERSONAL STATEMENT ON THE MOVIE
"CHRISTMAS ON EARTH CONTINUED"

written by: Barbara Rubin

1. as a 35mm color feature length film to be translated and distributed internationally.

2. to be directed by Barbara Rubin and with the help of other desired directors : Fellini, Ingmar Bergman, John Lennon (and any other people who together will work constructively and beautifully).

3. to be photographed by several desired camermen including myself; Jonas Mekas, Bob Whittacker, Harry Smith, Gerard Vandenberg, (again anybody else who will work together for the movies interest and Beauty).
Since the set will be so immense, the need will be for several cameras shooting at several different points.

4. to create Fairy City: Harry Smith, a great anthropologist and a genius film maker.

5. a special sound track created by the stars; Bob Dylan, John Lennon, Paul McCartney, George Harrison, Ringo Starr, Tiny Tim, Joan Baez, Donovan, P.J. Proby, Rolling Stones, etc.

6. and an LP and illustrated book with stills to be brought out translated and distributed internationally.

7. that Walt Disney will help in the vision to come true.

8. that everyone should be of the same mind and feeling to give the best to create a beautiful moment captured on film, that as one, the pure interest of the original idea of the movie is the formost concern, that commercial or any other notion to make money or abuse the film is not even an insey bitsey little way allowed to touch us. that if we are not all agreed, I will insist on strict rights and controls. AND THAT ALL PROFITS & AFTER ALL BILLS AND MONEY MATTERS ARE STRAIGHTENED AND EACH PERSON IS PAID ALL PROFITS ALL ALL PROFITS GO TO MAINTAIN FAIRY CITY AS A PERMANENT CITY FOR CHILDREN AND THAT A ROSEBUD FOUNDATION FOR DREAMS TO BECOME IS KEPT FRUITFUL.

9. that everyone hears me and this song, understands the meaning of it's realization and Know that I most of all want everyone to come and take a part and interest, to give till our gifts are eternal, and absolutely to much even for us.

SYNOPSIS OF THE MOVIE SCRIPT OF
"CHRISTMAS ON EARTH CONTINUED"

The story of the day God manifested Himself to Snow Queen, ruler of Fairy City, as she sat manifesting.
He tells her, that before "Paradise Come," He wants Jean Genet, (played by Jean Genet) saved. The proof to be in the beams of his eternal smile.
She calls the Fairies, (played by the heroes and stars of our time) and together decide how to save Jean Genet, (now a bowery bum).
What comes from their magic, is a coincidence of events that find........................
Macy's Christmas window displaying this year a miniature version of Fairy City, with a special visit from Santa Claus, who will stay over Christmas Eve and Day inside........
and Jean Genet, hungry and cold, to pass by Macy's and see advertised a job as Santa Claus, including foof shelter and warmth for one day and night.

POP!!!!!!!

We find Jean Genet as Santa Claus inside a miniature Fairy City, which comes alive at night and takes Santa through the city, the magic of which is: TO BECOME WHATEVER YOU DESIRE TO BE.
Santa meets and exchanges his desires, symbolized in each Fairy he encounters. (This is called The MIME, a new dance of our time).
They dance and sing, play, feast and drink
Till morning and exhaustion find Santa asleep
and Fairy City reassembled.
A boy watching but not being able to see the Fairies is so bewildered at Santa's distorted features and gestures, that when Santa awakes, the boy spontaneously sticks his tongue out.
Santa, who still believes Fairy City to be alive, responds....
and what occures between the two becomes horrid mockery
and delight
that cause
"a smile
whose beams bursts
a burst as such you wish
that lit
and more it paved the Heavens
with giggles

so that the Lord God
in Heaven on His throne
peered towards earth
before He came
and He saw a shimmer
THAT WAS SET A FLARE
OF THE NEON LIGHTS
MICKEY MOUSE WAS THERE" !!!!!!!

The idea of Fairy City &
the Fairies from Fairy City

Our Fairies from "Christmas on Earth Continued"
are the assimilation of all past Fairy Characters
alive through Mickey Mouse's eyes.
They dwell in Fairy City
here they rest
as God's will thru imagine
neither called on by their source of character:
man
in our dreams
or the desire of our need
here they have their visions
they manifest
thru God
between us
Fairy City is their home
It cares their souls in visions

As a City
It is the absorbtion of all past visualizations
of Fairy Tales
of Paradise
created from Walt Disney's eyes
laid in gardens, fountains and playlands
built in the structure of New Jerusalem
and using the synthetic materials of our time
To be born on the land where the King of the leprechauns sits in Ireland
I desire the Irish government to give me the land
to build Fairy City on
and from the profits of the movie I will give Ireland
money to maintain it as a permanent free city for children

It should be kept in mind that the story of "Christmas on Earth Continued" is written in the classical Fairy Tale concept.
Set in Fairy City, the epitomy of the classic vision of Fairy Cities and Paradises.
Played in costumes, designed in the classical style of the original Fairy Tale character.
The Hero is modern
The situation is present day.
The materials, ofthe costumes and Fairy City, are the synthetics, new rubbers, elastics and plastics (particularly airy, light and flowing) of our time.

Some of the list of desired Stars
Heroes and Heroines, who have received scripts
and are interested

John & Cynthia Lennon
Paul McCartney
Ringo & Maureen Starr
George Harrison
Lenny Bruce
Bob Dylan
Andy Warhol
Allen Ginsberg
William Burroughs
Jean Genet
The Rolling Stones...Mick,
Charlie,
Keith,
Brian,
& Bill

Tiny Tim
Marianne Faithful & John Dunbar
Joan Baez
Charlie Chaplan
Fellini
Kenneth Anger
Salvador Dali
Norman Mailer
LeRoi Jones
Gregory Corso
Andrei Voznesensky
Benito Carruthers
Pablo Neruda
Pablo Fernandez
Alex Trocchi
Lawrence Ferlinghetti
Donovan
Nicolo
Al Aronowitz
Peter Orlovsky

Al & Sally Grossman
Ernst Jandle
Allan & Ruth Sillitoe
Davie Graham
P.J. Proby
Bongo
Mr. President
Paul & Barry
Julie Felix
Jacque Ledoux
Doc Humes
Pasolini

IDEAS CONCERNING RAISING THE NECESSARY FUNDS & MATERIALS FOR:
CHRISTMAS ON EARTH CONTINUED

Using the construction of Fairy City as an example I will try to show one way of making this movie.

Fairy City, the set of the movie "Christmas on Earth Continued" and also a permanent city for children.

I desire Fairy City to be built in Ireland, the home of the leprachauns.

Knowing the abominable cost of the construction yet realizing the significance of a beautiful city for children and also the value in terms of tourist trade for Ireland, who I believe needs children as it dies of old age ... Fairy City and Ireland can care each other to build Ireland and flourish the city of children for Irelands hope and all childrens.

Therefore, if the Irish government will give me the land to build Fairy City, I will in turn give them Fairy City and help them to maintain it as a permanent city for children through the profits of the movie.

The whole movie: its construction, the actual filming, developing, prints, sounds and final distribution can also be worked on this basis. I did originally desire that certain stars and concerned people would together give money and work with me with an interest and say in the film, as long as the agreement is to the original beauty and truth of the film.

I am trying every possible way to have "Christmas on Earth Continued" made knowing the extreme expense of the cost and the amount of effort and time that must be given.

I am sorry for the inadequacy of presenting a possible budget with definite money and needs.

I lack the estimating ability and so much depends on how much is given, lent or donated and how much will need to be first hand, bought or made.

I need a producer and to begin the organizing for "Christmas on Earth Continued".

An open letter to Walt Disney

Dear Walt Disney:

I loved you as a child, who created a Fairy Tale vision for me in the presence of my own time. Now that I have grown to give birth to my own dreams and thoughts it is to you, the man who made me and all children of this age, a Walt Disney creation, that I return to.

I have written this movie, "Christmas on Earth Continued", as well as having completed one movie (for further information you can contact the Film Makers Co-Operative or Cinematheque C/o Jonas Mekas, Cinematheque, 83 East 4th Street, New York City.) "Christmas on Earth", a love story in the dreams and fantasies of man and I am in the process of completing "Allen for Allen", a film of Allen Ginsberg, America's greatest living poet, in London including the reading at The Royal Albert Hall; with Andrei Voznesensky Russia's great poet and Donovan, a popular singer and a special sound track now being finished.

I am now just turned 20 with the vision of "Christmas on Earth Continued" I have talked with many of the desired stars of the movie and have the wish of the list of stars I include in the synopsis of "Christmas on Earth Continued" to be in the movie, I am now getting in touch with Jean Genet who will star as Santa Claus. I would like you to consider this movie as something you would like to take part in (in any way you feel you can best give) I am now in London to return to America and can be reached at: 117-50 228th Street, Cambria Heights, New York 11, New York, (Telephone: LA 8-8176).

As you may imagine I need all possible help, love and finances to make "Christmas on Earth Continued" come true. Everyone's heart believes in miracles, but I know that miracles are the effort of how much you work and give to it. "Christmas on Earth Continued" could have only been dreamed of because of you and your visions; may they now bless and work upon the reality of it.

Love,

Love Barbara

Barbara Rubin

An open letter to Jean Genet

Dear Jean Genet:

Bernard Frechtman, has now opened himself to my calls for my movie "Christmas on Earth Continued" many times and suggested I write telling you my ideas and some background.

"Christmas on Earth Continued" is a movie dream. In my vision I saw you as the hero : Santa Claus.

God manifests Himself to Snow Queen ruler of Fairy City an imaginery city in New Jerusalem; home of the Fairies; and tells her that before "Paradise Come" he wants you saved and as proof he wants the beams of your eternal smile. All of the Fairies of Fairy City (played by the heroes and stars of our time) come together to save you.

It is through a series of events that Fairy City comes to be duplicated in a Christmas Macy's window display this year, and you a bowery bum, now, come to pass by and see advertized a job as Santa Claus, with warmth, food and shelter for Christmas Eve and Day.

You are now inside Fairy City as Santa Claus, it is Christmas Eve: midnite and Fairy City comes alive and the Fairies take you through the magic of their city. You become whatever you desire: you are a King of wishes come true and all nite,all the stars and heroes, dressed in their symbolic Fairy costume, exchange greetings and desires with you, entertain you, sing and dance, feast till all is merry and delight. In the morning when Fairy City is reassembled you are awakened by a boy who watching you but unable to see the Fairies is bewildered by your various distorted gestures; unconsciously sticks his tongue out. You respond and what goes between you and the boy is the love and magic of horrid mockery and delight that cause the beams of your eternal smile to burst upon the heavens in giggles to call upon God and "Paradise Come".

I am calling all the heroes and stars of my time together to play in this movie and the set of Fairy City I desire to be built in Ireland on the spot where the King of the leprachauns sits. I am now in the process of getting a producer, organizing the production for the movie and raising funds.

I have given the script and have spoken to many of the stars and many have the dream of playing Fairies to save you. I now turn to the hero, Jean Genet, Please come in the dreams and love of your wishes and to capture on film that moment when we go beyond ourselves and love.

The movie will be a 35mm color feature with a special sound track to be recorded by a conglomeration of great sound people: to be translated and distributed internationally. Also an L.P. and illustrated book with stills will come out internationally translated. Fairy City will remain as a permanent city for children and a Rosebud Foundation for "DREAMS TO BECOME" will be established and kept fruitful. All this I hope to do from the profits of the movie and the interest and funds of concerned people.

Jean Genet, I ask you again, to come, be the hero of "Christmas on Earth Continued".

Love,

Barbara Rubin

Christmas On Earth Continued
S C R I P T

The script for *Christmas on Earth Continued* reproduced is the version that Rubin distributed throughout London in 1965. It begins with her "calling on the heroes of my time" to "come, come monstrous." The title of her first film, *Christmas on Earth,* came from Arthur Rimbaud's[1] 1873 prose poem *A Season in Hell*:

"When will we go, over mountains and shores, to hail the birth of new labor, new wisdom, the flight of tyrants and demons, the end of superstition—to be the first to adore!—Christmas on earth!"

In this script, Rubin also quotes Rimbaud as a prelude to the action: "From the bosom of the high seas, you will rise up and give to the vast universe infinite love with its eternal smile!
The world will vibrate like an immense lyre in the trembling of an infinite kiss!
—The world thirsts for love! you will come and slake its thirst."

Like a strange mix of Alejandro Jodorowsky,[2] Walt Disney, and the Bible, the script is epic in scope but, except for a few detailed scenes with Jean Genet as Santa Claus, it's hard to imagine what the finished film could have looked like. As in the list of "Desired Stars," from the statement. Rubin's list of characters, including Babar the Elephant, the Greek Gods, and various American superheroes, is similarly excessive. Nevertheless, the idea of Genet playing Santa Claus or Tiny Tim playing Snow White is bizarrely fascinating. Most significantly, the script reflects Rubin's increasing obsession with various religious motifs and the ecstasy of faith.

1
Jean Nicholas Arthur Rimbaud, 1854–1891, French poet

2
Alejandro Jodorowsky Prullansky, b. 1929, Chilean-French filmmaker, actor, producer, novelist, and poet

FIRST CAME CHRISTMAS ON EARTH
ON FILM THAT IS
THEN WENT INTO LIVE ONE STRIVES

IN

CHRISTMAS
ON
EARTH
CONTINUED

written and directed by

BARBARA RUBIN

I am calling
The heroes of my time
In joy joy joy
With the glow of themselves
In love
On their faces
Come come come
Come monstrous

Rimbaud Rimbaud - Sun and Flesh III

"If only the times which have come and gone might come again! For man is finished! Man has played all the parts! In the broad day-light, wearied with breaking idols, he will revive, free of all his Gods; and since he is of heaven, he will scan the heavens! The ideal, that eternal, invincible thought, which is all; the living God within his fleshly clay, will rise, mount, burn beneath his brow! And when you see him plumbing the horizon despising old yokes, and free from all fear you will come and give him holy redemption! Resplendent, radiant. From the bosom of the hugh seas, you will rise up and give to the vast universe infinite love with its eternal smile! The world will vibrate like an immense lyre in the trembling of an infinite kiss!
- The world thirsts for love! You will come and slake its thirst."

CHRISTMAS ON EARTH CONTINUED

PROLOGUE:

Come out come out
You sitting in your head
Only thru the eyes of love
Can our dreams be put to bed

THIS IS OUR STORY

the situation ----------

"Lord's Museum"

an exact replica of
"God's Temple"

(the actualization known only in Heaven)

It's History began
nearing the approach
of

"HIS COMING
and PARADISE"

Fairy City
New Jerusalem, Heaven

then together we came
and gave memory a name

"MUSEUM
HOME OF DETAILED REPRODUCTIONS"

highlighting

"THE LORD GOD'S THRONE AND THE 24 ELDERS"

CHRISTMAS ON EARTH CONTINUED 2

(to be also used
on the high frequency as

"TEMPLE OF MANIFESTATI ONS"

AWARE ALL HOURS
TO ANYONE MANIFESTING)

The then Capital of Fairy City
Fairyland, the chosen,
was its landmark

Now this
crystallized told
of Snow Queen
when found
perched on "God's Throne"
UNCANNILY STILL
having a manifestation
(HEAR BELIEF REPEATS
- That Only -
"WHEN THE BLESSED ARE SEATED ON MY THRONE
WILL A MANIFESTATION APPEAR")

a sceptre

headed by a gilded mask

is held in her left hand
(this, the insignia of the Fairy,
is carried by all fairies here)

The Manifestation enters
SPARKLERS

bows

Dances
THE DANCE OF THE SPARKLERS

bows

exists

a moment

CHRISTMAS ON EARTH CONTINUED 3

SNOW QUEEN: Impossible, (flustered)

Impossible, (bangs sceptre three times)

Enter----------Peter Pan (a Flying)
Snow White (a Singing)
Seven Dwarfs (a Working)
Tinkle Bell (a Bursting)
Mother Goose (a Rapping)

Followed behind by the populace of Fairy City

SNOW QUEEN: impossible

THEY: impossible

SNOW QUEEN: "Ye Saviors, he says,
YE SAVIORS, I'M COMING
!!!!!!

THEY: "Ye Saviors, she said
Ye Saviors
He's Coming

SNOW QUEEN: (a full face stupor THAT SENDS TIME BACK)
"He says He Wants Jean Genet
jean genet
JEAN GENET

IMPOSSIBLE

THEY: Jean Genet
she says He Wants Jean Genet

jean genet

I M P O S S I B L E

SNOW QUEEN: (pleadingly) as proof He wants (pause)

THEY: He wants as proof

SNOW QUEEN: the beams

THEY: the Beams

CHRISTMAS ON EARTH CONTINUED 4

SNOW QUEEN: of

THEY: of

SNOW QUEEN: (her mouth agape and starry eyes) ----SILENT

THEY: (and Snow Queen joining)
HIS ETERNAL SMILE
He wants his eternal smile
eternal smile
as proof He wants the beams of his eternal smile
the beams of his eternal smile
the beams the beams

TOGETHER: IMPOSSIBLE
IMPOSSIBLE

impossible

she looks
they look

she flutters
they flutter

she winks, a cough, a moan, a sigh
they wink and cough and moan and sigh

all stop

Listen

take a glance

and one to the other

and other one

Look
and a nod
and a look
and nod and look
and
WOW!!!!!!!!!!

CHRISTMAS ON EARTH CONTINUED 5

Fairy City Bustles

Snow White strikes the first note

on her ukulele

Snow Queen nods
and does the shakes

Superhero's Legion (fly in)
Bizarro's Legion (back out)

Snow White sings

Fairyland Fairy City
Glows

And Dance do we Dance and Dance!!!

(simultaneously)

Tinkle Bell (suggest Sammy Davis Jr.) Bursts
The Songs Finale
Superhero's Legion fly
Bizarro's Legion dive

a sign

"WANTED"
SOMEONE WHO LOOKS JUST LIKE SANTA
INQUIRE WITHIN

And all of all this
was one of our trips

(Macy's Xmas Window Display)

"FAIRYLAND, FAIRY CITY
HOME OF THE FAIRY
WITH A SPECIAL FROM SANTA CLAUS"
(all Children welCOME)
Tours Between 2-5pm

Now who do you think
engrossed in his drink
was put on display
for this Christmas Day?

A light ripples
As this window plays
A midsummer's night beam
The bed of every
Fairy tale's dream

Macy's is Closed
reaching behind his throne
he takes
50¢ port and guzzles it down

snore snore uh uh zzzzz snorrrrrrrrrrrrr

Tinkle Bell lifts an eyelid
peers
the Seven Dwarfs rustle
fairies awaken
and
(we set off a glitter bomb)

TO MAKE SUCH MUSIC PRETTY

(Tuned to "The March of Smile")

"BEAWARE"

ALL ENTERING THESE IMMORTAL GROUNDS
LEAVE YOUR IDENTITY HOME
WE WILL NOT BE RESPONSIBLE
FOR CONSEQUENCES CERTAIN

UPON ENTERING YOU WILL BE SUBJECT TO LOSS
OF WILL

"ANYthing you are and want is yours
whether you say so or not
WE ARE MINDS"

Santa is greeted
his sceptre received
begins the night
of this Xmas Eve

NOTE -------

rules concerning the event that takes place
ALL actions are subjects of MIME
(a new dance of our time)
the tour Santa Experiences
with all of us
will be left to the order of variance
the chance at the time of shooting

conducted FLEACINGLY

At the foot of Fairyland
spread before in a horse's shoe
THIS IS THE NATIONAL PARK OF FAIRY CITY
CONTAINING THE MOST FANTASTIC PLEASURE PLAYLAND
WITH SWINGS, MONKEY BARS, ROLLER COASTERS AND GAMES
FLOODED IN GARDENS AND FOUNTAINS, LIT TO SPIN YOUR FOCUS

A Feast has been laid
During which
Snow White
High Priestess
leads a chorus number
singing her original medley
(accompanied by the Fairy Chorus)
then
joined by
THE BEATLES
JOAN BAEZ
BOB DYLAN
ROLLING STONES
MARIAN FAITHFUL
DONAVAN
FREDDY & THE DREAMERS
HERMAN & THE HERMITS
THE KINKS
AND SUPREMES

CHRISTMAS ON EARTH CONTINUED 8

TO SING DANCE ENCHANT AND PLAY
TO TAKE OUR VERY BREATHS AWAY
OF SUCH SPLENDOR JOY HILARITY
BEYOND ALL
EVER
POSSIBLE
IMAGINABLE
LOVE!!!!!!!!!!!!! LOVE LOVE
YEAH YEAH YEAY YAEA AYAEA AYEAH YEAHYAEHYEAHYEYA

CLIMAXING in
a SPIN
JERK
and SHAKES
(and our dance
THE SPIRAL & MIME
THE DANCE OF OUR TIME)

MEANWHILE --------

Tinkee Bell bursts
and Fairy City NODS
and reassembles

A young lad watching
has been bewitched
his face against the window

a smashed tongue protruded
(SUNRISES)
Santa peeks from weary eyes
TO BEHOLD SUCH A FACE!

HIS TONGUE POPPED OUT

He crossed his eyes
I'll cross my eyes

I'll scowl and stare
stand up my hairs

I'll scowl and stare
stand up my hairs
and my ears and nose will wiggle!

CHRISTMAS ON EARTH CONTINUED 9

SUCH GRIMACES OF HORRIBLE DELIGHT
MATCHING MOCKERIES TERRIBLE SIGHT
OH---you wouldn't---
---you couldn't---
imagine !!!
imagine--------
tinkee bell did
fainted out in the dawning
---NOW---
light this Christmas morning

---AND---

a smile whose beams burst
a burst as such you wish

that lit
and more it paved the Heavens
with giggles

so that the Lord God
in Heaven on His Throne
peered towards earth
before He came
and He saw a shimmer
THAT WAS SET A FLARE
OF THE NEON LIGHTS
MICKEY MOUSE WAS THERE!!!!!!!!!!!

Christmas is the come of hearts
and this is the glow

CHRISTMAS ON EARTH CONTINUED 10

T H E S E T

I BELIEVE THIS AS A TEMPLE IN IRELAND
A FOUNDATION FOR ROSEBUDS
"TO THE LORD AND JESUS CHRIST, HIS CHILD
CHILDREN
OUR CHILDREN"

"Suffer children
to come to me
and forbid them not.
For of such is
the Kingdom of God."
Chapt. 18.15.

OUR SET IS FAIRY CITY
A CITY IN NEW JERUSALEM
ITS CAPITOL
FAIRYLAND (THE STRUCTURE OF WHICH IS THAT OF NEW JERUSALEM)
HOME OF THE "LORD'S MUSEUM AND TEMPLE OF MANIFESTATIONS"
AN EXACT REPLICA OF
THE VISION OF HEAVEN
THE DESCRIPTION OF WHICH
SHOULD BE STRICTLY FOLLOWED
FROM THE BOOK OF REVELATIONS
CONTAINED WITHIN FAIRY CITY ITSELF
LAYING BEFORE FAIRYLAND
IS HER NATIONAL PARK
PLEASURE PLAYLAND RESORT
CONEY ISLAND WITH SUGGESTED
PLEASURE ISLAND, FROM PINOCCHIO
------WHILE------
THE REST OF THE CITY COMBINEDS
NEVER NEVERLAND PETER PAN
EMERALD CITY OZ
CHESS BOARD WONDERLAND
AND THE QUEEN OF HEARTS' PALACE ALICE IN WONDERLAND AND THROUGH THE LOOKING GLASS
TOWER OF RUPUNZEL
ORIENTAL GARDENS OF EMPEROR AND THE NIGHTINGALE
SANTA'S LAND
SNOW QUEEN'S THRONE
GINGERBREAD HOUSE HANSLE AND GRETL
WITH AND ARABIAN NIGHTS THREAD
SPUN IN A SPIDER'S WEB
LIKE A MIDSUMMER'S NIGHT DREAM
LOOKING LIKE A NEON MICKEY MOUSE BEAM

T H E   V I S I O N   O F   H E A V E N

BEFORE MY EYES A DOOR STOOD OPEN IN HEAVEN AND IN MY EAR WAS THE VOICE WITH THE RING OF A TRUMPET, WHICH I HAD HEARD AT FIRST SPEAKING TO ME AND SAYING
"COME UP HERE AND I WILL SHOW YOU WHAT MUST HAPPEN IN THE FUTURE"

In my vision I saw

A throne had been set up in heaven
And someone seated upon the throne
His appearance blazed like diamond and topaz
All around the throne
Shone a halo
Like an emerald rainbow
And circled around the throne
Were 24 thrones
Seated upon them 24 elders
Dressed in white
With golden crowns
From the central throne
Come flashes of lightning
Noises
And peals of thunder
Seven lamps are burning before the throne
They are the seven spirits of God
In front of the throne appears
A sea of glass
As clear as crystal
On each side
Encircling the throne
Are four living creatures
Covered with eyes
In front and behind
First living creature is like a lion
Two is like a calf
Three has a face like a man
Four living creature
Appears like an eagle in flight

These four creatures
Have each of them
Six wings
And are covered with eyes
All around them
And even within them
Day and night they never cease to say
"Holy holy holy is the Lord God
The Almighty
Who was
Who is
Who is coming"

-oOo-

THE VISION OF THE NEW JERUSALEM

The Holy Jerusalem
Descending from God
Out of heaven
Radiant with the glory of God
Her brilliance sparkles
Like a precious jewel
With the clear light of crystal
Around her
A vast lofty wall
In which are 12 gateways
With 12 angels at the gate
Over each gateway
Is inscribed the name
Of a tribe of the sons of Israel
Three gates on each side of the city
The wall of the city
Has 12 foundation stones
Bearing the names of the 12 apostles
Of the land

The wall itself
Is built of translucent stone
While the city is of purest gold
With the brilliance of glass
The foundation stones of the wall
Are made of every kind of precious jewel
First foundation
Is jasper
Two sapphire
Three agate
Four emerald
Five onyx
Six cornelian
Seven gold stone
Eight beryl
Nine topaz
Ten green goldstone
11 zircon
12 amethyst
The 12 gates
Are made of pearls
Each gate is made of a single pearl
The street of the city
Is pure as gold
Gleaming like glass
There is no temple in the city
For the Lord
And the almighty God
And the lamb
Are themselves the temple
The city needs no sun or moon
For the splendor of God
Fills it with light
And its radiance
Is the lamb
The nations will walk by its light
And the kings of the earth
Will bring their glory into it
The city's gate
Shall stand open
Day after day
And there will be no night there
Into the city
They will bring
The splendor and honor

Of the nation
Nothing unclean
None who deals in filthiness
And lies
Shall ever at any time enter it
Only those whose name
Are written in the lambs book of life
Inside the city
Is the river of the water of life
Sparkling like crystal
As it flows from the throne of God and the lamb
In the middle street of the city
And on either bank of the river
Grew the tree of life
Bearing 12 fruits
A different kind for each month
The leaves of the tree
Were for the healing of the nations
And nothing that has cursed mankind
Shall exist any longer
The throne of God
And of the lamb
Shall be within the city
His servants shall worship him
They shall see his face and
His name shall be upon their foreheads
Night shall be no more
They will have no more need for lamp light or sunlight
For the Lord God shall shed his light upon them
And they shall reign as kings
For timeless ages

Measurement of the city

The city lies foursquare
Its length equal to its breadth
It is 12,000 furlongs in each direction
For its length breadth and height
Are all equal
The wall is 144-1/2 yards high
By human measurement

And he measured the wall thereof, an hundred forty-four cubits, the measurement of a man, which is of an angel.

-oOo-

DESIRED STARS & HEROS, HEROINES

My mother and father
and to all those I have not yet realized
Please Come

JOHN & CYNTHIA LENNON
PAUL MC CARTNEY
RINGO & MAUREEN STARR
GEORGE HARRISON
BRIAN EPSTEIN
LENNY BRUCE
MARLON BRANDO
ELVIS PRESLEY
FRANK SINATRA
BOB DYLAN
TINY TIM
SAMMY DAVIS JR.
JONAS MEKAS
AL MEKAS
BRIGITTE BARDOT
JACK SMITH
ANDY WARHOL
ALLEN GINSBERG
GERARD MELANGA
PETER ORLOVSKY
TULI KUPFERBERG
ED SANDERS
CYNTHIA MC ADAMS
STAN BRAKHAGE
SYLVIA
WILLIAM BURROUGHS
GREGORY MARKOPOLOUS
NAOMI LEVINE
MR. RONNEY
HARRY SMITH
LISA
ANNIE PLYMELL
GRETA GARBO
JEAN GENET
ROLLING STONES
DAVID STONE
BARBARA STONE
TONY BALCH
ELLIOT STEIN

HARRY FAINLIGHT
SZABO AND ELLEN
HUNKEY
HERB SHAPIRO
LAUREN BACALL
BEVERLY GRANT
JOEL MARKMAN
JIMMY SMITH
JERRY JOFFEN
LESLIE TRUMBULL
JANET FINK
LOUIS BRIGANTE
STORM DE HIRSCH
LOUIE BERTRAND
JULIUS ORLOVSKY
BILL HEINIE
FELLINI
SOPHIA LOREN
P. ADAMS SITNEY
RONNY TAVEL
MARIO MONTEZ
CHARLIE CHAPLAN
BELMONDO
TATAYANA
GEORGE ANDREWS
& 5 CHILDREN
JOAN BAEZ
ALLAN MARLOW
DIANE DI PRIMA
ELIZABETH TAYLOR
RICHARD BURTON
JEANNE MOREAU
ALAIN DELON
SOUPY SALES
TONY CONRAD
JUDY PEABODY
CARLOS
DALE
PAOLO LIONNI

JOHN FLES
KENNETH ANGER
BOB BROWN
MARCELLO MASTROIANI
PIERO & KATE HELICZER
JEAN MARLOW
STEPHANIE JANE LOVELACE
LAUREN
ISRAEL YOUNG
JASON ROBARDS JR.
GABRIELLE BETTINA CALFON
JAMES BALDWIN
SALVADOR DALI
NORMAN MAILER
ROBERT & MARY FRANK
STEVE KRAUS
AL LESLIE
RODALE
PAT GRADY
FLO & KEN JACOBS
HERMAN & THE HERMITS
LEROI JONES
FREDDY & THE DREAMERS
ANGUS & FRANCES
MARIAN FAITHFUL
MARLENE DIETRICH
RAY CHARLES
SEYMORE STERN
JASPER JOHNS
PICASSO
MICHAEL MC CLURE
STAN GETZ
GREGORY CORSO
BUZZ LINHART
ORNETT COLEMAN
WALT DISNEY
ROLAND KIRK
JOHN CALE
LOU REED

CHRISTMAS ON EARTH CONTINUED

ANDREI VOZNESENSKY
LITTLE STEVIE WONDER
AL ARONOWITZ
CONRAD ROOKS
SAL MINEO
BEN CARRUTHERS
THE KINKS
AND SUPREMES
BECKETT
STEVIE SMITH
DAN & JILL RIGHTER
MARDIE COWPER
JOHN ESAM
DORTH
NEAL PHILLIPS
THE ROYAL FAMILY
AL & SALLY GROSSMAN
SEYMOUR STERN
ROSEBUD
PAMELA BADYK
GERARD VANDENBERG
PIP AND ASA
BART HUGHES
GEORGE SOLOMOS
ROBIN ROCKMAN
HARRY BELAFONTE
KEN & BONNY RUBIN
DEBBI
MICHAEL HOROVITZ
MARTHA & THE VANDELLA'S
MARCUS FIELD
PHILIP LAMANTIA
LAWRENCE FERLINGHETTI

JOHN WAYNE
SIDNEY POITIER
RODDY MC DOWAEL
PETER O'TOOL
LAURENCE OLIVER
ALBERT FINNEY
DALI LAMA
HENRY MILLER
MAUREEN O'HARA
KATHERINE HEPBERN
ANN MATTINGLY
JANE ASHER
JEREMY & RODDY
NUREYEV
PAUL & JASPER VAUGHAN
BASIL BUNTING
PABLO NERUDA
JEAN JACQUES LEBEL
ONNO NOL
MARIO
FRANZ WEISZ
MARK EDEN
TOM PICKARD
JAN AND DEAN
MAGGIE ABBOTT
DAVID CHAPMAN
TWINKLE
CILLA BLACK
NICOLO
MILES AND SUE
ALEX TROCCHI
THE KENNEDY FAMILY

MAX VON SYDOW
PETER AND GORDON
FRANCOIS HARDY
ANTHONY NEWLEY
DONOVAN
GYPSIE
BOB WITTACKER
TOM MASCHLER
PADDY
SANDY SHAW
DUSTY SPRINGFIELD
SARAH ROSENBAUM
JIMMY WITHERSPOON
BURT LANCASTER
CONNIE FRANCES
PETER SELLERS
MARINA THOMPSON
PETER STEPHENS
FERRO
GEORGE MOORSE
MAC SCOTT
PETER BERGMAN
PEARCE PAUL READ
KEN [illegible]TOR GERARD
ERNST JANDLE
BERIS SULLIVAN.
JEFF NUTTAL
ALAN SILLITOE
RUTH FAINLIGHT
DAVIE GRAHAM
JOSE & ANSELM HOLLO
STEWART AND
DEIDRIE MONTGOMERY

Tom Blake

NATALIE WOOD
LUCY BALL
CHESTER ANDERSON
OMAR SHARIF
GARY GRANT
THE FOX
MICHAEL CANTER
ERIC DOLPHY
AMANDA FIELDING
ED WYNN
JULIE FELIX
THE ANIMALS
LITTLE RICHARD
FRANCOIS TRUFFAUT
JACK KEROUAC
KIM NOVAK
DEAN STOCKWELL
GRAUCHO MARX
PAUL NEWMAN
MONICA VITTI
BELA LUGOSI
HALINA KIRN
GLORIA SWANSON
THEM
BING CROSBY
PIPER LAURIE
CASTRO
GRETA GARBO
CHRIS WEST
ROBERT RYAN
CHARLIE PARKER
ANNIE ROSS
JENNIFER JONES
COWBOY
PAOLO JOHNNY LYON
ALAN WATTS
GUILLIETTA MESSINA
TENNESSY WILLIAMS
THE LONG HAIRS
RODNEY BULL
SHIRLEY ELLIS
NINA SIMON
SEEKERS
JOHN HOUSTON
P.J. PROBY
FRANKIE AVLON
TUESDAY WELD
ALEC GUINESS
SARAH MILES
MARQUEL PETIT
ROSEBUD'S SISTERS
JOHNNY GRIFFIN
MOSES VANDEREK
JANE
KLAUS LEA
INGMAR BERGMAN
ANITA EKBERG
ALAIN RESNAIS
NEAL CASSIDY
RICHARD HARRIS
BOBBY DRISCOLL
MICHAEL CHAPLIN
BARRY
ANNA KARINA
CAROLL BAKER
CORNELIUS CARDEW
GINGER ROGERS
THE WHO
GEORGE JESSEL
BUSTER KEATON
CASSIUS CLAY
MILES DAVIS
ADRIAN HAGGARD
FREDERIC MARCH
PATRIZIA
WARREN BEATTIE
JOSEPH COTTON
STEVE MCQUEEN
LUCIA CAMPERT
ANTONIN ARTAUD
ANNA MAGNANI
OSCAR WILD
J.R. TOLKIN
GENE PITNEY
MOODY BLUES
JACK ELLIOT
DOC HUMES
JACQUE LEDOU
BONGO
RUDDY & VALI
SANDRA DEE
ANTHONY QUINN
SANDY BULL
BUFFY SAINT MARIE
BLIND GARY DAVIS
DON
DARYL
EVA, EVE, EVEN
THE HOLLIES
SUSANNAH CAMPBELL
JEAN-LUC GODARD
PASOLINI
PROFESSOR HOLLEROR
RAY & BONNY BREMSER
MICKEY ROONEY
JOANNE WOODWARD
VINCENT PRICE
BORIS KARLOFF
JOAN CRAWFORD
BETTE DAVIS
FRED ASTAIRE
HOPPY
JACKIE GLEASON
PLATTERS
THELONIOUS MONK
MARCEL DUCHAMP
CHRISTOPHER TREE
LEONARD BERNSTEIN
LOVE TO - NATHANIEL WEST
LESLIE CARON
ORSON WELLES
KITTY COUBOIS
PROFESSOR LANG
OLIVER REED
JOCK LIVINGSTON
AUBREY BEARDSLEY
SALINGER
JEAN PAUL BELMONDO
BYRDS
PATTI BOYD
THE SHANGRI-LAS
INGRID BERGMAN

Harry Smith, you drunken lover
you with the beauty and genius to conjure
the vision of love into a fairy city.

CHRISTMAS ON EARTH CONTINUED 17

CHARACTERS

THE BIBLE

Messenger Angel
The Angel with the Little Book
The Dragon
The Gorgeous Mother of Evil
The Locust
- 24 Elders -

PINOCCHIO

Pinocchio
Jimney Cricket
Blue Fairy

SNOW WHITE

Snow White
Sleepy
Grumpy
Doc
Sneezy
Happy
Bashful
Dopey
Prince Charming

CINDERELLA

Cinderella
Fairy Godmother
Prince Charming

CHRISTMAS ON EARTH CONTINUED 18

PETER PAN

Peter Pan
Tinkle Bell
Tiger Lily
Wendy
Nanny
Wicket crocodile
Captain Cook

THE WIZARD OF OZ

The Oz as a Humbug
(the Oz costume will contain
magnificent head dress bearing
his four wizards disguises
the head
The Fairy
The Beast
The Fire)
Tin Man
Lion
Scarocrow
Good Witch Glinda From the North
The Wicked Witch of the West
Dorothy

ALICE IN WONDERLAND

Red Queen
Red King
Tweedledee
Tweedledum
White Rabbit
March Hare
Knave of Hearts
Humpty Dumpty
Cheshire Cat
White Queen
White King
Queen of Hearts
Caterpillar
Alice
Mad Hatter

CHRISTMAS ON EARTH CONTINUED 19

SNOW QUEEN

Snow Queen

MOTHER GOOSE

Mother Goose
Wolf

HANSL AND GRETL

Hansl
Gretl
Witch

RUPUNZEL

Rupunzel
Prince Charming
Witch

THE EMPEROR AND THE NIGHTINGALE

Emperor
Nightingale

SUPERMAN

Superman

WONDER WOMAN

Wonder Woman

CHRISTMAS ON EARTH CONTINUED 20

LEGION OF SUPERHEROS

Superboy
Chameleon Boy
Saturn Girl
Brainiac 5
Eleement Lad
Invisible Kid
Lightning Lad

BIZARRO LEGION

Superboy
Chameleon Boy
Saturn Girl
Brainiac
Element Lad
Invisible Kid
Lightning Lad
(duplicate Backwards of Superheros dedicated to creating emergencies)

JUSTICE LEGION

Aquaman
Batman
Flash
J'onn J'onzz
Green Arrow

IMMORTAL HEROS

James Dean
Rimbaud
Marilyn Monroe
Rudolf Valentino
Buddha

CHRISTMAS ON EARTH CONTINUED 21

SANTA CLAUS

Jean Genet
Rudolph the Red-Nosed Reindeer

JESUS

Jesus
GOD (SPARKLERS)

WALT DISNEY

Dumbo
Donald Duck
Mighty Mouse

Comedy Team
Laurel
Hardy
Chico
Groucho
Zeppo
Harpo

BABAR THE ELEPHANT

Babar
Elephants

CASPER THE FRIENDLY GHOST

Casper
Nightmare (Friendly Horse Ghost)

CHRISTMAS ON EARTH CONTINUED 22

BEAUTY AND THE BEAST

Beauty
Beast

LITTLE MERMAID

Little Mermaid
Three Sister Mermaids

ARABIAN NIGHTS

Ali Baba (holding the heads of 40 thieves)
Sherharazade
Dancing Girls and Slaves
Many many Kings and Queens

ALADIN AND PRINCESS JINNI

SLEEPING BEAUTY

Prince Charming
Sleeping Beauty

BABES IN THE WOOD

2 Babes

Lots and lots of LITTLE PEOPLE

Leprechauns
Goblins
Fairy Folk

CHRISTMAS ON EARTH CONTINUED 23

MYTHS AND GODS

Apollo
Zeus
Diana
Venus
Great God Pan
Prometheus
Pandora
Pygmalion & Galatea
Daphne
Psyche
Orpheus & Eurydice
Atalanta
Arachne
Idas & Marpessa
Perseus
Niobe
Hyacinthus
King Midas
Proserpine
Iatona
Odin
Freya
Narcissus
Icarus & Son
Sphinx
Adonis
Ulysses
Roland
Deirdre

CHRISTMAS ON EARTH CONTINUED 24

D E S C R I P T I O N S   O F   C H A R A C T E R S

MESSENGER ANGEL

I saw seven golden lampstands
And among these lampstands I saw
MESSENGER ANGEL---
Someone like the son of man
Dressed in long robe
And a golden girdle around his breast
His head and his hair
Were white as
Snow white wool
His eyes blazed like fire
And his feet shone
As the finest bronze
Glows in the furnace
His voice had the sound of a great waterfall
He held seven stars
A sharp double-edged sword
Came out of his mouth
And his face was ablaze
Like the sun at its height

THE ANGEL WITH THE LITTLE BOOK

He was clothed in a cloud
There was a rainbow around his head
His face blazed
Like the sun
His legs
Like pillars of fire
He had a little book
Lying open
In his hand
He planted his right foot
On the sea
His left foot
On the land
Then shouted
With a loud voice
Like the roar of a lion

THE LAMB

I saw a lamb
That seemed to be slaughtered
He had seven horns
And seven eyes
Which are the seven spirits of God
And are sent out
Into every corner of the earth
Then he came
And took the book
From the right hand of one seated on the throne

THE DRAGON

And then a sign became visible in the sky
And I saw that it was a huge red dragon
With seven heads
And ten horns
With a crown upon each of his heads
His tail
Swept down
A third of the stars in the sky
And hurled them upon the earth

THE PREGNANT WOMAN

Figure of a Woman
Clothed with the sun
With the moon
Under her feet
And a crown of twelve stars
On her head
She was pregnant
And cried out in her labor
And in the pains
Of bringing forth
Her child

THE GORGEOUS MOTHER OF EVIL

There I saw a woman
Riding upon a scarlet animal
Covered with blasphemous titles
And having seven heads
And seven horns
The woman was dressed
Purple and scarlet
Glittering with gold
Jewels
And pearls
In her hand she
Held a golden cup
Full of the earth's filthiness
And her own foul impurity
On her forehead
Is written a name
With a secret meaning
"Babylon the great mother of all harlots and of the earth's abominations"
The woman was drunk
With the blood of the saints
And of the martyrs
For Jesus

The fifth trumpet
The fathomless pit

THE LOCUST

I saw a star
That had fallen down
From heaven to earth
And he was given the key
To the fathomless pit
Then he opened the pit
And smoke
Like the smoke
Of the vast furnace
Rose out of it
So the light of the sun
And the air itself
Grew dark

With the smoke of the pit
Out of the smoke
Emerged locust
To descend upon the earth

They were given powers
Like those of earthly scorpions
They had orders
To do no harm
To any grass---
Green thing---
Or tree---
But to injure
Only humans
Who didn't bear
The seal of God
On their foreheads
They were given no power to kill them
But only to torture
Them
For five months
The torture
They could inflict
Was like the pain of a scorpion sting
In those days men will seek death but they will
Never find it; they will long to die but death will
Elude them
These locusts
Looked to me in my vision
Like horses
Prepared for battle
On their heads
Were what appeared to be crowns
Like gold
Their faces were like human faces
And they had long hair like woman
Their teeth were like lion's teeth
Their breasts were like iron breastplates
And the noise of their wings
Was like the noise
Of a host of chariots
And horses
Charging into battle
They have tails that sting like scorpions
They have as their king
The angel of the pit

-oOo-

S E T R E M I N D E R S

LORD'S THRONE AND THE 24 ELDERS

SEVEN BURNING LAMPS

FOUR LIVING CREATURES
(like a LION
MAN
CALF
EAGLE IN FLIGHT)

--suggest--
complete woodcuts of
Albrecht Durer
edited by
Dr. Willi Kurth
THE APOCALYPSE

donkey
goldfish
whale
mice
birds
roses
violets
orchard
other talking flowers
swans

-oOo-

C O S T U M E S

All costumes to be made from lace chiffon silky flowing material, patterned after the classic design of each character, with the color figured through the use of glitter sequences, jewels and feathers.

-oOo-

CHRISTMAS ON EARTH CONTINUED 29

S O U N D   T R A C K

THE SOUND TRACK
A SYMPHONIC MUSICAL SCORE
COMPOSED ESPECIALLY FOR THE MOVIE
INCLUDES THE TITLE SONG
CHRISTMAS ON EARTH
ONLY THROUGH THE EYES OF LOVE
SHALL I DRAW MY DREAMS
LOVE
THE MARCH OF SMILE
ME
AND TWO NEW DANCE CRAZES
THE SPIRAL & MIME   THE DANCE OF OUR TIME
AND A SPECIAL BALLET   THE DANCE OF THE SPARKLERS
ALL FOR US THROUGH THE GLOW OF
TINEY TIM AS SNOW WHITE
THE BEATLES
BOB DYLAN
JOAN BAEZ
MARIAN FAITHFUL
FREDDY & THE DREAMERS
HERMAN & THE HERMITS
SOUPY SALES
THE KINKS
& SUPREMES
ALSO PREMIERING "THE FAIRY CHORUS"

An LP of the complete film (music, dance and dialogue) will be made to accompany an illustrated book of the film. This is to be translated in all languages for children of all countries.

THE PREMIERE OF
"CHRISTMAS ON EARTH CONTINUED"
"RADIO CITY HALL"
DURING CHRISTMAS

CHRISTMAS ON EARTH CONTINUED 30

SPECIAL CHARACTER DEDICATED TO LENNY BRUCE

THE VISION OF GOD IN HIS UNIVERSAL FORM
FROM THE SONG OF GOD
THE BHAGAVAD GITA

"SRI KRISHNA, MASTER OF ALL YOGIS
REVEALED TO ARJUNA
HIS TRANSCENDENT
DIVINE FORM
SPEAKING FROM INNUMERABLE MOUTHS
SEEING WITH MYRIAD EYES
OF MANY MARVELOUS ASPECTS
ADORNED WITH COUNTLESS DIVINE ORNAMENTS
BRANDISHING ALL KINDS OF HEAVENLY WEAPONS
WEARING CELESTIAL GARLANDS
AND THE RAIMENT OF PARADISE
ANNOINTED WITH PERFUMES
HEAVENLY FRAGRANCE
FULL OF REVELATIONS
RESPLENDENT
BOUNDLESS
OF UBIQUITOUS REGARD

SUPPOSE A THOUSAND SUNS SHOULD RISE
TOGETHER INTO THE SKY
SUCH IS THE GLORY
OF THE SHAPE OF INFINITE GOD

"From the bosom of the hugh seas, you will rise up and give to the vast universe infinite love with its eternal smile! The world will vibrate like an immense lyre in the trembling of an infinite kiss!
- The world thirsts for love! You will come and slake its thirst."

Christmas On Earth Continued
A G A I N

The final *Christmas on Earth Continued* document is the most fascinating of all. It's called a "chatter on the movie," and is titled "Christmas on Earth Continued Again and Again and Again." It is undated but the handwritten notes on the cover imply that it was written in 1966 or even later. It's a rambling, stream of consciousness string of ideas, thoughts, and words. If one takes the time to read the document, it becomes clear that Rubin is imagining what the filming of the script would be like and, even at times, what it was like as if it really happened. She also comments on events at the same time as she recounts an internal monologue about her concerns:

"soo i managed to raise my camera over my head and shoot and let the good lord guide you. it was a rather bumpy trip which left me quite exhausted"

"hmmmm i feel sorta strange and all cocky, oh well maybe it will go away, any way lets get back to Santa and see what he's up to,"

After over a year of trying to secure financing, Rubin is clearly desperate to convey her ideas. If she can't actually film the script, then she will simply imagine what it would be like to do so. The "chatter" continues with little regard to spelling or punctuation, and with occasional repetition of individual typewritten letters which lends the text a dynamic graphic quality.

Perhaps the most interesting aspect of the document is the unfiltered honesty with which it reflects Rubin's conflicted state of mind at the time.:

"Oh oh my head my head, oh oh i'm falling falling [...] ouch [...] oh, oh where is my movie camra? Oh oh, it is very important, my movie camra, I must find it, I CAN'T SEE WITHOUT IT" and To N.Y.C. WENT & BURIBED THIS TRIP TRIP TRIP Along with

CHRISTMAS ON EARTH CONTINUED AGAIN and again & again

by barbara rubin

a matter on the movie

This is the AFTERMATH of LAST YEARS esp. EFFORT TO VISUALIZE LINES CHRISTMAS ON EARTH CONTINUED

to Federico Fellini "..........,.,.,., .blab blab blab.... BLAB .. ideal ... Blaaaa..., ... blab, ... bla,... ,..a,. a ,,, the .... blab .. .. , ... bLAB, reason ....??????

...........I mean I don't know what's ideal, maybe it's the contract i signed that day, ...blab.., blab BLAAAAAAAAAAAAAAb .....,...

blab......, b.... , a ., ...ll,,,...aaaa...........blaB.......

B L a b"

my DEAR? again Hm Hm AGAIN my my

TO EVERYONE YES? And the Singin' Poet who wants to make a movie is a movie and his friend

who said We all are movie Freaks!

COME WELL —— "I'VE GOT A BETTER ONE MY DEAR" & SO WE LEAVES

AND HERE IT IS BLOWN

BUT INSTEAD WAS THE ROYAL ALBERT HALL MY FALL.

DEAR PETER. THIS IS WHY ALL MOST BE ALWAYS CHRISTMAS

WE MUST HAVE

1

1

1

Now one day as I was conversing, as I was oft'to do

with the Fairies, they told me a story that I like to
think of as Christmas On Earth Continued, being a
favorite of theirs and soon mine, i promised them I'D"...
blab blab blab ... and tell the world our story...and tell
our story to the world...blab blab blab ... and, I know
I know, blab BLABBLABBBB. you see we had this agreement
goin' and all...
A N Y HOW A N Y W A Y
now knowing how i sometimes tell little white lies sooo,
that i come out lookin' like the hero and all on my own,
I decided that when i told this story, that they told me,
to you, i was goin' to tell it like i thought it really
happened!

Now it takes place in Fairy City, which they tell me was especially built for them, within New Jerusalem, so they could rest and play and communicate with God in peace. It is as beautiful as you can imagine, with gardens and parks, ponds and games, swings and playlands.
It also has a Museum, of course, home of the Lord God's throne
Now the Lord God often calls on the Fairies for help, when all other help fails and it is thru the Lord God's throne that HIS message appears one of the Fairies, usually Snow Queen, ruler of Fairy City, will visit the Museum daily, and if she should feel all funny inside she will know that the Lord God is calling her and she will go sit on HIS throne to await HIS manifestation.
it was on such a day that our story, one of many stories, begins
THESTORYOFTHEDAYTHELORDGODMANIFESTEDHIMSELFTOSNOWQUEENRULEROFFAIRYCITY ASSHESATMANIFESTINGONHISTHRONE.
He tells her that Paradise, what all good Fairies wish for so they don't have to work, is coming
but that first they must save Jean Genet, WHO I HAVE GROWN TO LOVE
and the proof I want hee hee is the BEAMS of HIS ETERNAL SMILE, WHAAAT?
now everyone knows, particularly the Fairy, that to Save Jean Genet is nearly IMPOSSSible nearly because he is so smart and c l e v e r too
and Fairies don't like to work hard, so to save Jean Genet will be more than hard for Fairies but then again if to save Jean Genet will bring Paradise and no more work WEEEEEEEEEEEEEEEEEEEEEEEEEEEEEEl
So Snow Queen gathered the other Fairies together and explained that if they save him, like the good Lord Godwishes, then YEEEEEES sir,
you KNOW WHAT THAT MEANS, don't ya?
BUT HOW??? h e i s s o s m a r t a n d c l ever toooooo.

now for your information, all they have to do is just but all their noodles which the Lord God gave them, together because they have something goin' like a very special magic, a matter of fact it is the

2

2 very magic of the city itself, that you know Who built for them. now
this very special magic not only gave them power over the imagination
which is their birth right anyway, but also gave them the ability to
beable to become what ever they imagine Hows that for one hmmmmmm?
hmmmmmmmmmmmmmmmmmm m m m except it only works when they're in
the city A N Y way gettin' back to that very special magic
let me give you an example, LET'S SAY Happy wanted to be Sleepy (of
the 7 dwarfs of course) so Happy would concentrate on Sleepy, givin'
him one of those very special looks that he saves up especially for
these occasions, if however Sleepy didn't want to be Happy then whoever
concentrated hardess and givin' out those special looks, would become
either Sleepy or Happy. U N D E R S T A N D ? ? ? .... O H H H H
D e a r meeeeeee I almost forgot, u n f o r t u n a t e l y that since
all the Fairies have the same power equally .... tttthen Happy
would be Sleepilly Happy and Sleepy would be Happilly sllSLEEpyyyyyy
oooooooooooooooh weeeeeeeeeeeeeeeelllllllllllllllllllllll you see it only
really works on non Fairies which reminds me of course How was Snow
Queen and the Fairies goin' to save Jean Genet without workin' to
hard?? of course, of course of course, they read each others minds,
of course, of course that obviously the only way, that ObViOuSlY the
only way ,,, to save Genet,,,,,,, was get him inside Fairy City, of
course of course Ha Ha Ha Ha H A HA so believe it or not this year
Macy's Christmas window was displaying a minature Fairy City and by
coincidence Jean Genet instead of being a famous writer in France is
a Bowery Bum in New York, who just so happens to be walkin' up 34th
street and passes by Macy's Christmas Window display advertizni' a job
for a Santa Claus with room and board for Christmas Day and Night?
WEEEEL How About That? so what do you think, with Jean Genet inside
a minature Fairy City for a whole night and day, would you do if you
were a Fairy?
wait. of course. u n t i l l i t w a s n i c e a n d d a r k
t h e n WAAAAAAAAAAAAAM BBBBOOOOOOOOOOM BAM give him the old one
two three routine Feast him, sing him, and dance him, ALL right TO
night, and everyone and thing he wanted to be or do he was (they had
everything didn't they, A Fairy City Paradise and anyone he desired
to be there was a Fairy who was it and every Fairy was more then willin'
to let you become him, I mean that is our secret magic, right? right)
sooooooooooo so? so so so they feasted him and sang and danced
and everything he wanted to do, Jean Genet of course, he did, even if
he really didn't want to and everyone he wanted to be he was and since
all the Fairies were played by the heros and heroines of our time, he
also got a chance to meet them personally so? sooooooo what more could
you ask for?
tired, till so tired he falls asleep.
Now the Fairies are all content and fix everything up just like before,
so nobody would suspect anything unusual was goin' on, because they
were so sure that just because they gave Jean Genet everything
imaginable, that they thought he'd want, that he would smile for them

3

3 so that his beams of his eternal smile would go burst on God's face
and Paradise would come, AMEN, like a reward or something, and that
3 would mean like NO MORE WORK FOR E V E R AND EVER and ever ever ever
ever oh oh oh oh oh oh ohhhhhhhhhooooooooooooooooooooooooooooo
Now this is where we disagreed, but I wasn't going' to tell them to
their face or anything, but let me tell you that little do they know
that if it wasn't for aaaa little kid who was jealous, who Jean Genet
pushed when he was passin' Macy's Christmas window display, on that
memorable day, that if it wasn't for that little kid bein' in the
way Jean Genet would never have seen the sign and be in there now
instead of me tttthe the old GOAT, the oLD GOat I HATE him and so
the Little kid, that little kid stood all night outside in the ccccold
watdchin' Jean Genet, mad and angry and very jealously hurt too, so
that he couldn't see the Fairies when they came alive, see the feast
hear the songs, or dance, so that he thought the whole thing was very
funny, and spent his time sayin' bad things about the pecular in
which tthat Santa Claus ha ha, who does he think he is God or
something?, was behavin'. makin' all those funny faces and doin' all
those silly things, he showww looks stttupid
so that when Jean Genet woke (and those Fairies were to busy cele-
bratin' to see) and saw that that that FACE? the face of someone
makin' faces at him, he just thought it was all apart of the beautifull
dream he was havin' (oh all right so you were responsible for that),
and that it was just another Fairy (all right alllll right) makin'
SILLY FACES AT HIM! (so there!) cooperati n', wasn't goin' to start
no fight with no Fairy, or anything, cooperatin' as I said he just
made the Face and then the other face and the other face and the
other and the other the other all of which surely woke him up, to
S U C H A F A C E !!!!!! WEEEEEEEEEEEEL I'll show that kid a thing
or two about faces......blab blab blab..... blab blab Yeaaaaaa?
you stupid jeerrrrrrrk, you big ffat stupid jeerrrrrrrk, yeaaaaaaaaa??
by now Santa had already givin' up wishin' him away, being' he was
such a smart man, and clever too, and was real competition for the
little kid, that is in the art of makin' silly faces and doin' funny
things. It's not easy you Know, no? no no no no A N Y YYYYYYY
way they made so many faces did so many things, wished so many
thoughts and felt, felt too many things, that the last trick each of
them pulled left them sore and aware of how tired they were. so they
decided to use a little strategy: like, they were goin' to see who
could stare the other out with a straight face by the process of who
could think the worst thoughts, worst I mean the kind that make you
embarasseed and all,. hmmmmmmmmmmmmmm This however didn't last very
long because neither of them had the energy to make it convincin'
enough... so they settled to just stare at each other and soon
thought ..... hmmmmmmmm, and ...... ha,.....oh..... oooooh., and so
forth ...... and .... my he looks awful silly, ha ha ha
hmmmmm your face's not so hot either, ho ho ho (and soon they were at
it again)

oh, I can do that
oh yeaaaaa?   yeaaaaaaaaa and this one hmmmmm how about this, ho ho ho
oh sure it's nothin'   ooooh I can do this better than you
oooo ooooo h I can do that better then this   WHAAAAAAAT wait a minute
there
no.
oh yeaa?
yeaaaaa
yeaaa yeaaa yeaaa ho ho ho   ho ho ho???? HOHOHOHOHOHOHOHOHOHAHAHAHA
HAHAHAHAHAHAHAHAHAHAHAHAHAHAHAHAHAHAHAHAHAHAHAHAHAHAHAHAHAHAHA etc etc
why that kids nuts a nut   hmmmmm a pretty good one hmmmm as good as
weeeeeeel just about , when I was his age
the old goat's pretty smart, I mean for an old goat an all
he's a clever kid, he learns real quick realll quick
my father, my father nev hey wait a minute do that one again, yeaaaaaaa
like this ?
yea, where'd ya learn that? never saw it before
oh it's nothin' just somethin' i picked up in my er travels
yea, show me some more
weeel here's one I picked up in bleb bleb bleb and blab blab blab,
it was somethin'.................................... else!
WOWWWW really????????
yea I was about .... blab blab blab etc dash dash dash tra la la
laaaaaaaaaaaa
geee I've never been nowhere
you will   sure you will   you know you remind me of when I was

yea,?
yea

do I have to say more? I mean what do you think would happen, have to
happen, I mean after all that and all, of course he smiled OF C O U R S E
of course of course   but do you know what? no? weeeeeel the you know
who, I'M not goin' mention any names or nothing, but those you know
who's, who thought they we're reaaaaal smart and all, they are still
workin' yeaaa still workin', they thought the Lord God said if they
saved Jean Genet, HE would bring Paradise, remember? a bargain a Bargain,
they thought our Lord God made bargains, BARGAINS, ooooh my, it's not
that HE lied or anything He just said Paradise is coming! HMMMMMMMMMM
HMMMMMMMMMMMMMMMMMMMM   I wonder HMMMMMMMMMM I wonder if HE often
says that!

Allll right Fairies, our agreement is kept

but you sure did start somethin'

*************** It all began many many moons ago 00000000000 0 0 0 0 0 0
as a little kid I told ya I often carried on conversations with the
Fairies (and thats how latter I came to tell you their favorite story
that I call Christmas On Earth Continued) but I never told you that
after we had finished talking and they had gone, I use to pretend that
I was Jean Genet in disguise, really. .. and everywhere I went and
what ever I did, I believed that, for some reason, some bigGG reason,
which I forget now, I had to keep my real identity as Jean Genet
hidden as a little kid, except of course when nobody was around.
As I grew up I use to day dream all the time that someday I would be
just like Jean Genet and that God would ask the Fairies to save me
too because HE loved me, and the Fairies would throw me a big party
and let me be King for a day. but when i mmmmmmmma t u r ed..... i just
wish i had been there; so i could of taken some movies to show to my
friends when they come over to visit me,
so I got myself a movie camera and made movies, but always in my head
I saw the movie, the only movie, I really wanted to make, Christmas
On Earth Continued. Now one day as I lay dreamin', me and my movie
camera, my movie camera and me, we're never very far apart, you know
just incase. some strange magical force came and lifted us up and
carried us away to the Heavens.................................
via helicopter, hmmmmmmmmmmmmm I say I like it, ooooh It's sooo exciting,
sooo beautiful,   when suddenly Iremembered my movie camra, "oh
where is my movie camra, Imust take some pictures, oooh I just
c o u l d n ' t m i s s t h i s f o r a l l t h e m o n e y i n
t h e w o r l d, besides who would believe this? oh oh   oh there
is my movie camra". gently I picked it up and winded it and put
it next to my cheek, so the both of us could look out for a suitable
cloud to take a picture of . . . when suddenly I saw W A Y   O U T
there color spots before my eyes. I decided to see if my movie camra
was seeing spots too. Oh, you see spots too, so I figured this
would be a good way to open my movie. I did not , rather WE didn't
realize that our magical forse helicopter was circlin' to go down,
because we were to busy shootin' and admirin' how the little spots of
colors were growin' larger and larger, changin' shape and becomin' all
sorts of lovely things, a flower ooooh, abird weeeeeeee, superman?
Wait a minute I could have sworn sworn I saw MICKEY MOUSE????????
WHAAAAAAAAAAAAAAAAAAAAAAAAAAT perfect perfect what, i says to
myself, for my sound track perfeCT and with Mickey Mouse on screen,
hee hee MICKEY MOUSE, hmmmmm mmmmm why i's think we're gonin' right
into Mickey's eye, ho ho ho? we're goin' down but it ain't into
Mickey's eye, no sireeeee, why we're shooting right along side close by
oh ohhhhhhhh no no oh ohhh yesssss oh oh ho ho ho ho what shots ho ho --
PLOOOOOOOP, ho ho we've landed ho ho POOOOOOOOP and what do you think
we're shooting? my LOVE, MY DREAM FAIRY CITY oh OH is it true, is it
really you ? tell me, speak to me FAIRY CITY oh boy oh boy am I
gona shoot you, everything, oh boy oh boy, yes sireeeeee
wait till they see this, hm hm, I'll just shoot around, lala la, up,
tra la hmmmm lovely lovely, we'll climb a little higher and get some
shots down   t h e re hmmm hmmm, oh oh and around and a r o u n d.

6
6 beautiful, beautiful. and now in slow motion ha ha, a few single frames, a little faster, ho ho, and now we'll just swing a bissel over and
6 shoooooooooo HEY HE EEEE Y What's goin' on?, WE can't see aaaa thing, HEY hey i think someone might just be breathing on us, nooooooooo oh no that's impossible, impoosible, maybe it's dirty, I'll just wipe the lens with my left hand, that's right, and keep shooting with my right hand, hmmmmm and what's this i shoot, my pointer fingure in an eye? IN AN EYE? in a biggg eye, weeel we'll just shoot from a step back, hmmm that face sure seems to be somewhere, "over the rainbow," SSSHUT UPPPP, hmmmmmm, somewhere else, as i was thinkin' before you rudely interrupted me. hmmm i don't think it even knows i er we exist (now i gota remember me and my camra is we, you know how temperamental it gets.) any wayyyy i thinks if we just move back a bissel, yeaaa, ho ho and a little more, sure the big face has a body too, of of Snow FLAKES and BUBBBLES? snow flakes and bubbles? and back more it's sitting on a throne of HALO LIGHT? halo light, why not? we are in Fairy City. let's get a few more shots closer, the Snow Flakes and bubbles with a bigg face, and then just the bbig face, oh, my oh my, you you must be Snow Queen, oh mighty ruler of Fairy CITY, forgive our rash intrusion blab blab blab (i know i said it out loud, i mean i figured if i buttered her up it would distract her while we crept up closer to shoot but i couldn't hear a word on my sound track) and i need not have feared because when i got as close as would be polite she was definitely in some other world, so we tipped toed closer, still and took a real close up of her EYE and by gosh, something shinny like was comin' out of her eye, her eye? her eye, her right eye to be specific, something reaaal shinny moved across her eye and stopped half way in the right eye and half way in the left eye yes sireeeee BOOOOOOOOOOM, got ya! got me nothing, but what!s this, those shinny things like sparklers, yea sparklers are many, thousands of them popped out of her eyes, dancing on her nose thru her teeth at her ears, reallY r ALLY! why of course, of course, how silly of me, she's mani oh oh don't g . don't go get, no y t BOOOOOOM , gone gone the sparklers i mean the manifest tion, oh oh i mean reall, kno wHO, has gathered and gone back in her eyes, gone, butttt i could have sworn they bowed, yessssss bowed before they disappeared. Bow? bow bow boW. What's this I'm We're being pulled away. oh no but WEEE we were helpless and all we were able to shoot was Snow Queen fading in the distance and OUCH!---------stepped on my toe OUCH! Fairies, Fairies like all of a sudden from nowhere their swarming all over the place, up down look around reaally. WEEELL thank G, we've stopped, why why we're miles from Snow Queen oh no oooooo and with all these fluttering Fairies, blurring my shots we eeeeeeeeeeeeeeeeeeeeeeeeeeeeeeeeeeeeeeeeee We didn't have a chance, soon we're coming into focus on the Fairies below because we're in the air, wouldn't you know, so i decides to turn and take a shot of my abductor, whyyyy Peter Pan, ain't that nice! cheeeeeeeeseeee now what's this going on down there, geeee i can sure

7
7 shoot some pretty things from up here, and Petee Pan's givin' us a tour and all the Fairies cooperatin' and looking up right into my
7 camra, hmmmmm i wouldn't want to spoil anything but i wonder if they're not just puttin' us on weeeeee, PLOQOOOP, heYYY why did you drop us for? heeeeeey OUCHHHHHHHH! hey watch out where you're steppin', FAIRY. yeaaa? yeaaaaaaaaaaaaa I mean we don't mind shootin' legs and feet or nothin' especially such nice ones but OUCHHHHHH, i think we best get up yesss? hmmmm that's better hmhmmm hmmmmmmm you know what we're goina do, little ole Movie Camra of mine? hmmmmm? Since all the Fairies seem busy, with what not, we'll just sneak around, just like this, and get some close ups of them, that's right, ooh there's Cinderella, don't he look nice, hmmmm and the Prince, such a lovely girl, hmmmmmm, i wonder where Snow ...... SHHHHHHHH sssssshhhhhhh, Snow Queen, is talking, sorry didn't hear it on my sound track, shhhhhh, maybe i gota turn the volume up, yea? i know sshhhhhhhhh, HEYYYYY shop pushin', your jerkin' my shootinnnnnnnnn, HHHHEYyyyyyy ouCHHHHHHHHH, watch where your goin' biggg Fairyyyyyyy, hey you're not listenin' i don't like that, none of you are, but then again i can't even hear myself on my own sound trackkkkk, yakkkkkkkiteeeeeeyak teeeeyakkkkkkkk kkkkk little bo peep, hey, OZ, ALICE, Donald duck???? i mean i don't mind shootin' you nice Fairies and all but your backs and reARS?, bad enough Snow Queens Talkin' and we can't shoot it, but realLly your r e a r sssss? and of course i wouldn't be tall enough, even on my toes, to shoot over you or use strategy or change lens oh, oh, there's only one thing we can do movie camra of mine, up you go, like that, don't be afraid I got you goin', the motor is on, and the rest, is up to YOU. GOOOD LUCK! shhhhhhhhhhhh. all right all right, i'll be quiet and listen, even though, sniff, sniff, only my movie camra will be able to see SHHHHHHHHHHHHHHHHHHHHHHHHHHH

Snow Queen: He was here (she must have looked up or somethin'
because suddenly all the Fairies
were lookin' up and We took the
chance to get some air)
Snow Queen: Ye Saviors, He says
Ye Saviors, I'm comin'
Fairies: Ye Saviors, she said, Ye Saviors, He's comin'
Snow Queen: (in a hushed voice) YOU KNOW WHAT THAT MEANS?
Fairies: NO MORE work
Snow Queen: RIGHT

(while they were enjoying the pleasures of such a thoughttttttttttt we thought we'd try to get a little clooooo, ooooh, come down little movie camra of mine COME TO ME QUICKLY, that bigggg Fairy over there is givin' me the eeeeee; want your picture taken MR. Fairy? that's right just stand there in my way,,, got ya, MR. Fairy now GET OUT OF MY WAY! SSSSSHHHHHHHHHHHH shhhhhh I'll shhhh and get back to shooting your reARRRRRS. HELLO you back again MR. FAIRY? Yesssss? shake your

8 camra, YEEEEESSSS? MR. Fairy just one more shot, that's a nice MR. Fairy, now get losssst, hmmmmmmmm weeell weeeelllll a rearRRRRR
8 hmmmmm a back hmmmmm some feeeeeet)

Fairies:	RIGHT
Snow Queen:	bbbbbut HE wants JJJean Genet
Fairies:	bbbbbbut HE wants JJJean Genet?
Snow Queen:	that's right
Fairies:	that's right??
Snow Queen:	and the proof
Fairies:	and the proof??
Snow Queen:	and, the proof is to be in the beams of his eternal smile
Fairies:	and the proof is to be in the beams of his eternal smile??
Snow Queen:	in the beams of his eternal .,. smile!

HMMMMMM, it's quiet all of aaa sudden, hmmmmm the feet are moving out of my range, maybeee we'll just follow them and see where they lead us in our shootin', heyyy? hmmmm hmmmm their walking' faster, hmm slowin' down, stopped weeeell will just bring you, my movie camra, up a bissel, to the reaaar again, himma shoulder, a neck, a head, hmmm lucky for us he's shorttttt, whhhy if it isn't Snow Queen herself, we're shootin' now, HELLO SNOW QUEEn, how're ya doin' hold it! Shot ya, hmmmm hm why does she always have to look like she's some place else for? it's disturbin' you know! REALLY? really! hmmm why she's flutterin' and lookin' r e a l h a r d errr at us, whyyy Snow Queen, WE'll have to get a close up of that, oh ohhhh, why there's something appearin' on your face, yes, yes, why it's a picture, oh OHOHHHH, why it's Jean Genet why he looks reaal cold and hungry, and all tattered and worn and there's snow fallin' on him, oh oh why of course, this must be that marvelous Fairy thinkin' process, everyone's talkin' about. hmmmm it's gone gone she's turning and we will and shoot on my HEAVENS ABOVE if it ain't Mother Goose, and Snow Queen's doin' areal fast look flutter at her and now she's Lookin' and flutterin' and there appears on her face just as on Snow Queens the picture of the thought that made her flutter, poor Jean Genet, but shoot again, why she looks again and right in to you my dear camra and now she winks? winks, why Mother Goose I didn't know, you too? weeeel nobody's gona say i didn't take a close up of you. but look what appears on her face so near, why looky looky we're on 34th street standing right in front of Macy's Christmas Window Display featuring FAIRY CITY? "an actual reproduction of the real one, which no man till now Has seen???" REALLY? hmmmm know wonder she winked ohhhh, it too has faded just as it was gettin' interestin', hmmmm she's turnin too, i wonder to who? TWEEDLE DEE AND TWEEDLE DUM? could it be? it must be because Mother Goose is givin' them a quick look flutter look winkhmmmmmm Tweedle DEE's lookin' and flutterin' and there was the thought that fluttered

9

9 on his face and then he looks again and winks and the winkin' thought.blab
...on his face and then he looks and turns to TWEEDLE dum who looks and
9 flutters at the thought that appears on his face and looks and thinks the thought that appears on his face that made him wink and looks again and my gosh there's JEAN GENET. instead of being a famous writer in France he just so happens to be a bowery bum walkin' up 34th street on a cccold day, and then tweedle dum turns to TWEEEDLE DEE who just so happens to have on his face a picture of Macy's Christmas Window display of Fairy City with a sign advertizing for a Santa Claus with room and board for Christmas Day and night and then we're shootin' something quite remarkable, even in Fairy Thinking, Jean Genet walks out of Tweedle Dum's Head into the door of Macy's department store on Tweedle DEE's face and comes out the window of the Fairy City display on top of TWEEDLE DEE'S nose, as Santa Claus. WEEEEELL ain't that something else, and then Snow qUeen and Mother Goose stand next to Tweedle DEE and Tweedle Dum and we're able to take a family picture, so far of the looks the flutter and thought on the face and look and wink at the thought on your face and then look and have Tweedle DEE and Tweedle dum explain in their own pecululiar way, how to put the flutter in the wink and chuckle! and we all turn to GRUMPY? not grumpy and everything was going along so fine who looks and blab blab blab and looks and blablablabalb and looks and b l a bbbb bla b b b and looks and boy what a party was goin' on, on his face everyone was havin' some orgy there, feastin' singin' dancin' feastin' feastin' feastin' feastin', i's think he's got hung UP, and boy did he have a suggested belly a c h, oh, oh, of course grumpy's grumpy cause he has indigestion, Alka Selza any one? Doc, Happy gooood to see ya, goood to shoot ya, what a shot! what a sight! Snow queen a flutterin', Mother Goose a winkin', Tweedle dee, and tweedle dum put the flutter in the wink and was a gigglin' and grumpy's grumpy and Doc had the Alka SElZa and Happy was Happy and on his face appeared a very happy thought, P A R A D I S E ! oh oh here comes Peter, Snow White, the March Hare, Red Queen, Prince Charming, Wendy, Hansel, Wonder Women? get back alittle they're crowdin' us oh oh look they too are flutterin' and lookin' and winkin' and the rest, hmmm why shhootin' around everyone, seems to be, I wonder if it's not some kinda new Dance, hmmm? oh oh i think we'll try it hmm, movie camra ? a look a a flutter a look a wink a look a chuckel and we all get belly aches. oh hooo my my everyones movin' about, come on Camara let's go, where the action is, oh h oooooo, my, my what a shot, just like Fred Astair, and Ginger Rogers, dancin' my, my, oh oh banGGG, sorry stepped on your toe, why not? one shot of a toe, hmmmm, i hear i hear comin' in on my sound track, a song, a song of, of, louder please, no not louder please, the sound louder, the song something like, when Paradissss ...... something and something it will be ..... something something ...ever, hmmthat's nice.sooo your goin' a be a toe forever? OH we're being pushed, hmmmm come up come up little movie camra, enough of a toe, overthere t h e r e

10

10 yes yes shoot down t h e r e there, they're doin' something, the
Fairies, formin' a line, circuling, and back and forth. i thinks
their writing something, don't you? no come down, silly not in the
sky, with their bodies on the floor. stupid! sure they are , oh get
out of our view Fairy, please, your elbow PLEASE, there there, on
EaR ER, no, no over over, that's right, no more maybe with your wide
angle hmm? that's better, see they wrote C H R I S T M A S O N
E A R H T F O R E V E R you'd know they couldn't spell, but Wonder-
full it's wonderfuuuuuuuuuuu uuu u No nooooooooo, it can't be,
you wouldn't do this to Christmas, no no get back Christ, don't go
as, m you can't, oh oh ooooh ever, left, what happened? the words,
the words they're havin' a rumble; no more Christmas no more Earth
no more ever oh oh, "Oh yeaaaa I'm goina be Christmas from now on
understand?" You, Christmas,? why you couldn't .... "take that back
or i'll belt, " Weeel if your gona a argue over Christmas I'll just
be EVeeeeeeeeee, OUCH, oh oh oh oh, but what's this comin' in, it's
a BIRD, it's a PLANE, it's SUPERMAN, to the rescue and out of the
debths of the crowd, there rouse, MIGHTY MOUSE, HURRAYYYYYY and
perched in his hand is TINKEE BELL HURRAYYY HURRAYYYY, hurrrrr
H E LPPPPPPPPPPPPPP! they're after usssss, HEY what did weeeeee e
we din't have a chance as a matter of fact we never seem to havea
chance, for Tinkee bell was sure mad comin' at us shakin' her fist
and next minute was B L A N K (here I'd like to enlighten you on the
said person who, plays Tinkee bell and also some of the other
"characters, now I dream't that all the Fairies were really the heros
and heroines and stars of my time, but really incognito, soooo
I didn't find it necessary or needed to sterotype them, I let them
choose with my assistance of course, it was in my domain, the Fairy
they wanted to be who they felt with.irrecardless as in some cases
whether female or male, in case point of Lenny Bruce I wanted him to
play Snow Queen a fittin' and proper part Howevereeee he opposed, on
simple grounds, so I gave him a part especially for him: Sir Krishna,
the vision of God in His universal form. but for tinkee bell my heart
was set on one an only Sammy Davis Jr. who regrets that due to the
numerous etc. obligations....but we still must hope ... so it was
really Sammy Davis Jr. who more as Tinkee Bell came after us). "I
mean the Fairies behavin' like that was enough but you standin' there
with that silly thing in front of your face or maybe it was your face,
that was too much so BAAAAAAAAAAGgggggggggggggggggggggggggggggggggg"
oh weeel never say die, that's right dust your self off, button up,
it's chilly outside, oh didn't you know? your on 34th street and it's
very cccold this winter with the snow and all. oooh quick, put that
movie camera to your eye and shoot because here comes Jean Genet.
oh yes so here comes Jean Genet, you say. shootin'. I mean I say
shootin', but I was goin' keep my distance, I mean I've heard about
him, how smart and clever he is, it's sure cccold and quiet.
A N Y W A Y

11

11

11 HMMMMMM, i'd rather shoot the street, yes, the huddled passerbys,
sloshing a round in the snow, pullin' their kids with runny noses
along, cars stuck or creepin' by, and the air, picking up dresses and
sneaking up coats, hmmm, hmmm, Hey Hey now listen, you and i know
your not suppose to shoot that, right? SOOOOOO GET YOUR .....CAMRA
BACK ON JEAN GENET. all right all right Jean Genet, huff, heeeeey i
can't shoot him, I can't find himm. OVER there, OVER THERE STUpid.
where? WHERE? WHERE DO YOU THINK HE'D BE ON 34th STREET, hmmmm? all
right all right, JUST GET OVER THERE, pleaaaase. here, all right?
NOOOOOO, NOT HIS BACK, YOU'RE SHOOTIN' HIS BACK, now get over
OPPOSITES HIM, SO YOU CAN GET IN THE WINDOW DISPLAY, THE MACY'S
CHRISTMAS WINDOW DISPLAY, OF FAIRY CITY REMEMBERRRRR? i know, i know,
but in the streeeeeeet? GET OVER THERE * AND ON WITH THIS SHOOTING
OR ELSE IIIIIIIIII, oh allright, gee you got no sense of humor, really.
what's this what's this Jean GENET pushed a little kid down, why that
lousy s.o.b., he he could have at least helped him up, you know.
I KNOW I KNOW, BUT JUST GET ON WITH YOUR SHOOOOTIN',???? hmmmmmm,
all RIGHT I'LL GET ON WITH OUR OUR SHOOTIN', SO THERE WE
WAS SHOOTIN', he had his back to us, because he was lookin' in
the window naturally, and the little kid too, had he's back to us
cause he too is looking in the window, only on the opposite side, he
was gona be CAREFULL. then there are some people passin', by real
fast, right in front of us and it's reaaaaaal cccold out and snow
is fallin' everywhere, and now there is a snow flake on my wide angle
lens and I am shooting this thru a snow flake --- because the man
said GET ON WITH THE SHOOTING OR ELSE! are you finished? all right?
feel better? now WIPE THAT DAMN SNOW FLAKE OFFFF. i's wipes the
snow flake off and i's sees we're shootin' moveeement in theeewindowww,
HEY CUT THE CRAPPPPP, SMARTY, hmmm can't win no how, oh well, Jean
Genet is looking right into my camra, but he dosen't even notice us,
nobody seems to notice us, why he turns back to the window and bless
my soul a man is a standing right up front, in the window and is
holdin' a sign, SANTA CLAUS wanted ROOM AND BOARD FREEEE FOR
christmas day and night, hmmm i quess Santa thought it over and
decided because he pulled himself up straight, pushed his crummy
coat down in the back, turned and gave a hUFF, to the little kid and
turned about and walkinside. WEEEELL, weeeell nothing, you just go
on and follow him and don't stop shootin' for a minute. SOOOO we's
follow him, and don't stop shooting, except i thought it would be
nice to get a shot of the little kid before we went in, oh oOOOOH,
that's not nice at all sticking' your biggg little kids tongue in
my lens. WEEEEELL, we just trotted right back in, to find Genet., hmmmmmm
i shot a sign, it shoots EXIT, hmm it also shoots KEEP PUt, DON'T
ENTER KEEP OUT hmmmm why this must lead to hmmm why we're just
takin' pictures that's alll, oh ah hmmm. made it ah. now we can get
some shots of Fairy City, I mean we won't hurt nothin' we just wantto
shoot around and besides we'll be all ready in position for Jean's
grand entrance as Santa Claus ha ha ah hmmmm quite remarkable repro-
duction, hmmm just like the time I went lookin' around the real thing.
hmmm hasn't changed much. hmm hmm my my, what is this i perchance

12
12
12
to shoot, a lovely cinderella my my what a remarkable
resemblance, even if it's a doll. my mym hm hm hmmmmm. what's that
noise, quick gota hideeee but have you forgotten that your inside a
window? OOOOOOH thanks for remindin' me oh it's nothin' . ah to
my relief as I turned and shoot it was night time with just a few
shadowy figures of huddled passerbyers, probably all goin' to their
nice warm homes and oh do those cars look spooky now, with their
lights throwin' shadows all over the place, ahhhhhhhh i thinks we
shot quite enough of this and will go back tooooo oh OOOOH to catch
a shot, ugh, w a y in the corner of the window aaaa monstrous face,
oh OHHHHH "CALM DOWN, TAKE ANOTHER SHOT" "SEEE IT'S ONLY THE LITTLE
KID" welll i mean he shouldN't scare me like that hmmmmm, i see
you've decided to stay right there and watch hmmmm? oooooooH well to
shoot, to shoot some moreoh my gosh just look who's comin' in focus
from across the window, weavin' his way hm hm, well, well, I'M not
makin' fun of you or nothin' (i think we insulted himm) he keeps lookin'
straight at us, comin' closer like that, oh! oh he's just comin' to
take his throne, of course it's right in front of us, WHY DON'T YOU
MOVE BACK A BISSEL AND GIVE THE MAN SOME ROOM? of ccourse of course.
why you sure look Happy MR. SANTA, and all rosy, and stuffed, put
on a little weight didn'ttya? shhhhhhhhhhhh, he's sleepin', all
slomped on his throne, shhhhh hmmmmmmmmmmmm it sure got quiet all of
a sudden, hmmm while Santa sleeps let's shoot alittle around the
city, hmmmm wait let's take a long shot of Santa against the CITYY
the lights, what happened to the lights all of asudden? hmmmmm isn't
that nice, the city's sleeping too. hmm it sure is nice and cozy. a
little dark for shootin' but weird, rather. hmmmmmmm I'm sorta
gettin' sleepy too hmmmmmm i can bearly stand up ohhhhhh, hmmmm, i
don't think i'm goina be able to shoooooooooooooooo, t, hmmmm w e
ar e v e r y y ys s s l e e e e ppp y l e e p y when suddenly
there was a tremble that shook my shootin' to no end, what
asssskaaaakinnnng woooooow weeeeeee i can only imagine what i shot
but when the tremble subsided and i had manuvered over to the window
for suport incase of what was to come i looked thru my lens the city
had changed, no longer was we shootin' sleepy city but light.it was
as if everything in the city was animated with it's own light that
was just burstin' with life, sprallin' all over burstin' burstin'
and then came a real whoooper i felt like i was in a vibratin'
machine the way we were shaking and shooting, i imagine we must of
looked mighty funny because what we were shootin' sure did. boy was
that city movin'. it was all very silly, but we just couldn't
aaaaaaaaaaaa stoppppppppppppp BOOOOOOM. well that's over with i hope.
oh what a sight what aa sIGHT to be shooting AAAAAAAAAAAH. FIREWORKS
FIREWORKS every wherE FIREWORKS . we were movin' in delighted we're
goin' shoot this thru FIREWORKS ooooh beautiful beautiful, we were
shootin' all over the place EVERYTHING when at close range we shoot
oh no you wouldn't believe it oh no you wouldn't oh oh it it wasn't
fire FIREWORKS, no no oh oh it was it was would you believe it no no

13
13
13
oh YES Fairies, fairies? Right Fairies Fairies faries. yes yes I'll
show you, look thru my camra, seee those color light burst seee? there,
fairies underneath WAKING UP. seeeee? no. look look, over there coming
in focus that stuffed doll that's right Goofy, yes Mickey Mouses
friend Goofey, well any minute now he's goin' burst. GOOFEY?
goofey's goin' burst. there there see seee how it's i mean he's movin'
boooooom seseeeeee see the color lights see see wait a minute, there
you are GOOFEY, alive. Goofey i wonder how come he's here? weeeell.
he seems to say. as he looks right in the camra WEEEELL. and walks
away. boy oh boy ain't that somethinnnn? hmmmm i feel sorta strange
and all cocky, oh well may be it will go away, any way let s get
back to Santa and see what he's up to, hhm stillll asleepy, hmmmm
he shoots so small, asleepy sleepy close up Santa OH he'stirs and
i's hearing' sweet music on my sound track, hmm seems to come from
o v e r there, well if it isn't the awaken Fairies, a procession of
them, weaving thru the city, it looks like they're comin' this way,
and the sweet music's theirs, a song, A March Of Smile, and they're
all glowin', i'm feelin' weak, and little and then inside me a
voice rouse and only i heard "hear me oh little one with your movie
camra, till now you've been a tourist, with your senses in your
movie camra, but now as all the forces come to life in these my
awakening Fairies and Santa Claus is exposed, so shall you be. No
longer will you be satisfied to live thru your movie camra, now you
will want to be there. and no longer a peepin' tom, so to speak.
YOUR EXPOSED, and all the forces are comin' after you, gET READY.
Like Santa everything you want you'll have, and you'll be all those
things you want to be , you'll meet your heros personnalyy, sing
feast and dance be serenaded and charmed, seduced and free,
everything you want is yours yours yours. except the forces of
life that you are from and who know your presence and who who you
will feel are interfering with you. It's now YOURS. SEE there is
Fairy City glorious and splendid and coming are the Fairies who will
open the gate, and there is Santa Claus awakening to a dream?
WEEEEELL you and he are like one. and if this is a dream it will
only matter if you believe it."
HMMMMMMMMM, HE has spoken. and it was as if i never shot before. and
when i saw what i was shooting, Santa, i sorta a felt very close to
him and could feel the funny premonition going thru him that some-
thing was going to happen indeed! the fairies YES! I quickly
turned towards them, a blurr? ooops, wrong lens, there my zoooooom
ahh! they're comin' closer, they are, and just look at those
dangerous faces a good thing for you my zooom, that i can keep my
distance, ahhhhhh they stopped, everyone is turnin' their attention
on Happy and Sleepy, who were doin' a solo, (demonstratin' this
secret weapon theyhad, that i was sure they were goina use on us)
I really didn t pay much focus on them as we were zooomin' in an
all, ooops tooo close, ah they're movin' again, heyyy comin' closer
heeeey??oh oOOOOOH, they're takin' us along, heeey what are ya push-
in' for, I'll get you, all right, just wait, you look mighty suspicious to

14

me. i thinks this calls for some good shots of you, just in case somethin' happens for hiSTORY, for the PEOPLE. I mean just look at your faces, quilt is written all over them. HAAAAAAAAA a WITch, another WITch, ha ha the wolf, MISS TIGER LILY, THE MAD HAtter, ahh such FACEs, hmmm so you don't like me heeey shootin' you heeeey?? tryin' to get rid of me ? Mad HAtter? heeeeeeey get back, get back, don't come any closer, your goin' out of focussssss plooooop !!!!!!!! we went blank, for a minute, picked ourselves up, and resumed shootin' .... T H E B I G MOM E N T..T H E M O M E NT everyone was waiting for. the Fairies had stopped right in front of Santa's throne, all was still, and tense i was anxtious, when to my relief Snow Queen stepped forward, her hand raised in peace. boy was i glad to see her and all ofa sudden i felt sorta silly at my paranoia and when Snow Queen royally bowed and walked to Santa's side, (and Santa's face looked like something else, and soon i was in giggles, though i forced my self and shooting to be quiet, since i realized the seriousness and hushness of the situation and i would certainlly need steady hands to shoot it.)
Snow Queen had taken out a scroll and began reading off the names of the Fairies, who then called, stepped forward, and bowed, to Santa Claus, stood still a good minute and then walked off bowing. unfortunately from where i was shooting their backs were towards me, so i couldn't see what exactly went on during that minute but, i could see Santa's face and it went under enough changes, that his face couldn't even keep up with the faces he was making. there he was, everytime a fairy was introduced and bowed; making those silly faces and strange things with his body, then i remembered the strange magical power that Fairy City had and gave equally to all the Fairies and everything came back to me, as there rouse just like in Fairy thinking, from what i was shooting the image of what i was thinking; only real real fast; first Snow Queen on her throne manifesting, when i first shot her with all those sparklers of HIM dancing all over her face and then of course Fairy thinking the shots of the Fairies looks and flutters looks and winks and how it appeared on their faces just as it was now appearing on Santa Claus and the Fairies introduction, and then the image faded as my thoughts wandered and when Happy was being introduced to Santa Claus there popped up on this shot Happy and Sleepy, when i was too paranoid to focus carefully on them as they demonstrated their secret which the Fairies were, right this very moment, performin' on Santa, and remember when Happy and Sleepy started pushin' me along with them as they continued on their journey to Santa, and i thought somethin' terrible was goin' to happen and wanted to make sure i shot their faces for posterity? remember the WITch and the Woolf and Miss Tiger LILY yesss their faces now appear too before me. and the Mad Hatter remember how i thought he was after me and i would not stop shootin' him till finally i fell and went blank and when i got up and started shootin' again it was with relief at seein'---Snow Queen in peace, introducin' the Fairies to Santa Claus and look who's bein' introduced now, if it ain't the Mad HAtter

15

herself, why Santa's face looks just like the face of the Mad HAtter i shot before. oh look, now Santa has a hat toooooo, hm hm now i know what they do in that one minute with SANta. hmmmmmmmmm how strange though to be shootin' these two faces superimposed, doesn't look as frightenin' now, as when i first shot the Mad HAtter, yet it's the same shot, I mean all i really did was wind it back and shoot over it, yet it's sorta SPOOOOOOOOky hmmmmmmm hmmmmm the Mad HAtter's left. geee it's takin' a long time for the next fairy to be introduced, he shoots like he's floatin' or somethin', ah, ah, ahhhhhhh i'm shootin' it in slow motion, know wonder, there that's better, we'll shoot it in real fast motion and get it over with already, cause there's a long long line of Fairies still waitin' to be introduced yet. and it'll take ages at the rate they're goin', and anyway i's tired of shootin' this and i's gettin' dizzy from all this multibule thinkin' and shootin', the marvelous Fairy thinkin' process or not. hmmmmmm little did i know then that someone else was thinking' these very same thoughts, this was   PAN   who was just gettin' ready to be introduced to Santa, weeeell thank G. for Pan. why right under everyones eyes and before anyone knew, he was in Santa's throne and had Santa on his way along with the Fairies already introduced, wellllll i says to myself, if tthat ain't an opportunity for me to get, i'm an idiot. and didn't the man say to keep my shootin' on Santa? i mean he said it. but i was to find that rather difficult, since the mob, of impetuous singin' Fairies were squashin' me, oooooh i can't breathe let alone shot. However i did feel "this would mean something latter", soo i managed to raise my camra above my head and shoot and let the Good Lord guide you. it was a rather a bumpy trip which left me quite exhausted and when i finally caught my breathe and could resume my normal camra position, in front of my eye, my heart broke, sob sob sob, you mean this is what you've been shootin' BLURRRRRR? and where were you LORD? never mind, we'll see what's come out latter at home, but right now hmm? let's get you in focus, HMMM? hmmmmmmm first a blurr, now a hmmmmm why it looks like a zoo, really? yea, take a look, hmmm, it does! but come on, get in focusssssss, why WEEEEEEEEELL WEELL DELIGHTFUL! A WONDERland of sights! I shot before me magnificence, and pleasure alive thru Fairy contact. and in the center of this splendor of activity, amidst what could have been a reproduction of the Garden of Eden, sat Santa Claus, eating the fruits of the garden, served and entertained by the fruits of our imagination? Everything was there that could please the appetite. in what looked like the result of all mans dreams ambitions loves desires and forefillments thru the ages brought together and packaged in a Fairy deal and given to Santa as a present, (of what they thought was the answer to his earthman's problems) it was breath taking, is all i can say. and so as not to indure the thought of spoiling your own imagination process, we'll leave it at that. create it yourself, for we shot enough as we could stand and decided to join and enjoy it. at first we shot slowly around shooting up all these treasures

16

16 in so slow motion (so this would last forever) ohh the things we shot and every where we shot there was music and dancing on my sound
16 track. aaaaaahhhhh, we must have come upon the playground, though you couldn't really tell except that we found ourelves on a sorta ride, it shot like a seesaw only much much more daaaaannagerous, after a momentary shock i got accustomed or rather adjusted myself to it when i saw that i was shooting from a much better view of things, i couldn't have shot otherwise, it was all very high and low stuff and i was gettin' dizzy and decided on the next low to get off. which instead flung me and my movie camra, (it was at this point i reacted with a whatever i didn't or couldn't see my movie camra would see and what ever i couldn't or didn't want to do my movie camra would do., wasn't this what a movie camra was for? actually, i decide to close my eyes, and if we came thru the air alright and landed safely, i could always watch what happened when i got home on my movie screen, rather then witness it, if it went wrong and something happened ugh to ussss) fortunately we landed safe in one piece and when i opened my eyes to see what we we er my camra was shooting i was happily surprised to see we were in the Garden, which reminded me "where was Santa?" ah he's probably eating something delicious, like one of these, that we were shooting. we walked and shot a little here and there, so plentifull, when i saw we were shooting Santa, who was a little w a y s in front of us. i wasn't scared or nothin' but shootin' him like that all dressed up like that so round and jolly looking, his mouth and belly filled with the delicious things around him and all the Fairies busy looking after him and entertaining him, him sitting there stuffed with that look of a satisfied man and all and i couldn't help remembering another look when he was a poor shivering hungry Jean Genet with snow all over him, so fixed was this picture of him that it rouse from my mind and came before my lens and I was shooting double again. and when the Jean playing Santa Claus under bowery bum Genet, with his big hearty grin, laughingly pushed a little Fairy in jest, his bowery bum image, on top, too pushed, only it was the little kid in front of of oh dear I know where I am of course of course why it's and we turned to shoot the window that would verify my hope when we were definitely interfered by some very determined Fairies with very determined faces coming at us. I quess I spilled the beans? ho ho . because these Fairies were ready at all cost to get rid of us, so we didn't ruin their spell with any of our high funooting ideas. I mean you could tell by their determinessim and we were not going just stand there or nothing soo off we were, running and shooting figuring this may be my last chance to shoot and so we better get as much as possible but in my eagerness to satisfy my last shot i made the mistake "of shooting towards the sight of my undoing" and saw more Determined Fairies at my rear and shooting to the left more and and the right more and up Tinkee Bell HHHHHHHHE E L p, we were surrounded and we were shooting our er er assailents? MURDER, murder

17

17 i was about to shout as they closed in on us, especially the one with the big nose in my lens, when slowly we were being raised and over
17 the tops of their heads i was able to shoot my Farewell long shoot of Fairy City, FAREWELL.

F A R E W E LL

what? what's this we're shooting now a s a a biGG Face AGAIN! oh oh It's Tinkee Bell my my she sure is madddd, great theatrics why, all the time she looked right in my lens, great shot Tinkee, great, now a little to the right that's right, ARE YOU CRAZY! STOP, IT STOP IT, this is no time to be funny, I' mean she is real mad, why just look at the way she swings those arms, why I even think she might think, that that's your face, maybe she thinks your from some other planet or something. sHUT UP. all right all right I was just tryin' to be helpful. Well i'll ask you to just mind my own mind and stop bothering me, look you see i almost forgot what I was shooting OH YES TINKEE BE L L, of course Tinkee Bell, she's pointing at me, but I don't know what she's saying, she's getting impatient, WHAT'll we dooooooo. go on shake your camera that's right yesss tinkee bell yessssss you see , you see she's gone, she just wanted to make sure you were goin' to be good. SHUTTTT UP. my goodness i really have to try and shut that mind of mine oFFFF. now, oh d e a r even though TINKEE's gone we're so far away, I mean how are we expected to shoot from this distance I mean even my Zoom ZoooooM, I'll just move in a little bit, ahhhh that's better with my Zooooooooo oh i seem to be shooting the face of a very determined Fairy, oh dear and he seemss very determined to stay determined and he's coming closer, a blurry determine alright alright, back i go and i'll be goooooo. ah at least he's determined face is gone, well i'll try my telephoto lens no back to zoom, ah we'll get a few wide angle and with this lens and a few shoots real far away. hmmm with the zoooming in. hmmm hmmm ho ho we can just about shoot Santa with this one. a little far but not so bad, at least we can shoot him a bissel? o la la, hmmmm everything seems to have quieted down hmmm and the Fairies are all gathering around Santa hmmm zooming back a little hmmm they're coming from all over hmmmm I wonder what's up hmmmm, ma y b e one little step forward hm hm two little steps forward hm hm hm three little steps f o r w ar d and i'm shootin' closer, four four boo boo on the fourth little step the determined face appears. one little two little three little steps on the fourth wouldn't you know it we takes a rest. hello, we er we thought we'd take your picture didn't we and i shake my movie camra shooting yes and he shakes his determined head no and i shake my shooting movie camra no and we both agree and we're shooting one little step. back, two little steps back, three little steps back and Fairy City is receeding, alright, alright a half a step back and shooting oh what we were shooting, all this time back and forth and now thru Zoom, was an interesting spectical, Santa who had taken a little nap, was being nudged, rather

18

18 gently by Snow White, all the Fairies had gathered around now and were waiting for Santa to get up so they could give him a tour of

18 their city, i gathered this much by the gestulations they were making and all the jumping up and down and pulling going on, on my sound track was vague sounds of moans and sighs and could it be? but soon there was too much activity going on to be listening too closely for i was much to involved with getting as much of them, so i could get in on the fun, even at my distance, on film, good old movie camra, if it wasn't for you i wouldn't even be able to see it. my zoom had brought the activity in closer so i could follow them as they started moving around the city, Santa and Snow White leading, they left the garden thru a pond and was walking on a path that reflected and glittered, they were going higher and higher, and i found myself shooting closer and closer, at one point i was shooting so close, of what looked like a spirallin' city......looked like a spirallin city? I wonder how i got so close, we turned around to shoot to see if that determined Fairy was still determined, but we shoot nothing but more Fairy city, where Santa's throne had been, we turned quickly back to shoot on, satisfied that everyone was too busy with Santa to bother with us, and I quess we just, in our eagerness shooting, we just kept moving closer in, i quess. a n y w a y we were shooting real good now, and it was real pretty shooting. we could shoot now close enough so we could get in most of the city lined with Fairies weaving their way along with Santa and still be able to shoot and see what Santa was doing and he sure was enjoying himself. for awhile we couldn't move, there was so much happening so much excitment evrytime Santa tried on something or played or swam went on a ride or took pleasure in something he saw and what ever he did the Fairies wanted to do and touch as if it was their first time lookin' and they weaved their way up , i really couldn't move, it all, i don't know but i must of been in a daze for i shot this a long long time then something came over me and i wanted to shoot it in slow motion, and then real fast still, single frames slower faster haaaaaa i was going crazy how wever i tried was n't enough, upside down sideways, stop, their still having fun, only where's Santa we shoot to the left right up down but still didn't move, was something the matter? and then i could have sworn someone kicked me, for we were joining the procession of Fairies. up in circules we went but fast i could hardly get a good shot before we were being pushed along higher. everything started to become a blurr until a Fairies face popped up to be shot it was like someone was spinning me and then stopped and there was a Fairies face oh oh oh and then everything stopped for a long while, though i was still shooting NOTHING, no no maybe it's dirty, the focus, another lens ah yes yes but i was all alone high up in the playground, but in my sound track i heard giggles GIGGLES? . from a w a y and down , i turned shooting down and shot ants? no fairies, moving alone the path going down, hmmm all the Fairies were in circles

19

19 around Santa in the Garden, from up here i couldn't exactly tell what they were doing but when i descended more and was just above

19 them i shottthat one Fairy i couldn't say who had walked up to Santa and whispered something in his ear. there was a hush and we quickly got to the ground and shooting made our way into the garden.all the fairies were seated except for a few of them who were dancin' , Santa was directly in front of us, between rows of Fairies. We tried movin' in, but they weren't very nice about it, i was a bit annoyed, at this lack of hospitality we were receivin' and would have trotted off, if Santa hadn't gotten up and started mimicin' Mother Goose. He was just like her, blablbablabblabblAB, it was very funny and everyone was in hysterics. weeeeell weeeell this could get inter- estin'. I'd like to see him do CINDERELLA, why he must have read my mind, for he stood up again and lookin' right into my camra, became Cinderella, whaaat a sight, now suddenly all the Fairies we're pushin' to get in front of Santa and with a little of their very own VOO DOO let him become them, so they could watch how funny he looks as them (though i must say, that if he wasn't wearin' that Santa costume, He could have convinced me) and soon everyone was makin' fun, fun of him, themselves, me, you and why not? make fun???? everyone was making fun, everyone was having fun, so what are you a schmuck? SHUTT, i know i know, all right, so i's asked myself am i a schmuck? could it really be? and suddenly i started feeling better, and braver, i too am going to have some fun, you and i are goina shoot fun, so we pushed ourselves among the fun and everyone was giggling and on my sound track i giggled too, louder, i shot around and shot funny Fairies dancing and singing, playing games and making fun of each other and drinking, drinking? DRINKING, and then i was drinking, wooops all over the lens it dripped and went and i was shooting everyone jumping, weeeeeeeeeeeeeeeee, dancing and falling all over the place shooting everyONE, i LOVE YOU ALL, i love you too, smooch ahhhhhhhh ohhhhh ooooo ah ahohahoahahoh spinning spinning spinning and on my sound track i heard laughter and smooching and singing my own real off and real loud and i flewww weeeeee shot peter pan oh oh oh and all the city and fairies under me and around swam? ooooooooooooooh hahahohaohaoooooooooooaaaaweeeeeeeeeee o o AH OH AH OOOOOH AH WEEEEEEEEEEEEEE OH OH O OH OH OH OH OH O O HO HO

HO HO HOHOH HOHO HO HO HO HOH HO HO HO HO HP AHHHHHHHAAAAAWEEEEE o o h

plooop. oh excuse me Santa may i have this Dance? oooooh do you believe it we were dancing Santa and me and my movie camra and it's all been shot to prove IT oooooo and on my sound track louder came in the song I LOVE IT

i love it i love it i l o v e it iloveit iloveit
I LOVE IT IT IT OOOOOOOOO WEEEEEEEEEEE love it WE love it WE LOVE
LOVE LOVE it it? it AAAAAAAAAAAAAAH we LOVE it we LOVE it LOVE LOVE

20

20 LOVE it it? it it it IT IT IT TITITIT TITIT IT IT IT IT IT IT ITIT IT IT IT IT IT IT IT IT IT IT IT IT LOVE it, etc. cut.

20 oh oh my head my head, oh oh i'm falling falling f a l l i n g o o h

hmmmmmmmmm, hmmmmmmmmm, ouch ouch, oooooh my head m y h e a d, hmmmmmm

but what a time hmmmmmmmmmm, opps my movie camra and all my lovely film, oh where is my movie camra? oh, oh where is my movie camra? oh oh, it is very important, my movie camra, i must find it, I CAN'T SEE WITHOUT IT. oh OH my eyes, my movie camra, there you are. i thought i lost you, for a moment, hmmmmmm, you look all right, a little dirty, hmmm, there now, that's better. Now let us see, shoot, WHAAAAAT what what's happened to m y F a i r y C i t y somethings cooking,it's too quiet and still, what's happened to the PARTY, or was it all a dream? no no NO we shott a desolute city, ordered and clean without life empty, But for dolls, hello goofey, peter, cinderella,what happened to you? where is the light LIGHT light? light? we're shooting light, no no we shoot and run towards the light light light SUNLIGHT, NO NO, yes. oh oh Santa dear Santa, and we turn around and shoot Santa slumped on his throne snoring, Santa dear Santa you look so different, so small, and i remembered and thought of how different he looked before, (hmmmm I seem to spend all my time remembering) and on my sound track i chuckled as the image of him as bowery bum Genet appeared on top of his sleeping face, how afraid i was of him, because i was told how smart and clever he was too and then remember his face? yes it too appears now on him, when he played Santa for the first time after he had eatened and drunk and was fairly pleased with him self? and then his face so surprissed when he awoke to see all those strange Fairies coming at him and when they were introduced how he had to be-come all of them in a minute and how he had to make all those faces and do all those things, and he couldn't stop, that's the Face yes, yes I'm shooting that face too. and on my sound track i laughed at how we thought, that was a conspiracy and then I was beginning to believe i was Santa Claus, and became jealous and saw his face in the garden stuffing itself with food, drink and the attention of the Fairies and we laughed again as we thought of how the Fairies tried to get rid of us, so we er i didn't spoil anything with my jeaulousy and when we recovered and with the zoom we saw his face napping oh that face is on his now, yes and then you went thru the city and enjoyed yourself, your smiling, yes you sure was smiling and how we just couldn't shoot it straight and shoot it fast and slow upside down, over, under and backwards, and then all the faces you made in the garden do you remember that, yes mother goose cinderella yes, yes i'm shooting those faces too and when i asked you to dance, you looked so beautiful and high high and then now sleeping so small, yes all those faces are yours and now sleep, i sorta like you now. now, now,

21

21 and for now we shott him. goodbye Santa good-bye

21 we shot moving slowly away of this our last thought and the sun rouse full in the sky and light poured light on his face and all was still and we were going.
bang!
the window, opps sorry win d o w d i d n ' t s e e e e e youa WHAAAAAT? ARE YOU DOING. no no the little kid, we're shooting the little kid, whose making a face at me, as if i didn't see enough, shot enough faces. look kid why don't you take that horrible expression off your face like a good little kid, pleaSE not so early in the morning k i d. ha he popped his tongue in. good little whaaaat crossed his eyes and stuck now, his twisted tongue out and thenHUFFED, HUFF HUFF at who? ho ho NOOOOOOOO and turning shooting quickly Heavens above Santa Claus
REALLY, crossing your eyes and twisting your tongue out and scowling, huff huff huff NOOO NOOO to shoot the little kid yes? cross eyed twisted tongue out scowl and his nose wiggled too? to Santa we shoot crosseyedtwistedtongueoutscrowlnoseANDEAR wiggles? ho ho from then on it was waR. Santa versus the Little KId via me and my movie camra. it was on Santa the little boy, Santa the little boy the little boy? Santa! Santa! little BOY! back and forth we shot this spectical on and on won't this ever stop? no. they did everything, stood on their heads, made noises, did tricks jump boy, jump, good boy. it was terrible it was hilarious, I couldn't believe it couldn't believe it. there in Fairy City was Santa, Santa Claus, no, yes, oh, oh ho throwing his legs in the air doing the CAN CAN! TRA LA LA BOOM DE A? no. no? NO. POOP he's landed, on the floor but that won't stop him, up he comes brushes himself off and turns to see what the little kid is going to do, we turn and shoot; little kid stops laughing by holding hand over mouth, then turns and does cartwheel on street on 34th street, at 5 o'clock in morning, it is cold morning and slippery, boy slips and trips passerby, both fall to ground, both get off ground both rub back side boy looks at Santa rubbing backside, we turn and shoot Santa looking at boy rubbing backside both sore and tired, rubbing backside, we turn and shoot boy, nothing happening except run backside, we turn and shoot Santa, nothing happening except rub backside. both rub backside, I've been watching too many movies.
i was back on Santa shooting, his face seemed like it was falling apart? yes i turned to shoot, little kid and yes nothing happening except rub backside. but turning to shoot Santa, something was happening, i mean like on my sound track i was hearing churkle, churkle, gulp gulp churkle churkle gulp gulp, Santa was laughing in hysterics, the little kid i shott was laughing, i was laughing, i got to sit down this is too much, and sitting down i shot Santa who was on the floor now holding his side kicking his feet in the air?

22 ho ho and shooting the little kid hmmmm a group of people have
gathered around him, hmmmm, they look sorta bewildered, i wonder why,
22 the little kids in stiches, Santa's on the floor already, and i could-
n't stand up, soooo??? so. hmmmm more people are crowdin' around,
their stoppin' traffic, drivers are leavin' their warm cars to stand
in the cccold. hmmm you don't realize how many people are out in the
cccccold on a cccccold mornin' willin' to stand in the ccccold to
see what's sooo funNNNNY. i turned to shoot if Santa sees what's
happenin' outside, hmmmmm still on the floor, but his head raised
and he is lookin' outside. hmmmm he's stopped laughin'. "what a
curious group of people watchin' me,,,,,,,," he seems to say.
oh all right, i'd rather not say what i think he said, but there
was a smile on his face, that's for sure and his eyes seemed to rest,
turning i shott, on the little kid.they sure had something going,
for next minute they were laughing like their sides were goina
burst and in Santa's eye and in the little kid's, there was a twinkle,
and like it was contagious because soon everyone outside was laughing
too, with twinkles in their eyes, and everyone was in on the joke?
whaat joke, what are THEY laughing at, their nuts, a bunch of nuts,
churkling and gulping giggling like that Santa, little kid, but
they were too busy laughing to answer when I shot them and before
i knew what was coming off, the roof flew off and, NO N OOOOO, NO I
W WON'T GOOOOOOOO no no N OOOOOOO plEASEEEEEEEE not yet, another
minute, PPPPPPLEASE no no HHHHHHHHELLLLLLLLLP, HELPPPPPPP, hhheeeeeeelp,
but on my sound track i only heard laughter from everywhere; above,
below and around me, but even though i was being transported on my
magic helicopter i couldn't resis a last shot, so i turn's my
camra towards earth to shoot good-bye, and here in all honest i must
say that you all just got smaller and smaller and faded away, but in
my song of this i saw a shimmer that was set a flare, of the neon
lights MICKEY MOUSE WAS THERE! er: how about: I saw a shimmer that
was set a flare,
by your laughter, MICKEY MOUSE WAS THERE!????

A N Y W A Y good-bye

nooooooooooooooooooooo
i wasn't satisfied, that night i had a night mare?
and it ended like this;
oh all right, I rather not say what i think he said, but there was a
smile on his face, that's for sure, and i was able to shoot his
resting eyes on the little kid they both had twinkles in their eyes,
bigger than all the sparklers that manifested in Snow Queens eyes,
and strangely, shooting out in the crowd, the sun rouse higher and
it got warmer all over, and all the faces in the crowd began to look
weird. even the little kid's. first shadows of the sun's light made

23 shapely suggestions on their faces, particularly around the mouth,
i turned to shoot Santa to see if he also was going thru some of
23 these changes, but he was just back in his, all over the floor, holding
his sides, kicking his feet wiggling and giggling position. I shoot
back outside, and believe me I swear it, they all started growin'
ears, was i halucinatin'? i shook my camra to see maybe it would
go away, and it did, but just for a moment, for their noses grew
longer and curled at the tip and their ears grew large and wiggled!
and everyone was laughin' hysterically. and then i'm bein' lifted
off the ground by some strange magical force again, and i turn
towards the earth, on my way up, for my farewell shot, FAREWEELL,
shootin' you fade in the distance, when suddenly you rise, all you
people down there who i thought were passerbys, rise, and fly! and
all your winter clothes fall off and your long round wiggly ears
and curled buttoned noses, just like you know who, drop and it's
Happy, Sleepy, Crumpy and all, what are you doin' up here? Tinkee
Bell why Sammy Jr. and Frankie, bobby and Alllllly, Peter Pan!.
Hey what's goin' on here? why your not a little Kid, and Santa you
can't fly, Mother Goose, REALLY, PAN, PAM, STORM, AND JONAS, ANN, BILL,
JOHN, LOUIE, ANGUS, THE FUGS, SNOW QUEEN, PIERO, PAUL, JERRY, MARION,
SALVADOR?, LESLIE, BILLY GERARD, LENNY, BONNY, ANDY, NIAMI, GRETA, FOXY,
ANNIE DAVID TONY ELLIOT LIZ RICHARD HUNKY BEVERLY RONNY TATAYANA, THOR,
GEORGE JOAN DONOVAN BRYDS RODDY DALE PAOLO MARCELLO STEPHANIE TINY
ISRAEL JASPER MICHAEL PICASSO AND CHAPLIN? STAN BUZZ WALT ORNET, ERNST,
ROLAND THE VELVET UNDERGROUND THE MIDDLE CLASSKINGBEES CAROL GEORGE
SAL SALLY AL ALLEN AL AL ROBIN BOB JASON BOB MARTHA PHILIP LARRY, JACK,
MARCUS AMANDA PETER ROSE BART DAN DALI LAMA HENRY PABLO JACK MARIO
MARTY NICOLO ALEX JACQUELINE GIULIETTA MILES SUE ELLEN LISA SZABO
TOM JANE RINGO? FRANZ JEREMY MARIANNE RODNEY NINA SELMA OSCAR ORSON
JEAN PAUL INGRID BONGO MOM AND DAD, YOU TOO? BUFFY P.J. ANNA LEONARD
STEWART KITTY OLIVER JOCK CHRISTOPHER MR. X MARCEL BETTI BORIS JOANNE
MOSES DARYL FRANCIS VINCENT CARY MICKEY OMAR SUSANNHA SANDY SARAH
GINGERSYBIL DOC JACQUE STEVE FREDERIC BUSTER CAROLL BARRY NEAL, MIRON,
ANITA INGMAR LARRY ALEC CHARLIE SHIRLEY WARREN MARGARET MARCEL, ELAINE,
BRIDTTE ROMAN JEAN BURT FRANCOIS PADDY MAX GYPSIE SEYRIL PRINCES, EDIE,
QUEENS KINGS PRESIDENTS I'm goininininin'''' crazy, but but JEAN, JUDY,
GENET TOOOO, YOU UP HERE TOOOOOOOOO OOOOOOOOFFFFFFFederico0000000000?
tony brian mick penelope/ ??????? HELLPPPPP, NOOOOOOO, YAESSSSS U YESSS
Why Bing, Dean, Jeanne oh ho ho, David, Barbara, P. Adams! ho ho!
of course OF COURSE O F C O U R S E THE LONE RANGER, ADRIENNE,
SARAH, ANDREI, PAT, SCOTTY, JOEL ISABELLE BRYDEN JANET JULIUS RICK ION
DANNI BERNARD O F C O U R S E ! ! ! NOEL PIERRE
DIXIE LIZA JULIE GARY HARRY LE ROI JEFF STANLEE KIRBY GREGORY MISSY
"The closer he gets, the better you look. Suddenly inside, you have
a new confidence." JORDIE ELVIS RUDOLF HENRY CYNTHIA TULIE MORTY
"It's what Supp-hose does to your ego." GERTRUDE ED RUTH

London,
Summer 1965

I was thinking of approaching Bobby Dylan, Beatles (maybe in N.Y. when they'll be together) to give together or individually or any other interested parties. The money to be returned with an interest in the film which I hope to be Radio City distributed all over the world and a book of illustrations and stills to be translated to all over—if the Irish government gives me the land I will give them Fairy City and from the profits of the movie, money to maintain it since I'd prefer it charge-free for visitors. Is *Christmas* copy wanted? What does David feel about Producing? I feel I need to return to N.Y. and if David wants to produce to write up this memorandum, to see Bobby and the Beatles and go to speak to Walt Disney. I'm hoping any money from "*Allen for Allen*" will help. My visa runs out the 26 of July and unless I have the money to put in my account (I opened an external bank account with Chase Manhattan) I won't be able to get a renewal if the check doesn't come through. I hope Granada will buy some of the film either theirs of them or Allen to show and return to N.Y. I want definitely to be in N.Y. in August. (Dear Jonas I feel that *Christmas* must be done this year or *Christmas* will be here. Timing is essential for the right feeling.) Fairy City will be a city for children to be in, maintained through the profits of *Christmas* by Ireland. I will establish a Rosebud foundation[1] for money to be given for people's beautiful creations and after paying back all money and bills to build and make money from the movie including the LP and book and movie. As for me I just want complete rights on movie, book and LP so no one will dirty it or use it. Dear Jonas how do you feel about this? Is it not the time, the moment to excel ourselves.
I will write soon and tell you more give you more, love more more
love Barbara

1
In "An Open Letter to Jean Genet" from the statement, Rubin pitches her script to the French writer. She refers to the establishment of a "Rosebud Foundation" for "DREAMS TO BECOME"

London,
Summer 1965

Dear Jonas—
I am including in this letter a form of application information concerning a visa for Pamela Badyk as a temporary worker. She needs someone/employer, agent, to file a visa form 11296 "Petition permission to import non-immigration aliens" indicating she is being employed in the U.S.A. for a prearranged job. Is it possible for you or Film-Makers' Co-op Cinematheque to file such a form stating Pam Badyk is working on a film *Christmas on Earth Continued* and *AAA*[1] (name of the new movie of Allen Ginsberg, Andre Voznesensky,[2] Albert Hall), that we will be scouting for *Christmas* location, people etc. and filming Allen in America. That I am a member of the Co-op Cinematheque etc. and that we will be supporting her trip, etc. We would like to return to U.S.A. as soon as possible this summer so I'd appreciate quick action on this. If you feel Jonas that you can't do it or that it wouldn't be good please ask around for someone to do this. Please send me information on this soon.
Love love love Barbara

1
AAA, could be a working title for a planned film about Allen Ginsberg and Andrei Voznesensky at the Royal Albert Hall

2
Andrei Voznesensky, 1933–2010, Soviet and Russian poet and writer

Background image: from reel A of Barbara Rubin's double projection film *Christmas on Earth*. 1963-1965.
Foreground images: Barbara Rubin dressed as a nun, December 1965. Photos: Adam Ritchie

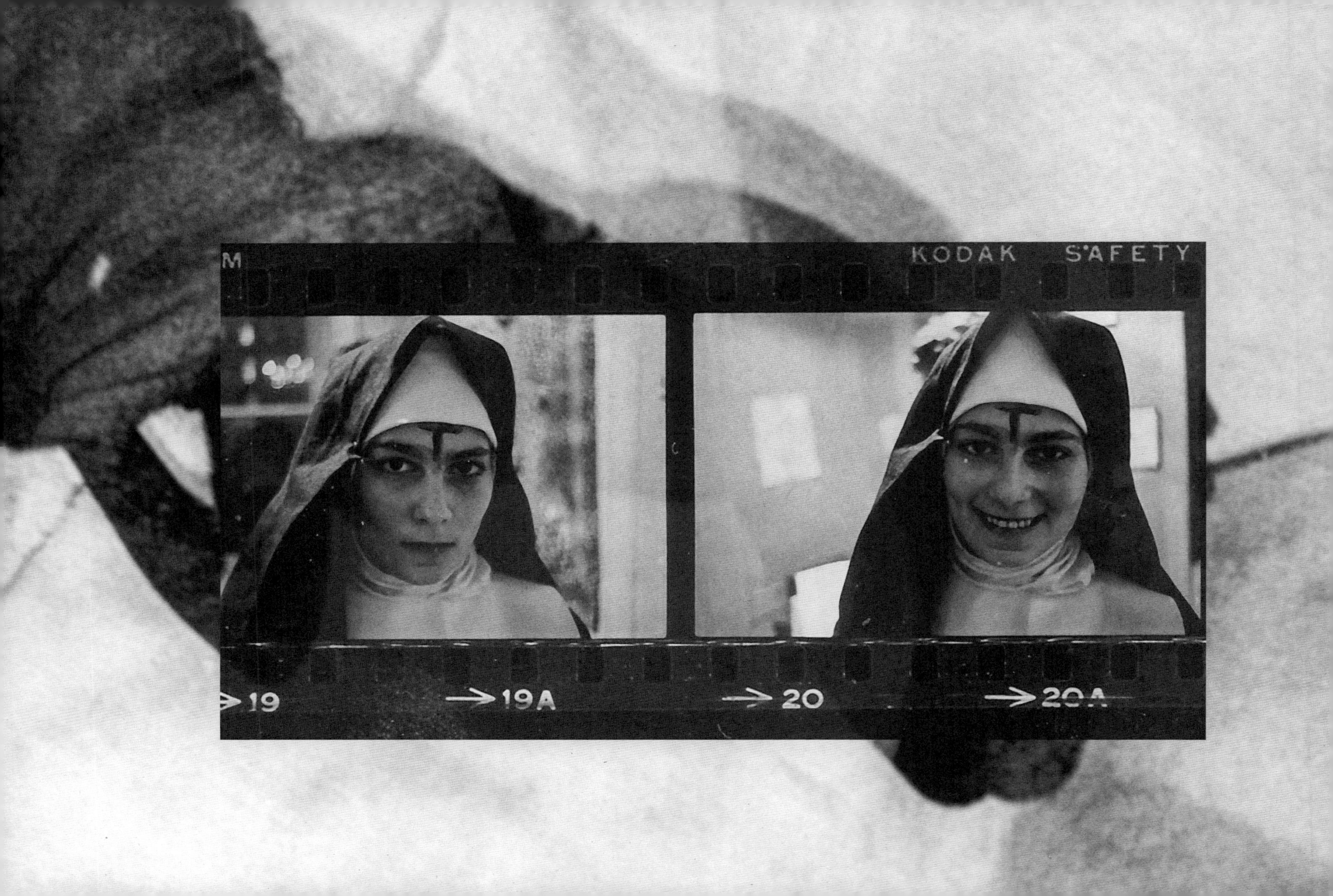
KODAK SAFETY
M
→19
→19A
→20
→20A

CHRISTMAS ON EARTH CONTINUED AGAIN

by barbara rubin

a chatter on the movie

to Federico Fellini "..........,.,..,., .blab blab blab.... BLAB .. ideal ... Blaaaa...., ... blab, ... bla,... ,..a,. a ,,, the .... blab .. .. , ... bLAB, reason ....??????

............I mean I don't know what's ideal, maybe it's the contract i signed that day, ...blab.., blab BLAAAAAAAAAAAAAAb .....,...

blab......., b.... , a ., ...ll,,,...aaaa............blaB........

B L a b"

And the Singin' Poet who wants to make a movie and his friend who said We all are movie Freaks!

Dear Jonas and David,

I am writing to you both, after reading David's
letter to me.
mad angry hurt and plainly not understanding your
position.

David you write telling me there is nothing constructive
you can add especially to raise money. That I am to approach
it on a charity basis. do you mean that you don't want to
involve yourself when if everyone just did and gave a liitle
the movie would have been made already. that you haven't
done anything but tell me so are you patting me on the head
so as not to concern yourself when basically all I ask is
your help ; to produce the movie, tobe the producer , to
get it made in definite constructive ways that all things
particaully films are done in . literal hard work patience
belief and time.
Does it matter on what basis or form the momey or materials
come when they will only be the outcome of the setup
(and what setup or organization is there but me?) ~~and the~~
and whatpeople like yourself give of your time efforts to promote
it. Is this what you would say to Jonas concerning a film or anything
jonas wanted to do when all he needs and asks of you to be constructive as
a producer? I need a producer . organization , a paper made up telling
of the ideas, necessities funds particulars (like what you originally
wanted) to be given to bussiness men, stars, walt disney, backers , interested
people, and the Irish government as constructive plans for it's reality.
Am I suppose to do all the work ? are you crazy? or don't you think
it worthy enough or maybe you just don'tbeleive it see it or isN't it
commercial enough? I just want to Know how you feel and how you could
possibly beleive this or anything eles can be by me alone?
do you not see that in "Christmas on Earth Continued" i am presenting to
you the profecy of the future or the present that is coming. that Christmas
has always been here but that now we will realize it. That in as short a time
as a year the movie will have missed it's moment. that we are on the verge of
realization andthat the way in which this movie is born ignored or dies
will be the life of its passion in us? That "Christmas on Earth Continued"
is the baby sent to profit the ~~[illegible]~~
INFINITY OF THE POSSIBILITY OF FEELING THE BEAUTY
REALIZING THE TRUTH AND GIVING IT THE PASSION OF CONSTRUCTIVE GLORY LOVE
if the movie is not made because of the lack of belief and the energy love
time and effort of everyone then how will we know christmas in our hearts
now
what possibly could you feel and think to treat this as you do?
If you think I'm unrealistic how realistic are you to image this could
be done by me alone. to make the movie , buildthe city get the stars
raise the funds and charity , gracious aren't you , when this must come from
all of us . i will go on whether you or anyone believes because i am
the realization of this truth but tell me you andJonas how you feel
whatever your reasons are but don't bullshit.
I may have not understood fully what to do and may have taken trips

influencing you and maybe even putting you thru some but I was in the vision of this.but where were you and now? You've let the glory ofthe moment when it was at its height to the wind for lack of strenghth

and now when the mome nt depends on it's birth you freak.
I believe in what iam doingin the attempt I make as a person and artists to give birth and struggle to become in beauty and truth and love. life is and is what you or do I do to realize ourselves and dreams depends on the strangth persistance and in truth and constructivness beauty we give and the work we are
In "Christmas on Earth Continued " i wanted to creat a moment when we were the realization on it's highest level of a state of being that always existed that will exist because it is happening. It will happen but the beauty of it's feelingwill depend on our realizing it belief and work together which The Movie will be the outcome of. on how much we give and work.
I will return to New York because it is ridiculous to go to Ireland or do anymore than the first stages (what I have benn doing) (spreading the news joy and possibility in the movies and City's idea) Without some constructive plans on paper to present andthe beginning of cooperation and organization to show the proof of it's reality.
I can(t do it alone How can I when it must come from all besides the pysical PRACTICAL WAY IN WHICH ANYTHING TO BE REAL IS DONE.

I spoke with Bernard Frectman, Jean Genet's personal manager who told me to see him in Paris/befor the end ofJuly.
I will go to Paris for a few Days return to London andFly home as soon as possible.I entend on giving all my breath and time energy love to

attempt "Christmas"and the City for Children to live, to get organized properly with producer, staff, production, plans and fund raising and want to know if you will be apart of it and in what way for iwill go on whatever. This is all a natural outcome of the beauty and constructive part of me and anyone andwill either exist thru all or ignored to death. It is life, my life ,if you denyit you deny me, and your own experience.

love barbara

London,
July 1965

Dear Jonas and David[1],
I am writing to you both, after reading David's letter to me. Mad angry hurt and just plainly not understanding your position.
David, you write telling me there is nothing constructive you can add, especially to raise money. That I am to approach it on a charity basis. Do you mean that you don't want to involve yourself when if everyone just did and gave a little the movie would have been made already. That you haven't done anything but tell me so are you patting me on the head so as not to concern yourself when basically all I ask is your help; to produce the movie, to be the producer, to get it made in definite constructive ways that all things particularly films are done in. Literal hard work patience belief and time. Does it matter on what basis or form the money or materials come when they will only be the outcome of the setup (and what setup or organization is there but me?) and what people like yourself give of your time [and] efforts to promote it. Is this what you would say to Jonas concerning a film or anything Jonas wanted to do when all he needs and asks of you [is] to be constructive as a producer? I need a producer, organization, a paper made up telling of the ideas, necessities, funds, particulars (like what you originally wanted) to be given to businessmen, stars, Walt Disney, backers, interested people, and the Irish government as constructive plans for its reality. Am I supposed to do all the work? Are you crazy? Or don't you think it worthy enough or maybe you just don't believe it see it or isn't it commercial enough? I just want to know how you feel and how you could possibly believe this or anything else can be by me alone? Do you not see that in *Christmas on Earth Continued* I am presenting to you the prophecy of the future or the present that is coming. That *Christmas* has always been here but that now we will realize it. That in as short a time as a year the movie will have missed its moment. That we are on the verge of realization and that the way in which this movie is born ignored or dies will be the life of its passion in us? That *Christmas on Earth Continued* is the baby sent to profit the INFINITY OF THE POSSIBILITY OF FEELING THE BEAUTY REALIZING THE TRUTH AND GIVING IT THE PASSION OF CONSTRUCTIVE GLORY LOVE if the movie is not made because of the lack of belief and the energy love time and effort of everyone then how will we know *Christmas* in our hearts now.
What possibly could you feel and think to treat this as you do?
If you think I'm unrealistic how realistic are you to imagine this could be done by me alone. To make the movie, build the city get the stars raise the funds and charity, gracious aren't you, when this must come from all of us. I will go on whether you or anyone believes because I am the realization of this truth but tell me, you and Jonas,

1
David Charles Stone, 1932–2011, sometimes David or Charles, American producer, distributor, and exhibitor. He and his wife Barbara Stone were key figures in art house cinemas and film distribution in England in the 1970s

how you feel whatever your reasons are but don't bullshit. I may have not understood fully what to do and may have taken trips influencing you and maybe even putting you thru some but I was in the vision of this. But where were you and now? You've let the glory of the moment when it was at its height to the wind for lack of strength and now when the moment depends on its birth you freak. I believe in what I am doing in the attempt I make as a person and artists to give birth and struggle to become in beauty and truth and love. Life is and is what you or I do to realize ourselves and dreams depends on the strength persistence and in truth and constructiveness we give and the work we are In *Christmas on Earth Continued* I wanted to create a moment when we were the realization on its highest level of a state of being that always existed that will exist because it is happening. It will happen but the beauty of its feeling will depend on our realizing it belief and work together which The Movie will be the outcome of. On how much we give and work.

I will return to New York because it is ridiculous to go to Ireland or do anymore than the first stages (what I have been doing) (spreading the news joy and possibility in the movie and City's idea). Without some constructive plans on paper to present and the beginning of cooperation and organization to show the proof of its reality. I can't do it alone. How can I when it must come from all besides the physical PRACTICAL WAY IN WHICH ANYTHING TO BE REAL IS DONE.

I spoke with Bernard Frechtman,[1] Jean Genet's personal manager who told me to see him in Paris before the end of July. I will go to Paris for a few days, return to London and fly home as soon as possible. I intend on giving all my breath and time energy love to attempt *Christmas* and the City for Children to live, to get organized properly with producer, staff, production, plans and fundraising and want to know if you will be a part of it and in what way for I will go on whatever. This is all a natural outcome of the beauty and constructive part of me and will either exist thru all or ignored to death. It is life, my life, if you deny it you deny me, and your own experience.

love barbara

1
Bernard Frechtman, 1914–1967, translator from the French into the English and the most prominent translator of Jean Genet's writings

In the Fall of 1965, Rubin moved back to New York City from London. Besides working with Mekas at the Co-op, she was helping her filmmaker friends like Jack Smith, Jerry Jofen, and Piero Heliczer with various films, plays, and multi-media projects such as the *Rites of the Dreamweapon* event, an early "happening" that combined films with live music performed by The Primitives, later The Velvet Underground. By late 1965, Rubin was spending a lot of time at Andy Warhol's Factory. She was also helping The Velvet Underground promote their music. In mid-December, she brought Warhol to meet the band at the Café Bizarre and he immediately invited them to rehearse at The Factory. For the next three to four months, Rubin drove the band to rehearsals at The Factory and helped Warhol devise the multi-media stage show which she dubbed *Uptight* and which would later become *The Exploding Plastic Inevitable*[1]. Rubin and Danny Williams[2] were responsible for the visuals of the show, projecting films both before and during The Velvet Underground's performance and using various gels and projector techniques to add to the mayhem. By April 1966, The Velvet Underground began to focus on producing their first album and going on tour, at which point Rubin's association with the EPI dissolved.

In May 1966, she gathered all her New York City friends, such as Allen Ginsberg, Ed Sanders, and

1
The Exploding Plastic Inevitable, sometimes *Plastic Inevitable* or *EPI*, was a series of multi-media events organized by Andy Warhol between 1966 and 1967

2
Danny Williams, 1939–1966, Andy Warhol's lighting engineer, filmmaker and editor

Tuli Kupferberg from The Fugs,[3] Peter Orlovsky, Andy Warhol, and Jonas Mekas, and formed a group called the Kreeping Kreplachs.[4] The purpose of the group was to coordinate crosscutural, inter-city exchanges of artists and musicians who would organize non-profit multi-media events that would bring a new consciousness to the world.
The first planned event was to take place in London at the Royal Albert Hall exactly a year after the poetry event of 1965.
In the following letters, Rubin reports to Mekas about the project.

3
The Fugs, American band formed in New York City in late 1964 by the poets Ed Sanders, Tuli Kupferberg, and Ken Weaver

4
Kreeping Kreplachs, sometimes referred to as creeping Kreplachs

New York,
May 1966

[Incomplete: starts on p. 2, mid-sentence]

...proper hands lawyers have Our Rosebud's Foundation is in the process of forming and towards its formation.

We are being sponsored by the International language the Esperanto Foundation, founded by Bernard Stollman,[1] owner of E.S.P. disk, and a lawyer in his own, though not ours. We're talking with who else but the Beatles' American lawyer! Other than the already known fact of the Royal Albert Hall sponsored by the Esperanto Foundation in agreement with our Rosebud's Foundation's forming arrangements and you will be kept posted are being made for its transportation (films) and of course, to be shown at the Royal Albert Hall, then it will be, with the aid of Indica,[2] Miles, and money from this shown at the theater Mile's friend has rent-free for a year if we are lucky in our permission to get into London and perform (our approach is exchange from the City of New York to the City of London by the respected mayor of both). We might be able to arrange on time a continued tour thru the continent, based on the same approach. Of course we want and always do, as a part of anything we do, want to show movies and have their film-makers.

1
Bernard Stollman, 1929–2015, American lawyer and the founder of the ESP disk record label

2
Indica Books and Gallery, founded in London, 1965

We will let you know of this plan and let each film-maker decide. Most likely this will be simultaneous with the showing at the theatre in London. That's what each film-maker must decide. For our tour we pay expenses but no direct profit, since we're non-profit can be gotten, though we could give a grant to the Co-op!! But in London's theater a special arrangement like for rentals in U.S.A. will be made.
Now most important for all you to know is WHAT can "Our Rosebud's Foundation" do for you??? It's yours, it's your Rosebud's, that's what it can do!! Do through the procedure and functioning of a foundation. I'll keep you posted. Love always, Barbara

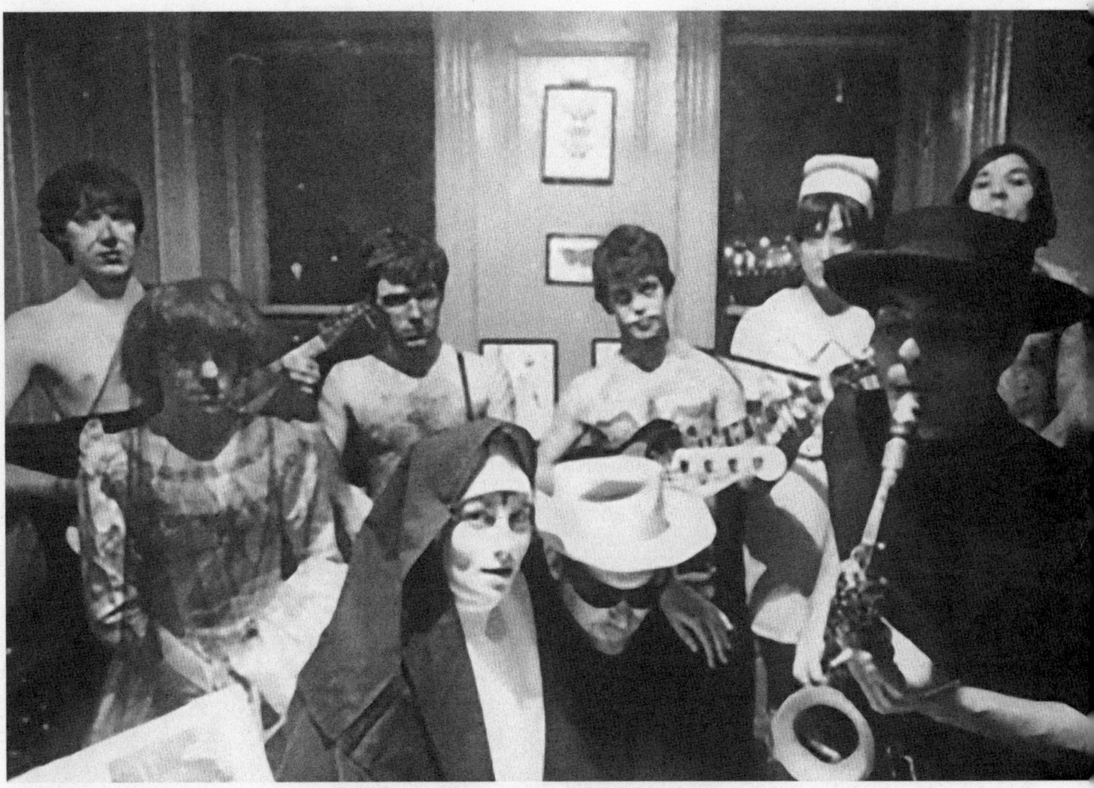

From left to right, back row: Sterling Morrison, Maureen Tucker, Bobby Ritchkin, Lou Reed, Margaret Boyce Cam, John Cale. Front row: Barbara Rubin, Al Aronowitz, Piero Heliczer, New York, December 1965. Photo: Adam Ritchie

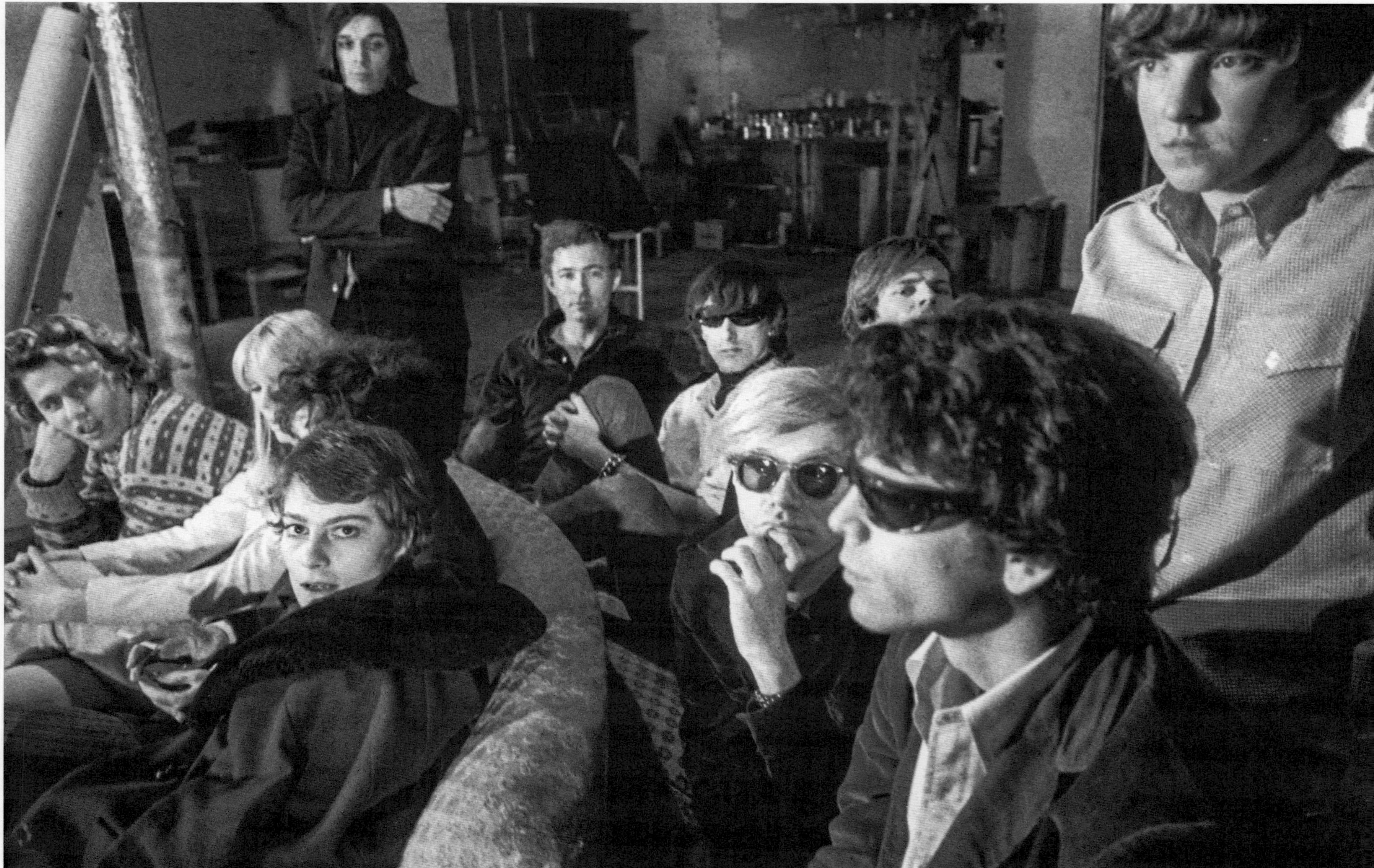

From left to right, on the sofa: Gerard Malanga, Nico, Donovan, Barbara Rubin.
First row behind the sofa: John Cale, Danny Williams, Sterling Morrison, Andy Warhol, Lou Reed. Last row: Paul Morrissey, Maureen Tucker, New York, 1966. Photo: Nat Finkelstein

New York,
late May 1966

Dear Jonas,
This beautiful lady Robbin 565-6746 will be coordinating the American end of the Foundation. (We've got one called Esperanto Inter national Language that's sponsoring our London trip.) The films will enter as part of the cultural trip. She will contact you etc. tentatively on June 20th-26th with option for longer will be the first program for them on a bill with the Fugs at the 400-seat theater at 7 tonight. I'll be at E.S.P. records 924-7660 call me later I'll be home, must talk to you for I'm leaving for London around Weds/Thursday this week.
Love Barbara

Miles
c/o Indica Bookstore
6 Mason's Yard
Duke Street Saint James
London SW1

Remember the publicity I'd like to have it before I go. How would you like to come over to London for June 16 & 17 & longer, all expenses paid? Let me know. I think it would be just what's needed if you're there you could make sure everything was set up right for London's Co-op.

The planned Albert Hall event was going to feature films as well as performances by The Fugs, The Chambers Brothers,[1] The Velvet Underground, and Bo Diddley.[2] But Rubin and the Kreeping Kreplachs couldn't raise enough money and the event never took place. In June 1966, however, Rubin went to London anyway to see what she could do to raise interest in the idea of a broader cross-cultural exchange of Underground films and music.

1
The Chambers Brothers, founded in 1954, American soul band

2
Ellas McDaniel, 1928–2008, professionally known as Bo Diddley, American singer, guitarist, and music producer

London,
July 8, 1966

Letter I

Dear Jonas, here I am and here things already have gone ahead. Harvey Metusa,[1] from U.S., is setting up the co-op here with Miles and Jim Haynes[2] of the Jeannetta Cochrane Theatre[3] and Bob Cobbing of Better Books. He's also helping put out the paper to *EVO,*[4] the fortnightly weekly and is running around interviewing the Bertrand Russells[5] and art counsel souls. He also wants to open up an all nite restaurant with something more like food. London is in a peculiar situation now of being almost completely overrun by people from everywhere else. Soon the citizens of London will be those deciding to make their home here rather than born here. The few English stuck in the midst, Miles, happy. Mike Boyland, the runarounds are establishing museums to the beings overrunning them for money. Already the result of last year's people who came here and left myself and particularly Allen, can see the effect which is not the center of anything except London. It's running around in the commercial field of investment and losing financially, Miles complains of thefts ruining Indica and can't understand why people steal from Indica. He's gonna prosecute anyone caught. It's very sad Jonas. They have no imagination and no effect more than a museum. I don't complete their function because their source of art poetry books life Underground high life is the people passing thru a difficult way to make a profit continuity. I'm sorry we didn't stay longer and help its life direction bloom. Now already it's a material

1
Harvey Matusow, 1926–2002, FBI informant who collaborated with Joseph McCarthy's communist witch-hunts in the 1950s. He later lived in London, where he got involved in the founding of the London Film-Makers' Cooperative in 1966

2
Jim Haynes, b. 1933, founder of the Arts Lab, an important film screening venue and events space in London

3
Jeannette Cochrane Theatre, founded in 1964, is a receiving and producing theater situated in London. It was run by Jim Haynes

4
EVO, abbreviation for *East Village Other* was an American Underground newspaper founded in 1965, and ceased publication in 1972

5
Bertrand Russell, 1872–1970, British philosopher, mathematician, writer, and social critic

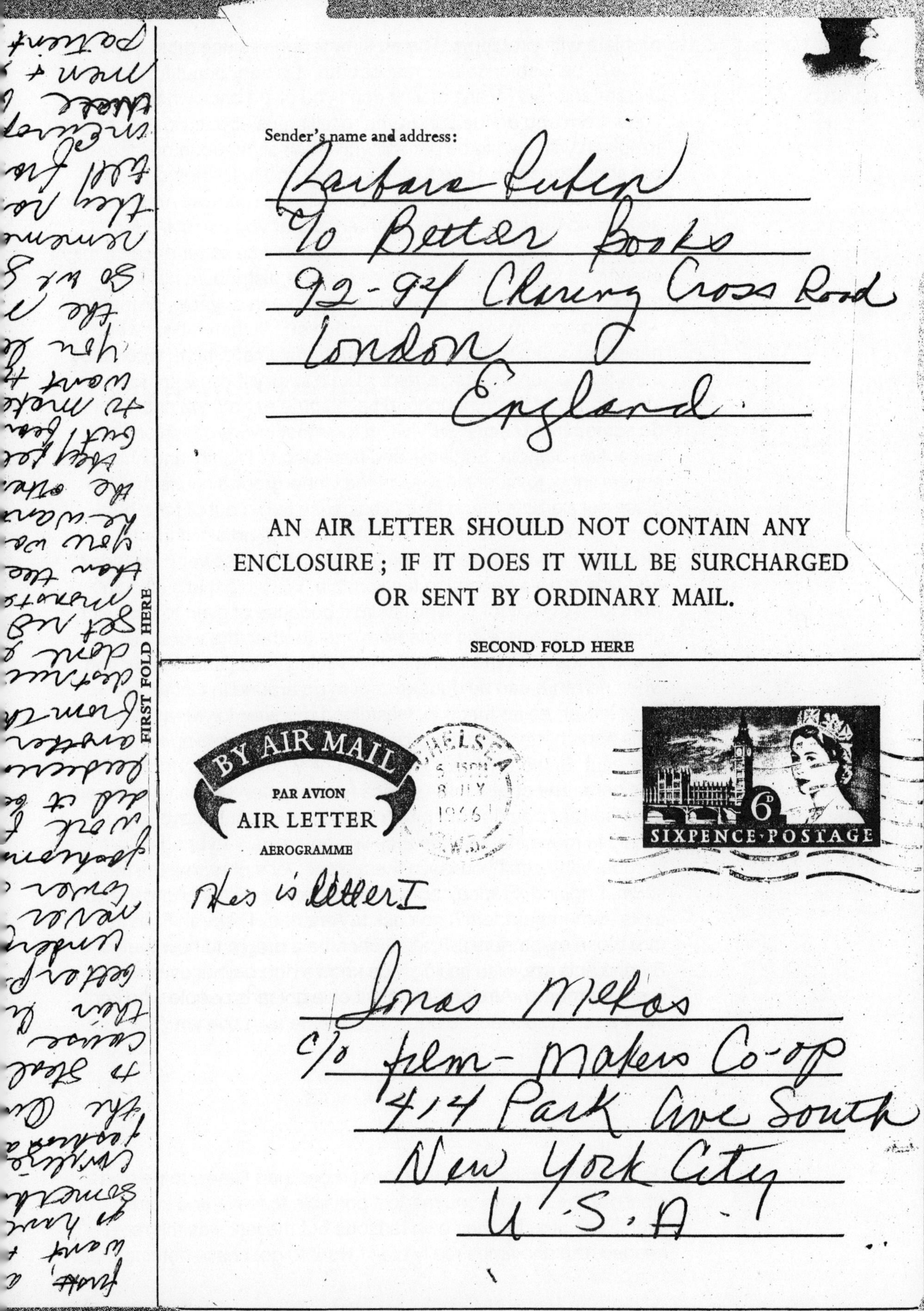

Sender's name and address:

Barbara Rubin
c/o Better Books
92-94 Charing Cross Road
London
England

AN AIR LETTER SHOULD NOT CONTAIN ANY ENCLOSURE; IF IT DOES IT WILL BE SURCHARGED OR SENT BY ORDINARY MAIL.

SECOND FOLD HERE

FIRST FOLD HERE

BY AIR MAIL
PAR AVION
AIR LETTER
AEROGRAMME

CHELSEA
8 JLY
1966
S.W.3

6D
SIXPENCE·POSTAGE

this is letter I

Jonas Mekas
c/o Film-Makers Co-op
414 Park Ave South
New York City
U.S.A.

TO OPEN SLIT HERE

problem with problems. The artist here is null since most people come to be fashionable or rest or both, it is very beautiful and very understandable feeling of why don't you all go back where you come from and do the things you're telling us about. So the creeping Kreplach will have to be patient while their sister countries found out about themselves so they can know and fulfill their own destinies. I'm telling everyone here especially the runaway Americans to go back to the life structure of America that you can still affect into non-existence. The creeping Kreplach was so far ahead it might even need to exist as such, movies will be distributed here and music heard and the poetry and beauty seen anyhow, probably, when it means money. Jonas, how do you tell them about what happens in New York that can happen anywhere, here, when they think first to survive first, after it's like a luxury if you want to create or strive or if you happen to have some extra drive and want to do something, but first survive, in the most civilized fashionable apparition of India, England, and the Queen? Dignity and at all times appearance, to steal the reason the Underground cause that the place our parents made their lives cause to get out of for a better place for us, is the home of the Underground artist living with those who never had a chance to get out of the Lower East Side? And now too it's becoming fashionable. We stole that's all didn't work for it or wait for it. We just did it because of even to the heights of ludicrousy where we stole from one another, the worst perversion coming from this being the very thing it was and destruction when no more can be done except to go around in circles, get rid of it. Serves no function, wasteland monster for whatever reasons none better than the other. Get rid of it and salvage what you want. England? Piero's here and he wants to rest, that's why he's here. The others left America for whatever they felt destroyed them so they couldn't but bear witness, what could have happened to make that change that we should want to bring it over to Europe. Why don't you leave them alone, let's preserve the museum, England, France, the rest so we got to wait til all those expatriots (remember them?) go back to America. They ran France thru those ex-patriots til France became a drag and now they're in Europe and who else has Europe known but celebrities, tourists, businessmen and ex-patriots. So we've got to be patient, Jonas, there's no more room so open the other letter. Love you, Barbara

London,
July 8, 1966

Letter II

Dear Jonas, I think you understood more than I knew to be true when for the 3rd time you made it possible to leave and come over. Each time for their own reasons but the last was the most needed, the one time I really didn't want to go; I have nothing more to think I can do here than I can do in America except luxuriate or stimulate myself by change but things change with you by you as you decide you need a change. Europe knows about that well. The creeping Kreplach was like ambition, understandably, but here too there's the ambition, taking off and Jonas do you know what, forget about all them Americans coming here now, let's bring everyone to America. London doesn't even have a functioning mayor, you see and since you need more to get into America financially, as well as Visas, etc. it's a luxury or a theft or work for them to come over there, like all of us Americans the way we come over here reverse inside out upside down turn it around and there's the scene, the desire and the possibility grande[u]r says more than all the talk about what's happening in U.S. by wanting to bring them over to see and we're ready to show it's for the kids. I haven't met anyone new here, English and younger than me. Strange isn't it: where are they and what are they doing and at the same time in Amsterdam a wide range and ages of people called the Provos[6] got one of them elected to office on the statements of Provo the white cop. The white bicycle, the White House, the white wife etc. White, the color white the sea green sky blue the white bicycles. Bikes you pick up where you find them and ride them to your destination and then leave them, White House, houses vacant anyone can live in free. White cops carry not guns but food and medicine for the sick and hungry more like nurses and docs! Etc. I'm not quite sure of the white wife. (Maybe like you don't have to divorce etc.) & strange political structure always structure better or worse structure should we take them more seriously? Or still don't they know structure breeds structure needs structure problems & problem structure & the more structure the more structure. They say, the Provos, they'd clean the center of Amsterdam from all traffic, no one would be allowed to drive a car there, so what happens if someone doesn't ride a bike? Or wants to drive a car there or does… prosecute him? So we still need functioning cops besides white cops? Or they say well everyone understands traffic jams and wants to prevent them so they'll obey and not drive their cars in the center, so why aren't they doing it now? I see that but everyone generally thinks it interesting and exciting just that they exist and have power organized rather than what they stand for. Sooo they don't think much, don't think it means much, it's the way things are, all that matters is how much you can get for yourself. Jonas, I wonder is it too soon to wonder, when we become fashionable here and earn our luxuries in America, will we forget, or are we just saying it's our chance to call the shots, make the money, spend the money on the habits we like, read *EVO* instead of the *Times* til *EVO*'s the *Times*. You're made aware of these things more than ever here, where in London the profit on our fashionableness where they have more structure, equipment available, not even antique not even struggled with lived with, not even the result of anything but the machine.

6
Provo, Dutch counterculture movement in the mid-1960s that focused on provoking violent responses from authorities using non-violent bait

result & his interest got mad. now she comes offering nothing
all she seems willing to pay is 10 pounds for this place to
have it in. We could have put up that for something
completely our own while in one week, freaking these asses
off for no money, for someone else's freak which has
nothing to say cause it doesn't exist, while they have
much to say, & they elect Pierro. typical. So that's me
here Margaret Eva Katy & Pierro, & we're gona put on the
happening for no money in one week. who needs it.
did we ever look for ideas or things to do or not do things
for lack of money like $30 borrowed stole or given anything
you wanted to do could get done somehow someway
in a week a day. a happening? I don't even know
what it is so she can do a movie about a happening
that didn't exist so she had to make it exist so
she could do a film about something showing somethin
what? let her do it. etc. etc. it was a little more
difficult, nay it's so easy to get lazy! If it happened in
New York I wouldn't have thought twice I wouldn't have
even listened probably she wouldn't never have approached
me, but here you see, the magic affect it produced
something was finally gona happen. I asked
Pete the Rat, an enthusiast about the Happening why
he was willing to do the Happening!!! When if all that was

London,
July 8, 1966

Letter III
This lady from Italy comes to London and finds a happening preferably Afro/European theme for this film unit to film. She gets here and discovers that nothing is happening. She's told by her film unit to get some people to put on a happening preferably with 250 black people and 250 white people by next week and that they'll pay for it, but not more than £150 for everything, including them. So she calls us together and tells us of it and everyone's excited and tells her there will be no problem of making it happen in a week, all one needs is a week anyway, and they tell her that they'll give their time free except they said she'd have to pay those professionals they could get, but not the poets, film-makers, or anyone else who doesn't have an agent. And who should direct this grand happening, Piero they decide Piero he can do it, so me who's been trying to get things done for the creeping Kreplach ever since I arrived and got no result and no interest and got mad, here she comes offering nothing, all she seems willing to pay is 10 pounds for this place to have it in. We could have put up that for something completely our own while in one week, breaking their asses off for no money, for someone else's break which has nothing to say cause it doesn't exist, while they have much to say and they elect Piero, typical. So that's me, Irene,[7] Margaret,[8] Eva, Katy, and Piero, and we're gonna put on the happening for no money in one week. Who needs it. Did we ever look for ideas or things to do or not do them for lack of money like $30 borrowed, stolen, or given. Any-thing you wanted to do should get done somehow some way in a week a day. A happening? I don't even know what it is so she can do a movie about a happening that didn't exist so she had to make it exist so she could do a film about something showing something. What? Let her do it, etc., etc. It was a little more difficult, nay it's so easy to get lazy! If it happened in New York I wouldn't have thought twice, I wouldn't have even listened, probably she would never have approached me, but here you see, the magic effect, it produced. Something was finally gonna happen. I asked Pete the Rat, an enthusiast about the Happening, why he was willing to do the Happening!!! When if all that was required was ten pounds for the place, since that is about all she was paying for, we'd get a place to do our own thing. Pete the Rat said, 'Well, she had the ten pounds.' I had suggested everyone wear robes before they entered and we planted 250 people black and 250 people white. She said her film unit couldn't afford to spend too much money on the Happening!! I went to a meeting of the film-makers to form the Co-op. Wow! A bunch of pompous asses, we spent over 3 hours talking snobbery? Stupidity? Idiocy? Could this be a cooperative of film-makers, yet? "You pay 5 pounds to become a member of the

7
Irene Nolan, b. 1947, appeared in Piero Heliczer's 1965 films *Dirt* and *Satisfaction*

8
Margaret Boyce Cam, plays the nurse in Piero Heliczer's 1965 short film *Venus in Furs*

film-makers Co-op." "Should we judge the films I mean, not everyone makes good films you know." "I think we should maybe censor." "But what if you don't have 5 pounds?" I said, and a Co-op is based on the cooperation of all film-makers—anyone who gives a film, finished or not, one foot or a head given to the Co-op to distribute is an automatic member and benefits. Wow, there they were talking of how much equipment they had among them. Cameras, [...] tape recorders, film and film stock, use of film school's equipment and they said they need more equipment especially if others wanted to use it. How can you let anyone use your equipment.

Even though she had suggested and helped promote the idea of a London Film-Makers' Cooperative in the Summer of 1965, Rubin felt increasingly ostracized when the Co-op was then formed in the Summer of 1966 and the founders seemed less interested in her input.

London,
July 8, 1966

Letter IV
Cooperation? When I told them of how the N.Y. Co-op (by the way they weren't too eager to bother about distribution esp of other Co-ops like America's films, so Miles, Jim Haynes of Jeanette Cochrane Theater, and Bob Cobbing of Better Books are handling distribution and showings. They said this isn't N.Y. this is London [and] commenting that I thought the distribution side was equally important and that the film-makers must always themselves deal in distribution and the renting and showings so that all possible effort should be made to pay for a theater separately from the money made at film showings, so that only certain films and get-togethers more profitable than others would show, they didn't even listen, just say I was talking nonsense and that I didn't know what I was talking about and that it was up to the English film-maker to decide. I asked them who were they. I was told these were a few but the purpose of the Film-makers Co-op is to get interest going about films and film-making. It just seemed they had a very rigid view of what those future film-makers would be like because I suggested my views could be that of one of those future film-makers, so they should listen and consider what I was saying. I got the feeling I probably wouldn't be one of those future film-makers of this London Co-op. We had supper last night with Ravi Shankar[9] and Alan.[10] We sat on the bed wanting to smoke, they sat in chairs

9
Ravi Shankar, 1920–2012, Bengali Indian musician and composer of Hindustani classical music

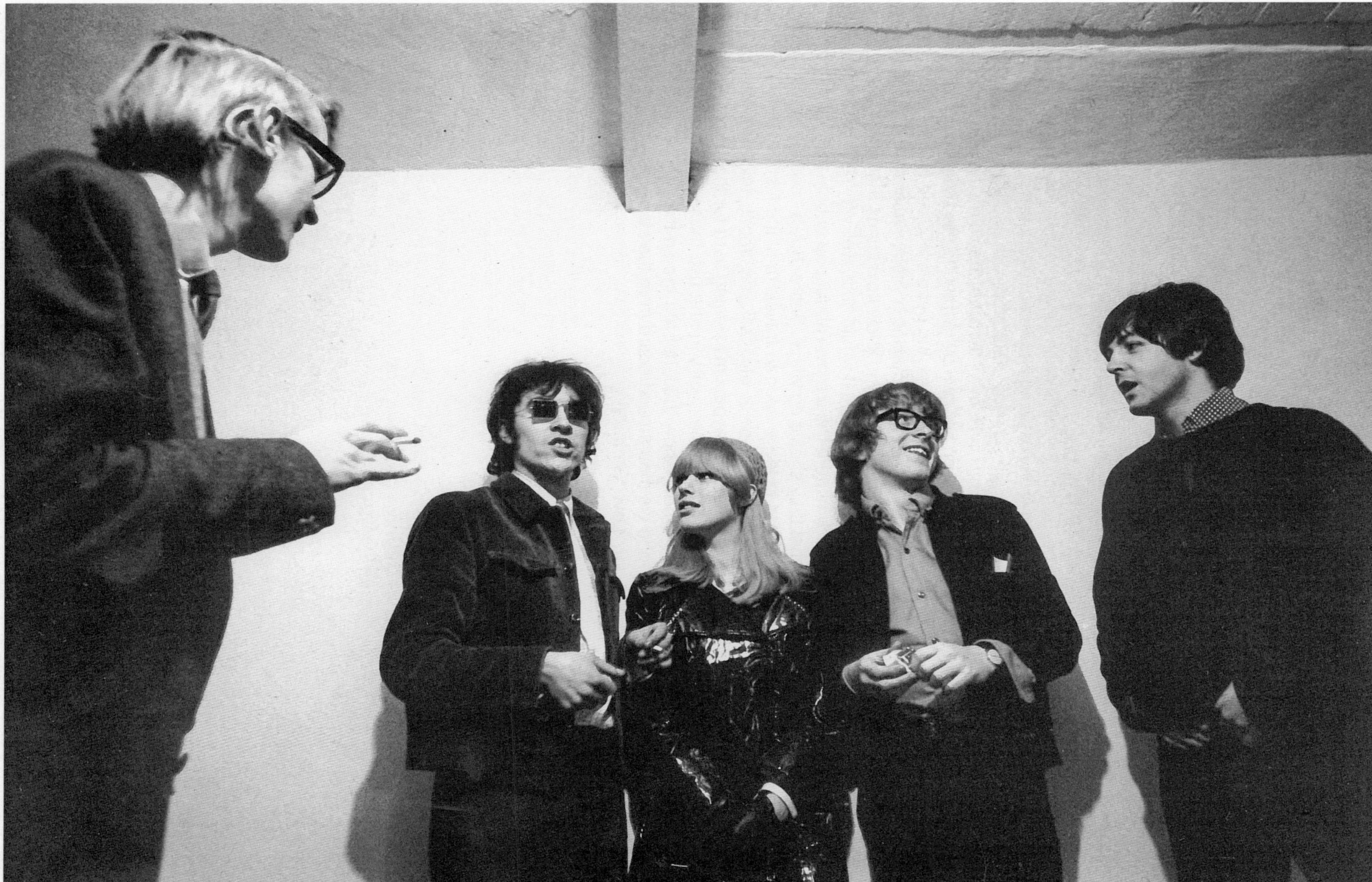

From left to right: Barry Miles, John Dunbar, Marianne Faithfull, Peter Asher, Paul McCartney, London, 1966. Photo: Graham Keen

and drank whiskey. They don't believe in smoking. They think there's too much smoking going on in India. We underwent a reality change, flew our minds as the India we dreamed from what we took to be wasn't. Donovan and Ashley[11] are very beautiful and the untimely arrest for drugs was a bring down. I think they'll get off but it makes a lot difficult for him to do things. They've invited me to the Awards for the pop people and I've written the story for the movie *The Gilded Year* about all of the pop stars becoming thieves, Jonas I believe all arrangements should be made with the mayor's office about beginning the Twin City Cultural interchange in N.Y. this fall. Speak to Jim Marcus,[12] it's time for us to take the initiative at home. Let me know as soon as you're able to c/o Better Books. We're at the irony of being kicked out of our apartment and the living space here is already over-saturated, Eva and I are planning to go to see Fellini[13] in Rome. I think he should do the movie of this life of the girl today on her own by recreating the situations most memorable, making the places and people involved restage it, what was and what will come… the making of history has formed to the recently remembered and you know how things metamorphize with time and memory. I want it would help, well why not make a movie to precede the future like a movie about pop people making money and what they should do with it. Satire. Buy a house in every country in the world to leave open to travels, a plane just available for use by anyone wherever, etc. I ask you, Jonas, tell me if more can be done directly, maybe. I'm listening hard for the circle of 21 is completed. Let me hear you and use these words for the ears waiting to now, show the letter around so they can evaluate the world we thought and heard from the stuckness of its reality, London. Love, Barbara

10
Alan Watts, 1915–1973, British thinker who played a big role in popularizing Eastern spiritualism for the 1960s counterculture

11
Ashley Kozak, ca. 1930–2008, British jazz bassist, record producer, and artist's manager. She is best known as having been Donovan's manager

12
James Lewis Marcus, 1931–1988, was an aide to Mayor John Lindsay in New York City and, in 1966, the City's Commissioner on Water, Gas, and Electric

13
Federico Fellini, 1920–1993, Italian film director and screenwriter

Sender's name and address:
Barbara Rubin (in candle lite)
c/o Better Books
92-94 Charing Cross Road
London
England

Do you still want to get the 8mm Frankel send - is there still the 8mm?

AN AIR LETTER SHOULD NOT CONTAIN ANY ENCLOSURE; IF IT DOES IT WILL BE SURCHARGED OR SENT BY ORDINARY MAIL.

Jerzy Tatayana & their 5 children Andrew's

SECOND FOLD HERE

BY AIR MAIL
PAR AVION
AIR LETTER
AEROGRAMME

PADDINGTON W.2.
12 45PM
22 SEP
1966
B

SIXPENCE POSTAGE

Jonas Mekas
c/o Film-makers Co-op
414 Park Ave South
New York City
New York!
U.S.A.

FIRST FOLD HERE

Dear Jonas

guess who?

Who says you comin' to London

Could this be true?

Oct. or November Please Come Soon

All activities say God please save the Da

We will wait a delay a good shove to the w

For Jonas is coming He'll figure it out

To concur the forth coming — obscure the stumbling forth crumbling

I'd like to se

you

Please send sweet sleep fleet — sweet sweat sweet sweat

and a song come your feet

says on

to you

So here we must meet — lear

Sweet Jonas

A little tune awaits the Fat

If find rythms your time

sent forth just less than a line to me

I'D LIKE to joy WITH YOU

Love you, Barbara

London,
September 22, 1966

Dear Jonas,
Words says (guess who?) you comin' to London.
Could this be true?
(I'd like to joy with you)
Oct. or November please come soon.
All activities say God please save the day.
We will wait a delay a good shove to the way
For Jonas is coming, he'll figure it out
To secure the stumbling forth crumbling
To concur the forthcoming
(I'd like to see you too, says me to you)
(sweet sweat sweet sweat)
Please send sweet sleep fleet
And a song come your feet
So hear (here) we must meet Sweet Jonas
If find rhythms your time
Sent forth just less than a line
To me
A little tune awaits the fate
Love you, Barbara

Rubin's Summer in London in 1966 was frustrating. None of the events she was planning had taken place, and her ideas about the London Film-Makers' Co-op were mostly ignored. Undaunted, she returned to New York in late 1966 and began spending time at the Chelsea Hotel with the filmmaker Shirley Clarke,[1] her daughter Wendy, and Harry Smith. By early 1967, Rubin resurrected the idea of a huge multi-media event that would include films and music. Instead of trying to stage it at the Royal Albert Hall, she would do it this time on her home turf in New York City. In late February 1967, she and a group of friends including Gordon Ball and Mekas organized a two-week long multi-media show that she dubbed *Caterpillar Changes*.

1
Shirley Clarke, 1919–1997, American independent filmmaker, member of the New American Cinema, and co-founder of the Film-Makers' Cooperative in New York

New York,
Fall 1966

Dear Jonas,
Being a morning's leaving rush. Beg a last favor's
request. If upon leaving I forget please mail
these letters quickly for me and I leave here also
last night's lost reel (excerpt for Suzy's)
Suzy's # 677-2029.
And on another dawning of soooo many new mornings shared I
want to say thank you Dear Jonas, simply Thank you for being here
and near. Take care and thank you and peace with the
ladies fleeced.
Love Barbara

New York,
mid-February 1967

Dear Jonas,
A busy note and early morning snow. Nam June Paik's[1] case was dismissed. Charlotte Moorman's[2] charged with indecent exposure, she's out on parole. The Cinematheque got summoned. The Free Spirits'[3] sound technician got arrested too. Tonite we all met at nite court. *The Butterfly*[4] will be ready. Here is a bad printed copy of one and some things for you from Susanna[5] and please wake me up when you get up for I must tell you of the person we found who wants to give us the cash for the Emmanuel Brotherhood Building. It's been very busy.
Love Barbara

1
Nam June Paik, 1932–2006, Korean American new media artist; instigated Fluxus

2
Charlotte Moorman, 1933–1991, American cellist, performance artist, and advocate for avant-garde music

3
The Free Spirits, 1965–1968, American jazz-rock band

4
The Butterfly refers to the poster for the *Caterpillar Changes* event

5
Susanna de Maria Wilson, b. 1940, performer in the Underground arts scene, Andy Warhol took a *Screen Test* of her in 1964

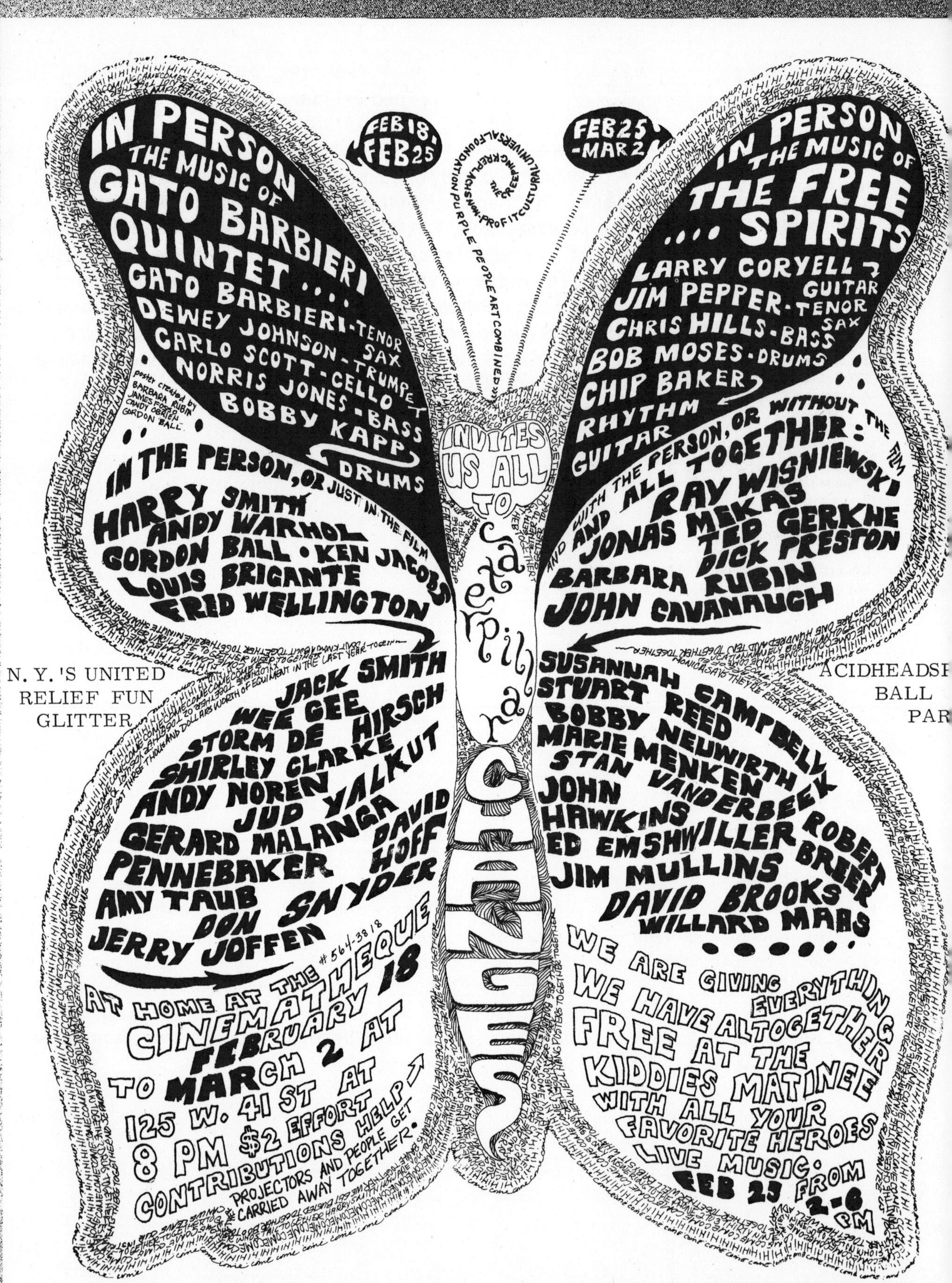

Poster for Barbara Rubin's mixed-media event *Caterpillar Changes* at the Film-Makers' Cinematheque, New York, 1966

CONVERSATION 1

THE VILLAGE VOICE, February 9, 1967

CONVERSATION WITH BARBARA RUBIN AND JOHN CAVANAUGH FIRST PART

I have good news. Change is taking place in the Underground. The youngest generation, a generation that grew up with Bobby Dylan, with LSD, with Allen Ginsberg, with Stan Brakhage—this generation is entering the field of action.

The people involved in this conversation are: John Cavanaugh, who had his first one-man show at the Cinematheque last Saturday; Gordon Ball, whose first film, *Georgia*, was premiered at the *National Magazine* photographers' gathering two weeks ago; Barbara Rubin, whose new film, *Love Supreme for the Free Spirits*, will be shown at the Cinematheque later in February; and Susanna Campbell, who also worked on *Love Supreme*. The other voices are those of friends.

CAVANAUGH I'd rather make my movies in the country, not in the city. There I'd have only trees, and beautiful girls. Then I wouldn't have to stop and to select anything. I could just move constantly, and all would be completely beautiful.

QUESTION Why should there be that difference between the city and the country! Why can't you just...

CAVANAUGH Because you haven't got the freedom of movement, the space isn't the same. Here we are in a multidimensional space.

RUBIN Yes, but that's all we can do, we shoot. In the city. Everywhere we go. He's just into the dimensions...

CAMPBELL Seeing pretty girls and brooks... He could go stay with my grandmother. She's got all these brooks.

CANDY Grandmother could go naked.

CAVANAUGH That would be a good idea. You wouldn't have to stop moving. 'Cause everywhere you move you have something beautiful.

QUESTION You mean, there are some things in the city that you wouldn't select, as you shoot, because they aren't beautiful?

RUBIN He means, when he shoots a flower, he is shooting only a flower, while in the city there are all these multiple meanings...

CAVANAUGH Like, say, to make a movie in here, in this place. Whenever you move around, everything is so multidimensional. If I'm in the woods, like, I have plants up there, millions of spaces that I can move in and out of. I have the whole cosmos. Because I have the sky, and the earth, and the water, and the trees, everything. Whereas here there's nothing. I'd have to frame. That's what I mean. I got to frame...

QUESTION You have to compose? What about your current film?

CAVANAUGH I'd say there was no conscious planning. I just try to be as... I don't know... as like, conscious... not in the conscious way... as conscious as possible, when I shoot... so that I shot what was there at the time...

JONAS In the lobby of the Cinematheque, he used to practice, to "shoot" with an empty camera, moving around. People thought he was crazy.

CAVANAUGH What's so crazy about that? I wish someone would make films with round screens.

CAMPBELL Man... if you could have movie theatres like planetariums...

CAVANAUGH We could have movie theatres like rocket ships, we could really take people places. The screens could be like the portholes.

QUESTION **Could you go back to what you said about structuring and picking out what you want? About being completely free?**
CAVANAUGH **No... I am much more interested in... I am not interested in that at all... less and less. I am interested now in using camera as an energy-transforming machine, to bind kinetic energy sequences. That's to me the important thing, to do this, to bind the kinetic energy... I think that's what I'm interested in.**
RUBIN **This is the kind of film Gordon is filming around the room... looking at each other...**
JONAS **That's what we mean by home movies...**
CAMPBELL **That's wherever I go in the streets, I want to take a picture, like of that spade lady, who was turning around. I just say, "Hey, I'm making a home movie, would you please stand in the light."**
QUESTION **You say that?**
CAMPBELL **Yes. Lots of people go and stand in the light. I'm serious.**
A VOICE **That's nice, and soft, and warm ...**
JONAS **You see, we always said that we are closer to the sun than to the...**
QUESTION (TO BARBARA) **You don't dig his kinetic energy scene?**
RUBIN **Of course I do. I'm just thinking... I sit there and I marvel at what he's doing. But I, like, like I am at the point when I just... you know... I am emanating feeling...**
JONAS **His movies for you are too intellectual...**
RUBIN **Well, how do you like that? I think *Empire* is my favorite... the most beautiful movie I've ever seen, even though I know exactly what he was doing. He was shooting still camera life... but it's really, really beautiful. I'm waiting till we project it in the sky.**
JONAS **When you are shooting... you are all emotion... your mind is no longer there, it seems. And when Cavanaugh shoots, he seems to combine both...**
RUBIN **If you'd ever believe that! It's not true at all. It's not true. Because to get to the point where you can be free is far more... I mean, to understand that concept of free... is not just, you know, it's almost as if, you know, like it's somebody else, something else shooting, it's not me.**
JONAS **Still, it's the emotion that predominates in your work.**

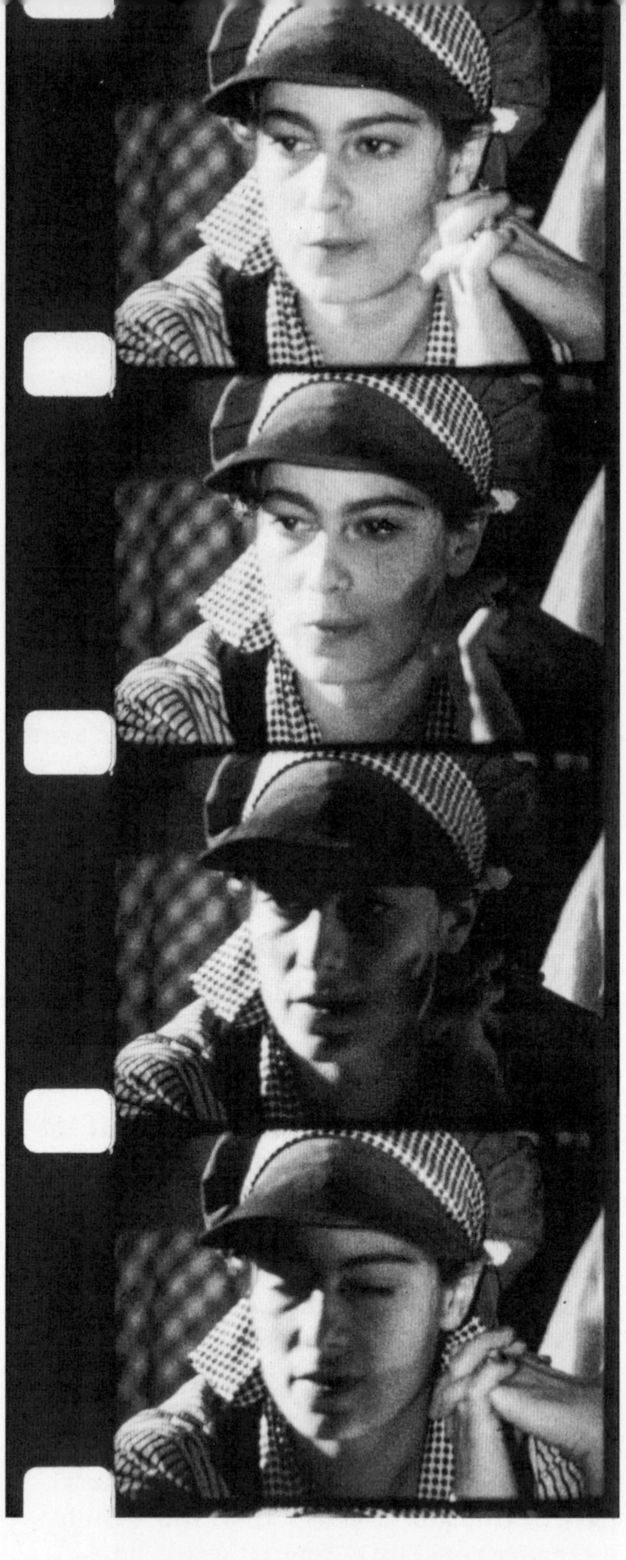

Barbara Rubin, after Kreeping Kreplachs, New York, 1966. Film stills by Jonas Mekas

RUBIN But it's not even my... just my emotions... it's magic, it's just pure magic. It's the spirit other than myself. It's maybe the whole thing that I am rather than the emotion.

JONAS All I'm saying is that it seems that the mind is more at work in John's case than in yours. But then, I could say, the difference between Barbara's movies and John's movies is the same as is between them as people.

QUESTION Is John more interested in formal stuff?

JONAS Well, you see, he went through a stage when he was interested.

RUBIN We are exactly the same, like the opposite sides of a coin. Exactly. Exactly the same.

JONAS The only thing is that you'd never read books on craft and theory, and John reads, or has read, them.

RUBIN But that has nothing to do with it. One side heads and one side tails, but they are still the same two sides of the same coin.

A VOICE You are tails, he is heads ...

RUBIN Now let's not get into that one... it switches all the time. One day he won't even be a coin. He will be a star.

JONAS Anyway, I don't know what other film-maker besides Brakhage has read so many books as John Cavanaugh.

CAVANAUGH Yeah... but, of course, now, I'd say that that was... that was just a tremendous waste of time.

JONAS Now your word has no value. You ain't pure any longer because you went through it.

RUBIN Oh, this is one of those arty conversations between film-makers. I want to do it in the sky. John will probably be there first.

A VOICE He's taller...

RUBIN And believe me, I'm just beginning to appreciate the value of being so many feet above people. Maybe I wouldn't have so many faces. Imagine the different movie I'd make if I were taller. What a different view of the world he has. (Cavanaugh is six foot five).

THE VILLAGE VOICE, February 9, 1967 SECOND PART

This is the second part of the conversation on what's new in New Cinema.

JOHN CAVANAUGH It seems to me that what the cinematic process is, like where it has value, is in directly expressing certain things that are going on in the body, which I take to be an approximation of certain kinds of magnetic energies, magnetic currents. I want to delineate this subtle magnetic process, because I think that's like the essence of mind. In other words, like the mind isn't the symbol program (Cavanaugh here opposes Stan VanDerBeek—JM) but the mind is like an energy structure. So what I'm interested in doing in cinema is directly delineating mind, rather than delineating mind by way of any kind of symbols. I see mind as a very definitely shaped pattern of energy fields. You know, I'd like to directly express that with the camera.

QUESTION You think that Barbara Rubin's movie is a freer movie than yours?

CAVANAUGH Yeah... but not... You see, it's a matter of degrees. Like my movie is free too, but the point is to be totally free.

RUBIN The only difference between you and me is that you use all those big words, and I'd need a dictionary. I didn't understand one word you said. Not one word you said.

QUESTION Would you say you are completely free when you are shooting?

RUBIN You have moments.

QUESTION Do you care if you have those moments or not?

RUBIN But that's my joy, that's where I am. I didn't know what it was like, I started with 16mm. Wow, and I went through a trip with that one! The whole beautiful setup, sound, and motor, and I couldn't move, I couldn't move! And I said, NOOO, this couldn't be where it's at, it's too much. So

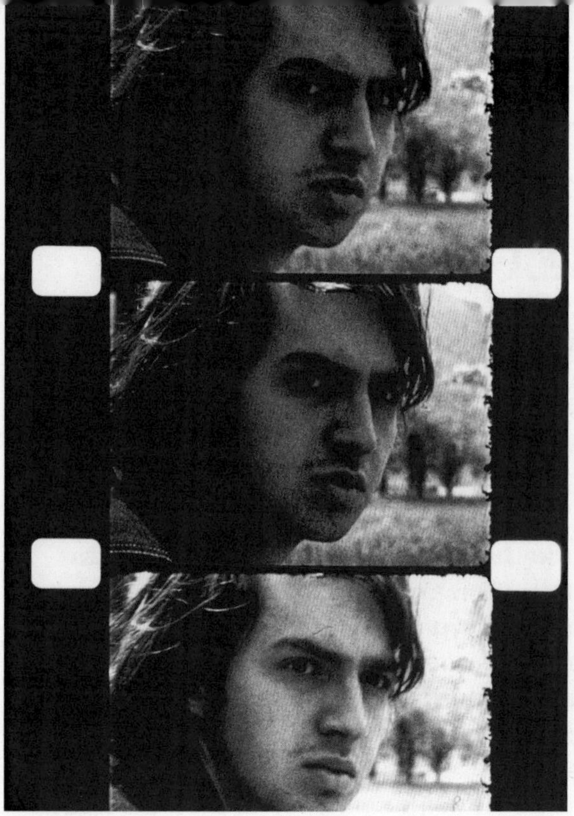

John Cavanaugh, Assisi, 1967. Film stills by Jonas Mekas

when I discovered 8mm it was like... I have to be careful, because, you know, if I'd had the opportunity to have enough film, it would be like a hand with me, I'd just carry it around all the time, shooting all the time. If they'd make anything smaller... like eyes... eyes...

CAVANAUGH **I'm like really interested in mind.**

RUBIN **I think you should give classes to the Puerto Rican kids of the Lower East Side, on film-making. As an eighteen-year-old film-maker I think you should endow some of your intelligence...**

CAVANAUGH **I'm nineteen.**

RUBIN **Pardon me, nineteen.**

QUESTION (TO GORDON BALL) **And you haven't said a word. You just kind of sit taking it all in...**

GORDON BALL **I know very little else.**

RUBIN **He makes beautiful movies.**

JONAS **There is no city in his work... peaceful...**

CAVANAUGH **I'm concerned with tuning the positive-negative symbol systems back to the body, which is where I think the intelligence is. I don't think that intelligence resides in the symbolic mind. In other words, if somebody just has intellect, he isn't intelligent. Intelligence, literally, is in the body. So that my concern is to get away from the symbol mind, which I feel is like stupidity, you know. Let's say, I have been taking LSD now, for the last few months, and, according to the Tibetan religions, what it does to you, it liberates the life flux, the basic life flux, the swirling energy patterns that make up the actuality of life... and that to me is like pure mind, intelligence. So my concern now is to deal directly with that, and trace out with my camera the life fluxus. And the reason I said (see last week's column—JM) I have to be out in nature to do this, is that that's where the natural energy is, which is based on the same types of energy structures as I'm dealing with, like directly, perceptually.**

QUESTION **What happens to the energy in the city? It gets perverted?**

BALL **Organized humanity always does.**

QUESTION **The drift of all modern civilization has been to imprint your mind, no?**

CAVANAUGH **True, very true. But not anymore! Me and William Burroughs will rub out all mind imprints.**

QUESTION **What happens when you start "de-imprinting" the mind, like "de-imprinting" the astronauts, you know?**

RUBIN **Then they set fire to the capsules, right?**

QUESTION **How far can you go with "de-imprinting" the mind?**

BALL **All the way.**

QUESTION **How far is "all the way"?**

BALL **I don't know, whatever you can think of.**

QUESTION **Why is film so important in this whole process?**

RUBIN **Because of the reflections. We are going through the reflection age. Living through the subjective reflections.**

CAVANAUGH **To me, cinema is the yoga of getting the patterns of direct energy organized. Burroughs has a conception of the image virus. I'm beginning to understand what he means by that. When I was stoned on acid, I found out just what it is. Like Burroughs** says that a virus is a two-dimensional entity, that it needs a three-dimensional being to operate through. And he says, the virus enters the three-dimensional body through the cardinal points, which are, which is like any habit, like it can be as simple a thing as a certain style of body movement, anything that's part of a controlled situation is a cardinal point.

RUBIN That's the whole beauty, the whole prophecy of films. That's why we are making films now. That's why all our saints today are the artists. Because it's the whole creating of that, the backwards living we are going to do now. Now we are going to spend all our time watching what we are doing, we are not going to live it. We are going to reflect it, project it, then we are going to re-hash it, re-edit it, and then we are going to throw it back out, just like the flying saucers. We are going to go through it. Here in America today all those young kids who are turning on and everything, they are all doing the tribal scenes, taking Eastern cultures, you know, doing that whole thing, and there will be little communities in America, Independent States of Mind, and they will make the United States. Until one day, we realize we are not really in America, but we are flying saucers from outer space. Everybody's making movies. Everyone. Even my uncle had an 8mm camera, before I had one.

QUESTION About this backward living. You aren't going to live it, you are just going to reflect it?

RUBIN It's much swifter. Imagine if we'd have to live through all that?

JONAS What she means, I think, is that we have collected too much dead matter. In man's development, whenever he has to make a big step forward, he looks back and drops the dead matter, he becomes very conscious of his past and sees that's like nothing, not worth keeping—compared with what's coming.

RUBIN The biggest problem with films like this is that you need a trained eye. It's the whole backwards thing. We are getting to the point where we're just doing blinks, more in film than we do as human beings. How many people do you know who go out in the street and blink?

BALL Twelve-frame-per-second blinks...

RUBIN Like Brakhage, he's still such a problem, the man has such a trained eye. It's like sitting and listening to music and being able to hear the gut outside of itself. That's the whole beauty of films now. And now we have Andy Warhol.

I was thinking, while watching John's movie, listening to the Velvet music. They are like Buddhists, like Zen Buddhists. The kind of person who might, years ago, have gone out and dug that kind of state of mind, living in that, you know, kind of mystery and feeling, that whole generating quality. Now, you understand, he's making movies or playing this music. The Velvets—this tape... it's a meditation. They are sending me in that kind of feeling... which is just sitting and being very quiet.

e lection day

Dear Arlene McElroy, Arthur Knight, Hollis Al^D^bert (sorry) and Playboy

I'm sending you all**God's maya rosary of strawberries**

stillies from Christmas on Earth, it's here you know
seen in the lord's year 1963
I'm also still reading your letter

you tell me
As you may be aware,(I8m not) Playboy is in the process of publishing "
not THat? that ? no ? not what?
The History of Sex in Cinema"?(what's that)which is a continuing series
dealing with censorship in films(censorship ? sex? in Cinema?) and the
(it's devoted
the upcoming chapter will be devoted(i's glad) to experimental and under-
opps
ground films. i'm also unawares of who Sir Arthur Knight and Lord
Hollis A L PPert are, sorry you tell me Sir Arthur is writing the chapter
on experimental films, and will be discussing one of my films and you
would appreciate etc. blab de da blap w h aaaaat? pictorIAL applicableee to the sexcensor sh
now all that really bugged me so i sat down and i and i a nd i i i he did
give you God's maya rosary of strawberries holy holy strawberries
didn't you here hear ear hear i had a vision it was a vision it is god
CHRISTMAS ON EARTH C H R I S T M A S O OPPS N E A R T H is
YOU8ll be discussing one of my films?
have you known Christmas on Earth Continued, or, Christmas On Earth Continued
Again, or, Trip Trip Trip Along With Christmas On Earth Again and agin
now have you?
i mean i don't know but you really did do something T H E
the history of sex in cinema
the history of sex in cinema
the history of sex in cinema H I S T O R Y O F S E X
THE HISTORY OF SEX IN CINEMA i mean really
the history of sex in cinema N O christmas on earth do you hear
the history the history history history aren't you listening christmas christmas
christmas christmas on earth ON EARTH CHRISTMAS GEEEE CHRISTMAS CHRISTMAS CHRIST
MAS ON EARTH and your talking of the history of sex in cinema so you didn't hear
it's always been hear but you ain't soooo i sat down and He gives you His own
GOD's
maya rosary of strawberries c h r i s t m a s o n earth
i'm sorry it's in the air air i thought you had ears here to hear but you seem else

where where? where where where ?????

try eyes heart soul nose or toes fly rise and cry but please i's only alive
i ain't history
please see that film is god's tree of lifeliving L O V E sighing cry
lovelovelovelovelovelovelovelovelovelovelovelovelovelovelovelovelovelovelove

please let me know how long you'll be holding God's maya
the rosary of strawberries for they're his wedding
and christmas gift to my love

maybe you shouldshall chant sing dance ring

Hari Krishna Hari Krishna Krishna Krishna Hari Hari

Hari Rama Hari Rama Rama Rama Hari Hari=*LORD*

Barbara Rubin's letter to *Playboy Magazine* in answer to their request regarding a series of articles called *The History of Sex in Cinema*, *Film Culture* No. 44, New York, ca. 1967

After *Caterpillar Changes*, Rubin wrote a screenplay with Shirley Clarke and Lionel Ziprin[1] called *Sydney Arthur: A Musical Comedy*, which was never produced. By the Summer of 1967, she was living at Allen Ginsberg's apartment again and taking care of the drug-addicted Peter Orlovsky and his catatonic brother Julius.[2] During this time, she helped Robert Frank with the production of his film about the Orlovskys called *Me and My Brother*.[3] Rubin also participated in many anti-war protests both in New York City and Washington and she was arrested numerous times.

1
Lionel Ziprin, 1924–2009, mystic Jewish poet and a key figure in the Lower East Side scene of the 1950s and 1960s

2
Julius Orlovsky, 1931–2012, brother of Peter Orlovsky

3
Robert Frank, b. 1924, Swiss-American photographer and documentary filmmaker. *Me and My Brother* is a 1969 film

ca. 1967

Dear Jonas,
Foreboding thoughts of flames [and] smoke in this house to tell us watch safety precautions please before you go either yourself or I will speak to the landlord about lighting the stairs particularly.
Love Barbara

People coming to hear Lionel's poem tomorrow at 4 in the afternoon: and Storm, Amy[1] and Richard,[2] Shirley, Lionel and Joanna[3] and Lee their 13 year old son, Stuart Reed, Lynn, and maybe Harry and Mark.

1
Amy Taubin, b. 1939, American film critic and actress

2
Richard Foreman, b. 1937, American playwright, theater director, and founder of the Ontological-Hysteric Theater

3
Joanna Ziprin, 1919–1994, wife of Lionel Ziprin

New York,
Spring 1968

Dear Charles,[1]
Gordon Ball[2] and myself are working on a program of films specifically for college showing. One program is of poets, Allen Ginsberg, Andrei Voznesensky, Gregory Corso,[3] and others. It should run from an hour or more. We felt this kind of film is made for colleges rather than public theater paying audience. It would be nice if these could be shown without the discussion film-maker present scene. But if it has to be either Gordon or myself will be willing to go along. The material on the poets was shot with Shirley Clarke and any more information we can give you when it's completed. If you're rushed for time you can just put the description I gave you here, specifying that it was put together for colleges. The only other film (*Allen for Allen*, is incorporated in the poets "anthology") I have is *Christmas on Earth*. I would like to have that shown at colleges but I believe you'll have to investigate the legal problems involved in showing genitals, lovemaking, etc. You could discuss this with Jonas if you feel it would be possible to show I will send you a description of the film for your catalogue, unless you will use my own present one-liner, "a study of genital differentiation and psychic tumult"[4] and leave it at that. I would prefer that though I understand your desire for accuracy and precision. We don't care too much for biographies and photos, since the works "seem to be more important" unless you feel the photo background induces the sell, then I really rather be noncommittal and leave my chance to those who don't care.
Please write me and inform of what is absolutely necessary and what is not for your pitch-help. We do send you minimal statistics hoping this will cover it. The only consideration about doing the tour is both Gordon and I are a part of a foundation farm in the country and the best time would be in winter since it's snowbound.
The poets film should be ready this winter.
If this is all confusing please let me know!
For *Christmas on Earth* don't bother Leslie, write me if it's necessary for your catalogue for projecting explanations since *Christmas* is complicated to show requiring 2 projectors spaced properly and a radio hook-up. Sorry for so much.
Love Barbara Rubin

1
Likely referring to David Charles Stone

2
Gordon Ball, b. 1944 American avant-garde filmmaker and now memoirist

3
Gregory Corso, 1930–2001, American poet, youngest of the inner circle of Beat Generation writers

4
Candy O'Brien's quote about *Christmas on Earth*, that is still included in the Film-Makers' Cooperative listing today

RUBIN, Barbara:

CHRISTMAS ON EARTH 16mm. 30 min. Rental: $60.00

The exploit explain written for and about Christmas On Earth in the catalogue is disolving and as the cut up film version it referred to is, from the holeburnedscratches of stripping film peepers.

What you'll be renting now is just what was filmed, uncut, unedited. Made in 1963. "A study in genital differentiation and psychic tumult." -- Candy O'Brien.

(Projection Instructions: The film remains on two reels, requiring two projectors, to be projected simultaneously at sound speed. The film on the first projector fills the screen, while the image of the second projector is approximately one-half smaller and fills the middle of the screen, superimposing on the first image. This can be done either by using different lenses or by placing one projector closer to the screen. They begin simultaneously, though due to slight differences in speed of each projector, they end slightly different. I've added black leader to compensate for that. When both images are off, turn projectors off. I suggest if possible to use two of the same kind of projectors and check them before beginning.)

I also suggest since this is the first time viewing this, to put reel I (figures) on the larger screen, and reel 2 (images) on the inner smaller screen, making sure each film is being projected heads out.

To complete the cycle, a radio must be hooked up to your P. A. system with a nice cross section of psychic tumult, like an AM rock station turned on and played loud. Also (optional) colored gels may be used in front of the lenses of the projectors and moved and alternated by hand during the film.

PLEASE RETURN THIS FILM AS IT WAS SENT YOU, WHOLE.

Thank you,

Barbara Rubin

P.S. : <u>PLEASE</u> -- PROJECT MY FILM IN THE IMAGE IN WHICH IT WAS CREATED -- i.e., EXACTLY ACCORDING TO THE PROJECTION INSTRUCTIONS!

Barbara Rubin's projection instructions for her film *Christmas on Earth*, ca. 1965

By early 1968, Rubin was slowly losing touch with Mekas. In March, she convinced Allen Ginsberg to buy a farm in upstate New York near Cherry Valley. She lived there full-time in May with Ginsberg, Gordon Ball, Peter and Julius Orlovsky, and Ball's then girlfriend Candy.[1] Herbert Huncke,[2] Gregory Corso, and other of Ginsberg's friends were frequent visitors. Though Rubin only lived at the farm for the first six months of its existence, East Hill Farm, as it came to be known, became an important haven for Ginsberg and his friends for the next twenty years. It was the birthplace of Ginsberg's non-profit organization called the Committee on Poetry.

1
Candy O'Brien, medicine woman and former girlfriend of filmmaker Gordon Ball

2
Herbert Huncke, 1915–1996, American writer and poet, member of the Beat Generation

East Hill Farm,
July 1968

Dear Leslie,[1]
I send you new instructions and new words instruction for catalogue. I believe it is coherent and precise. I seem to have the misfortune of lack of clarity and spelling, so Candy did it for me. I believe her quote will do for a line explanation of *Christmas*.
Could you send me a copy of this in your own good time since typewriter broke no carbon paper and mass confusion am writing this in outhouse. I also send you a letter received from special events division of New York Film Festival. It's alright with me. Could you make arrangements for it to be sent to them with these new instructions. I wrote them too, explaining.
We just midwifed the first born goat on the farm while Gordon filmed. Unfortunately, it died from oversize.
Otherwise we work, work work always work and play soft ball, Sir Balls, sheriff insistence. Everyone and animals well and healthy. I'm in outhouse writing you, hiding since I'm sick, supposed to be in bed.
Love from all to you Love Barbara

1
Leslie Trumbull, 1933–2017, secretary and eventually the head of the New York Film-Makers' Cooperative from 1963 until the early 1990s

August 19, 1968

Dear Jonas,
Lincoln Center film
festival wanted
to show *Christmas*
at private screening
you have my per-
mission to remove it
if you feel we
shouldn't partake
or if you picket.
Come up.
love Barbara

August 19, 1968

Dear Leslie,
Please give Jonas
my permission
to remove *Christmas*
from Lincoln Center
showing (if they
take it) if Jonas etc.
pickets the festival
or if he feels we
shouldn't show.
Love Barbara

or le slue

Please give Jonas
permission to remove
us + mas from Lincoln
ter Showing (if they take
of Jonas etc. - pickets
Festival or if he feels
ashamed to show
love Barbara

Barbara Rubin
R.D. 2
Cherry Valley
w York 13328

CHERRY VALLEY N.Y.
AUG 19
PM
1968

ANDREW JACKSON
1c
U.S. POSTAGE

4c
U.S. POST

THIS SIDE OF CARD IS FOR ADDRESS

Jonas
note 4 Festival
to Festival
makers
175
Lexington
N.Y.C. 10016

By August 1968, Rubin had grown increasingly frustrated by life at East Hill Farm. Her vision of a healthy, self-sustaining farm dedicated to clean living was being ruined by Peter Orlovsky's drug addiction and Gregory Corso's drunken, harassing visits. Meanwhile, Ginsberg himself was spending less time there and Rubin's hopes of marrying him and having children were dashed. At the same time, Rubin began spending more and more time at a Satmar Hasidic community in nearby Sharon Springs. According to her friend Susan Brustman, one day in late August, she simply jumped out of the car as they were driving by the Hasidic community and said she was going to stay there and not return to the farm. Over the next few months, Rubin became an Orthodox Jew and disavowed her former life. By the Summer of 1969, she moved to Far Rockaway, New York to study with Rabbi Shlomo Freifeld.[1] In the following letter addressed to Leslie Trumbull, she writes of asking Jacques Ledoux to "burn" his copy of *Christmas on Earth*. Rubin's new life was based on repenting for past sins, and she considered a lot of what she had done to be sinful. Mekas recalls that she also asked him to burn her film but acknowledged its historical value.

1 Rabbi Shlomo Freifeld, 1925–1990, influential personality in the world of Orthodox Judaism

no date found

Dear Jonas,
Don’t be saddened—
give me time and
patience for it was I
who was exposed
also—no change, or
losing, just growth.
Love always
Barbara

DEAR JONAS,

DON'T BE SADDENED ———

GIVE ME TIME AND PATIENCE

FOR IT WAS I WHO WAS EXPOSED ALSO —

NO CHANGE, OR LOOSING, JUST GROWTH.

LOVE ALWAYS

BARBARA —

ca. 1970

Dear Leslie,
I just received a letter from Jacques Ledoux. I had wrote him to burn *Christmas*, as you suggested. He writes me he will be in town this May 15 to the 25th and wants to discuss this with me, naturally. Could you, or Jonas, give him my phone number here 518-284-8361 and if, as it can be, connections fail, could you, in the diplomacy you are known for, attempt my thanks to you dear Leslie and hope well the Spring's with you.
Love, Bashe Bruche[1]

1
Bashe Bruche, Barbara Rubin after becoming a Hasidic Jew. She experimented with different names and eventually settled on Bracha

ca. 1970

Dear Jonas
Thanking you very
much again for
your help.
Please show this
to Amy.
She would be my
choice for the lead
Shalom
Bracha

1969

Dear Jonas,
I want to thank you for the many good things you've been to me, to your many years to be, may G-d watch you in good health and strength in your kindness.
This is the spice of the coming of the Messiah, peace on earth, to the words of Malcolm X,[1] "Till all men acknowledge there is but one G-d," each in his own way, to His glory and the good of HUMANITY.
Love Brache Barbara

1 Malcolm X, 1925–1965, African-American Muslim minister and human rights activist

CONVERSATION 2

CONVERSATION WITH BARBARA RUBIN AND JONAS MEKAS

THE VILLAGE VOICE, March 2, 1972 BARBARA RUBIN TRANSFORMS INTO BRACHA RUBIN FIRST PART

Barbara Rubin, one of the most legendary figures of the early Underground film era, has surfaced again. She is going to make a film with Daniel Cohn-Bendit. At least, that's what she is trying to do, at this moment.

Where has Barbara Rubin been for the last four years? Those who lived through the most active days of the New York film Underground, between 1962 and 1967, miss Barbara Rubin. She was one of the four or five key figures of the period, and probably Number One Woman in the movement. Her work, her adventures, her influences, her true and invented stories reached the far corners of this and the European continent. Her name was connected with a variety of key names of the period, from Allen Ginsberg and Harry Smith to Roman Polański and Federico Fellini, from Lenny Bruce and Paul McCartney to Bob Dylan and Andrei Voznesenski. And then, four years ago, Barbara disappeared.

JONAS Let us begin with the beginning. What is your name now?

BARBARA RUBIN Bracha.

JONAS: You'd like to be called Bracha, instead of Barbara?

BARBARA Yes.

JONAS How come you changed your name?

BRACHA It's a Hebrew equivalent of Barbara.

JONAS I know that during the last four years you have become a very conscious and active Jewess. Could you describe the steps you have gone through since our last *Voice* interview, in 1967? If I am not wrong, very soon after that, Allen Ginsberg bought a farm upstate and you went to help him.

BRACHA I lived there for six months, prior to the Chicago convention. There was much talk about Chicago. I didn't think it was going to be peaceful. And I felt there was a lot of hypocrisy about what was going to go down there. In December 1967 some of the people came and we were discussing it and I just realized that they were going to create an either/or situation where you couldn't think for yourself. And I decided that the truth that I was looking for, this truth demanded that I act at this point. I am Jewish, and though I knew nothing about what Jewishness is, since my parents are atheists, I started looking into it.

JONAS Were there some people who led you into this active looking into your Jewishness?

BRACHA There were some people. Jerry Jofen used to be a rabbi. He used to be a Torah Jew. He comes from a very old line of Orthodox rabbis. He went through the war in Russia, in Białystok; left with his father, went through China, came to America, and after a while here, you know, he slowly went into another world. The same with Lionel Ziprin.

JONAS: The poet?

BRACHA He's everything. His wife, you know, was the one who helped Harry Smith on his *Oz* film. He also came from a very religious family from Israel. And he also went "away," and ended up in the drug, you know, art world, same as Jerry Jofen. And having met these people, and seeing how

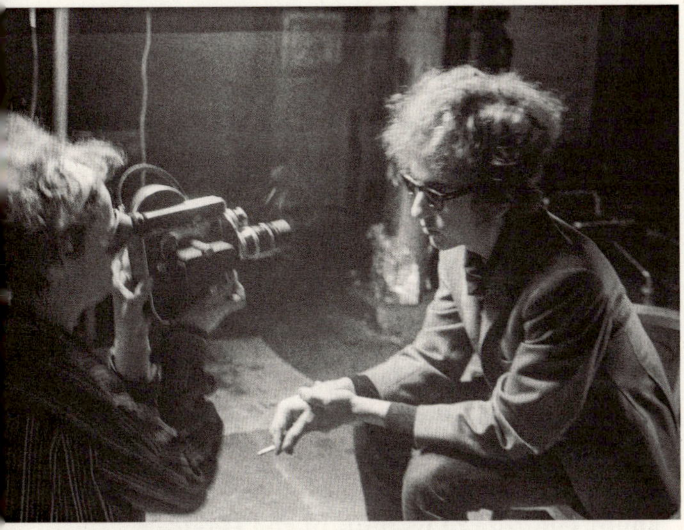

Barbara Rubin filming Bob Dylan at Warhol's Silver Factory, New York, 1966. Photo: Nat Finkelstein

different they were from everyone else, I realized that they had the answer. And it was a matter of finding the way back. A real way, not a hypocritical way. And that took four to five years. When I arrived, away from home, I believed you had to break every rule, create chaos, not order. And in the process of creating chaos, if one didn't pick up every stitch, the feedback was your payment. While we were doing "our scene," we didn't take care of it enough, we had no perspective of, you know, what eventually was going to happen.

JONAS: What was your next step, after you arrived at those conclusions?

BRACHA To act upon it, which is always the hardest. It just so happened, up in Cherry Valley, where Allen had the farm, there was a Hasidic group in the next town.

JONAS Jerry Jofen and Lionel Ziprin are not Hasidic?

BRACHA Lionel is part Hasidic and part from Israel, which doesn't have a name.

JONAS Could you sum up, in a short paragraph, what a Hasidic Jew is?

BRACHA Well, in the seventeenth century the Jews were divided into very poor, peasant people, who could neither read nor write, and the scholars. The scholars married wealthy women and were supported, and they studied and learned all their lives. And this dichotomy grew until the 1700s false Messiahs swept over Europe. And along came this very holy man called Ba'al Shem Tov and tried to unite all Jews. The scholars claimed that only sitting and learning was the way of God. Ba'al Shem Tov said that eating is learning, living is learning, work is learning, sleeping is learning, making love is learning—every aspect of one's life is the Torah. So he brought another dimension into life is the Torah which at that point wasn't there. Everything has the sparks of holiness in it. Say, if you are cleaning the top of the table, if you do it with holiness, you are redeeming the sparks in matter. You now, in the rock, in the table, in paper—everything—you have to do and handle it knowing that it's holy, not something just to...
You know, you are forbidden in the Torah just to take a piece of paper like this and fiddle with it, because it's destroying a piece of paper which was created... So this Ba'al Shem Tov Hasidism grew over the years and, of course, during World War II they were the people who were destroyed in the concentration camps, which, in the Torah, was like an act of holiness, because the Torah says, when you come upon somebody who wants to take your God away, and wants you to bow down to the idol, rather die than allow him to force you to do this. Only die knowing you're doing it for holiness. That's why the Jews were walking into gas chambers singing. They weren't sheep, like they say. Because, you know, the Germans were at the height of civilization, right? The Jews even thought the Germans came to liberate them. So if this is the height of civilization, technology, man, and mind, then it's worth dying because there is no living.

JONAS Maybe the reason to live would be to attempt to change it all?

BRACHA You see, but at that point, there was no possible way of changing it other than showing the Germans that they weren't going to fall to their level.

(... to be continued next week.)

THE VILLAGE VOICE, March 9, 1972 SECOND PART

I will continue my conversation with Bracha (Barbara) Rubin.

JONAS Are there many Hasidic groups in America?

BRACHA There are a lot of them. The biggest groups are in Williamsburg and Crown Heights. So one family said to me: why don't you come and live with us. I said, all right. And that was just the time of the Chicago convention.

JONAS Did you discuss Hasidism with Ginsberg?

BRACHA Yes, we spent some time talking about it. All his life he looked for truth too. Each person finds it in his own way. When I look at ten years ago, the way it was, and what the kids have today, to begin with—there is such a difference. But I was sitting in a pizza place, and a twelve-year-old turned to me and she said, "Doesn't that lady look funny?" And suddenly I felt like I was ancient. And I wanted to get up and say, "Who the fuck do you think you are?" But then... I thought... of course, she doesn't know at all what I went through. Her world is beginning in a completely different way. And she says to me, "I don't want to hear about any of your experiences; I have to do it myself." And I thought, what in the world did we go through, and some died, to break those walls, and yet everyone wants to go through and do it all again, everyone has to have that experience inside their being. Like I went through it.

JONAS They won't be going through exactly the same experience, though. Things have been brought to another level, be it in drug experience, politics, or cinema. So it's not exactly the same. That's why they have to go through it.

BRACHA When I went to the Hasidic group upstate in New York, I finally found out that I was just a spoiled American child and that I was totally incapable of changing. So, like I had to go through five years of this truth and find it myself. And then, like you found it, and how are you going to live it, right? This is the big thing, you found it, right, and suddenly you feel, I just want to break out. I want to go out! Because praying is greater than throwing a rock. But it's difficult when you are your rock and you are constantly fighting. Because we are the most spoiled children in the world. So it's been very difficult.

JONAS All kinds of rumors have reached me about the role of women in the Hasidic groups. How is it?

BRACHA Let's differentiate now between people who are so-called Hasids, and the Torah. What the Torah says is different from the way some people act. There are a lot of male chauvinist pigs in the Torah. But that doesn't mean the Torah advocates it. The Torah holds that the man and the woman are like a microcosm of the universe. And the Torah says the woman isn't the one of softness—it's the man. It says, a woman is hard, she's filled with judgment. In the Torah, the male is the external force, and the woman is the internal force. External meaning that the man's function in the universe is not going out and getting a job and doing all that; in the Torah, the woman does that. The woman takes care of the literal, physical world, and the man takes care of the spiritual. But without the interchange between the man and the woman, the spiritual world of man goes crazy, it flies away. Like men tend to fly away. And the female world, which is literal, tends to be harsh, and it gets so harsh that it's like nature, it starts to destroy. So there must always be that interchange, you see, between the two. And of course, there are situations which are not right.

JONAS Did your work in cinema stop with your interest in Hasidism?

BRACHA No. I abandoned cinema before that.

I realized I had to stop and take a good look at myself, or else it was going to be another game, all laid out for me. I had to go through five years of realizing that no longer would I create chaos, like I did with my other films. Now I want to create order. And that took five years, to break through that concept that I had: nothing is wrong, nothing is bad, nothing is evil, everything is good... except when you do something bad... and then you have to pay for it... because you're stupid, right? So now, what I want to do, I have these problems. I am a woman. I have to earn a living. Very, very complex, right? I never finished high school. I am not going to become a doctor or a lawyer. And all I can hope for is that I can offer another alternative. Some people went there, and I went here. All I can do is transmit it, to the best of my ability. This is all I can do. And it's time. Because I lived too long in a vacuum.

JONAS **What do you want to transmit?**

BRACHA **Where I am. Because I don't believe there is such a thing as objectivity. And all we can offer, if we don't grab too much—like to make a multimillion dollar movie—is just that. You know, just take a little, do what you have to do. Everyone has to say where they are at. There are alternatives of life. They are not all black or evil. Especially for women. What I'd like to do, at this point, I'd like to make a film with Daniel Cohn-Bendit.**

JONAS **I was under the impression that Hasidism forbids you to make films?**

BRACHA **No, not at all. They said it's very wonderful. All they said was make sure your motives are good. Make sure you're not personally gaining anything from it.**

JONAS **What about your early films? Will you show them again?**

BRACHA **Yes, but I have to reverse the process. Because that's what facing myself in the Torah was. It's the inverse of believing that there is a creator in the universe, there is order. And if one finds that order, in one's own way, one matches oneself to the order of the universe and helps the universe by every action one does, not working against it.**

JONAS **You have been talking to Daniel Cohn-Bendit about your next film. Could you say something about the subject of this film?**

BRACHA **I want to make a film dealing with the concentration camp experience. Every Jew, and every person, has to get that straight—what happened in Germany from 1939 to 1945. If we don't get World War II straight in our hearts and our minds, then it's all possible again. And it's an experience I want to live through. I want to go to the concentration camps, I want to feel the blood of the people who died, coming up from the earth, I want to have an integral part of that experience so I could learn from it, God willing.**

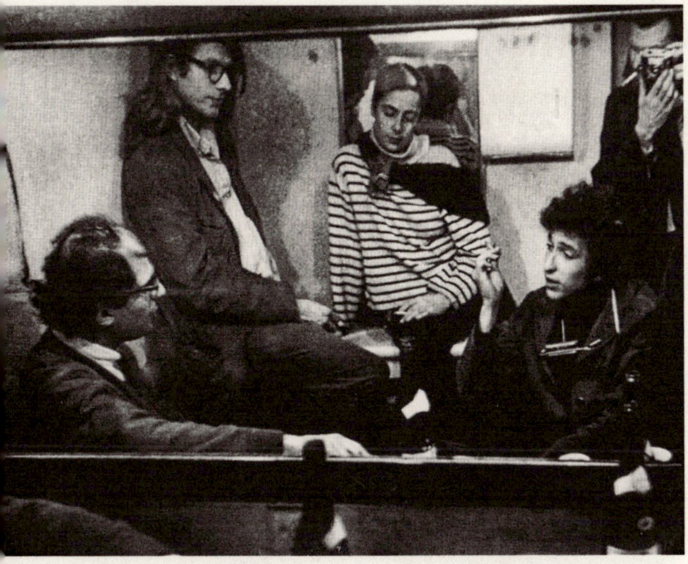

From left to right: Allen Ginsberg, Peter Orlovsky, Barbara Rubin, Bob Dylan, Daniel Kramer backstage at the McCarter Theatre at Princeton University, 1964. Photo: Daniel Kramer

Brucha Bloancor
(Barbara Rubin)
F.S.T.
50 Montée de la Reine
Victoria
Aix-les-Bains, France 73100

Dear Jonas Guess What I still don't have George Moorse's address & you take the print of Allen for Allen & the tape it ain't here so I guess you did so now I'd got to tell Pam because

P.S. LOVE LOVE LOVE? LOVE!

love love you

Don't forget I was sending you ... ain't coming to Stan the film's Oh Why Love

... Stan or by mail I'd rather use ... of something or other but I'd rather have her also know now

Chuck Smith
Barbara Rubin's Spirit

"Chuck, DO IT! Count me IN. jonas." That was the email Jonas Mekas sent me in January 2014 when I asked him if he would help me make a documentary film about his friend Barbara Rubin. Now, four years later, my film is done, Jonas is happy, and, thanks to many of Rubin's friends and relatives and all the scholars who came before me, I've learned a lot about her. The films and footage she left behind provide glimpses of who she was as an artist, but it is in her letters to Jonas Mekas, and her scripts and other writings—collected here for the first time together—that Barbara Rubin's true self is revealed.

It is divinely fitting that Barbara Rubin's letters to Jonas Mekas end with the word "HUMANITY." Above all else, Rubin believed in the power of humanity to change the world around us. She plunged deep into everything with a curious eye that was supremely human. While making my documentary film, *Barbara Rubin and the Exploding NY Underground*, I encountered many aspects of her humanity that I couldn't include in the film. While I could never find any evidence that she held a 9-5 job of any kind, I did discover that she was the "best babysitter" ever, "like a Mary Poppins on acid!" as Brett Aronowitz (the daughter of Al Aronowitz) once exclaimed. Rubin also seemed to be extremely caring and mother-like to all damaged souls whether they were suffering in a hospital from a mental breakdown or just having a bad drug trip at a party. Her experiences with her schizophrenic brother Kenny, with Peter & Julius Orlovsky, and with her own manic states of mind gave her a keen sense of the vagaries of mental illness and awakened a strong sympathetic response that was remembered by all who knew her. As Jonas Mekas remembers, one night a group of friends from the Cinematheque were debating who would have the compassion to truly adopt and take care of a homeless man that they saw rummaging through garbage in the street. "Barbara would," they all agreed.

By all accounts, as Rubin moved from her filmmaking world to her Orthodox Jewish world, she took her compassion and belief in humanity with her. She was an extremely caring mother of her five children and an integral part of the community that she and her second husband, Yitzchak, joined in Aix-Les-Bains, France in 1973. According to Rubin's aunt Selma and other friends, Barbara and Yitzchak were a perfect match who had both studied with Rabbi Freifeld and were "on the same path." While her Orthodox life in France was vastly different from her life as an Underground filmmaker, she did not lose her outspoken personality and her taste for life's joys. The Breslov Hasidic sect that she became a part of believes in a joyous relationship with God that is exemplified by ritual dancing and music. Contrary to certain perceptions of Hasidism, Rubin did *not* become a quiet, subservient wife and mother. And she did not disappear. Her children are all still alive and are Orthodox Jews with children of their own. She would be proud of them all.

Throughout the 1970s Rubin would occasionally write to Amy Taubin, Allen Ginsberg, and other old friends. Taubin recalls never writing back. To die-hard, secular New Yorkers, Rubin's new life was too hard to imagine and too challenging to connect with. So, by the time of her tragic death in 1980 after giving birth to her fifth child, she had drifted into the realm of mystery and legend. The only evidence of Rubin that remained were a few rare screenings of *Christmas on Earth* organized by those who couldn't forget its power. But Jonas Mekas never forgot his friend and the inspiration she had given him. It was he who saved all the letters that form the basis of this book, and it was he who spared his copy of *Christmas on Earth* from the flames. This book is Jonas's tribute to Barbara's spirit—a divine spirit that lives on in all of life's wonders.

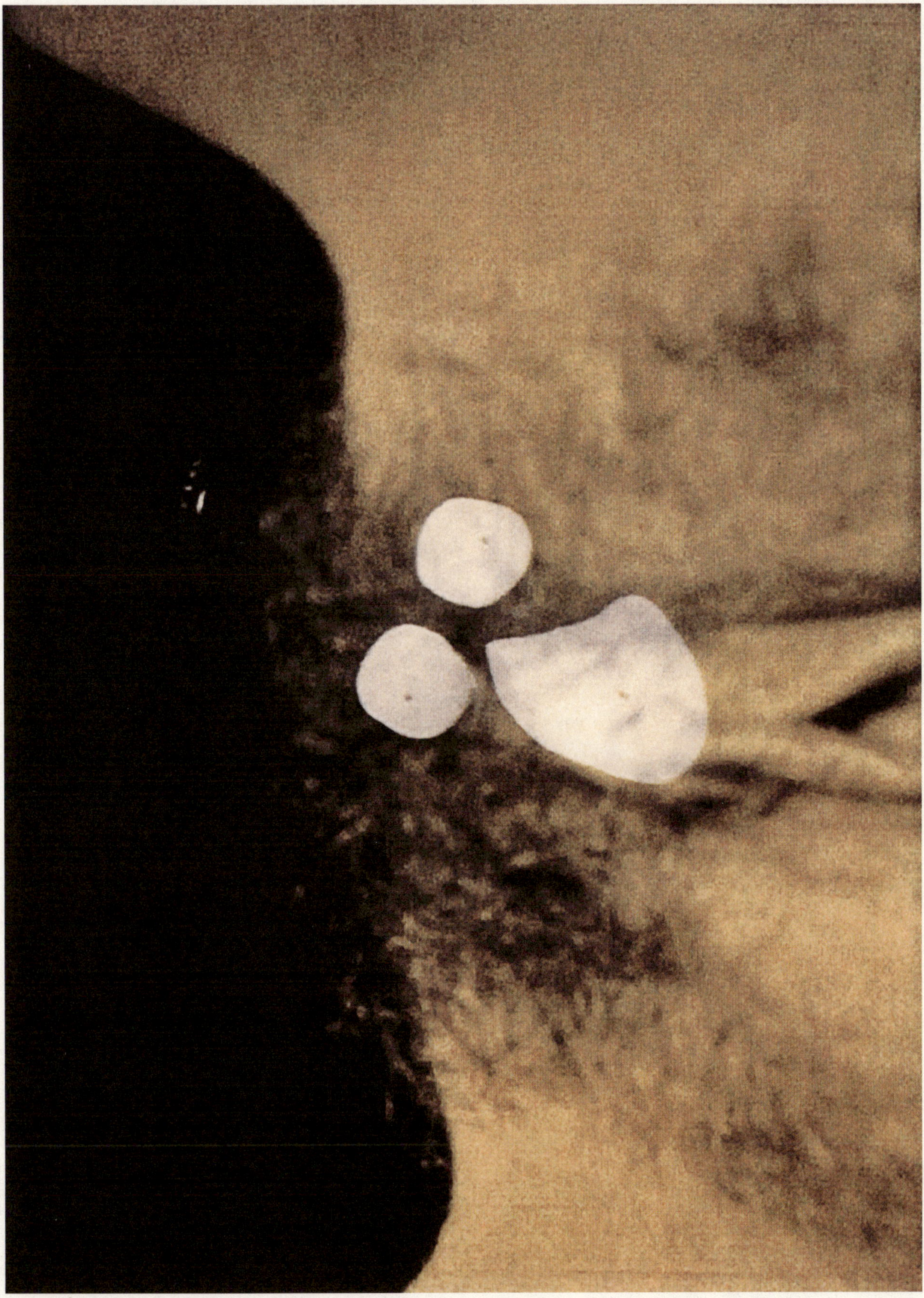

Film stills from *Christmas on Earth* a dual projection film
by Barbara Rubin, 1963–1965

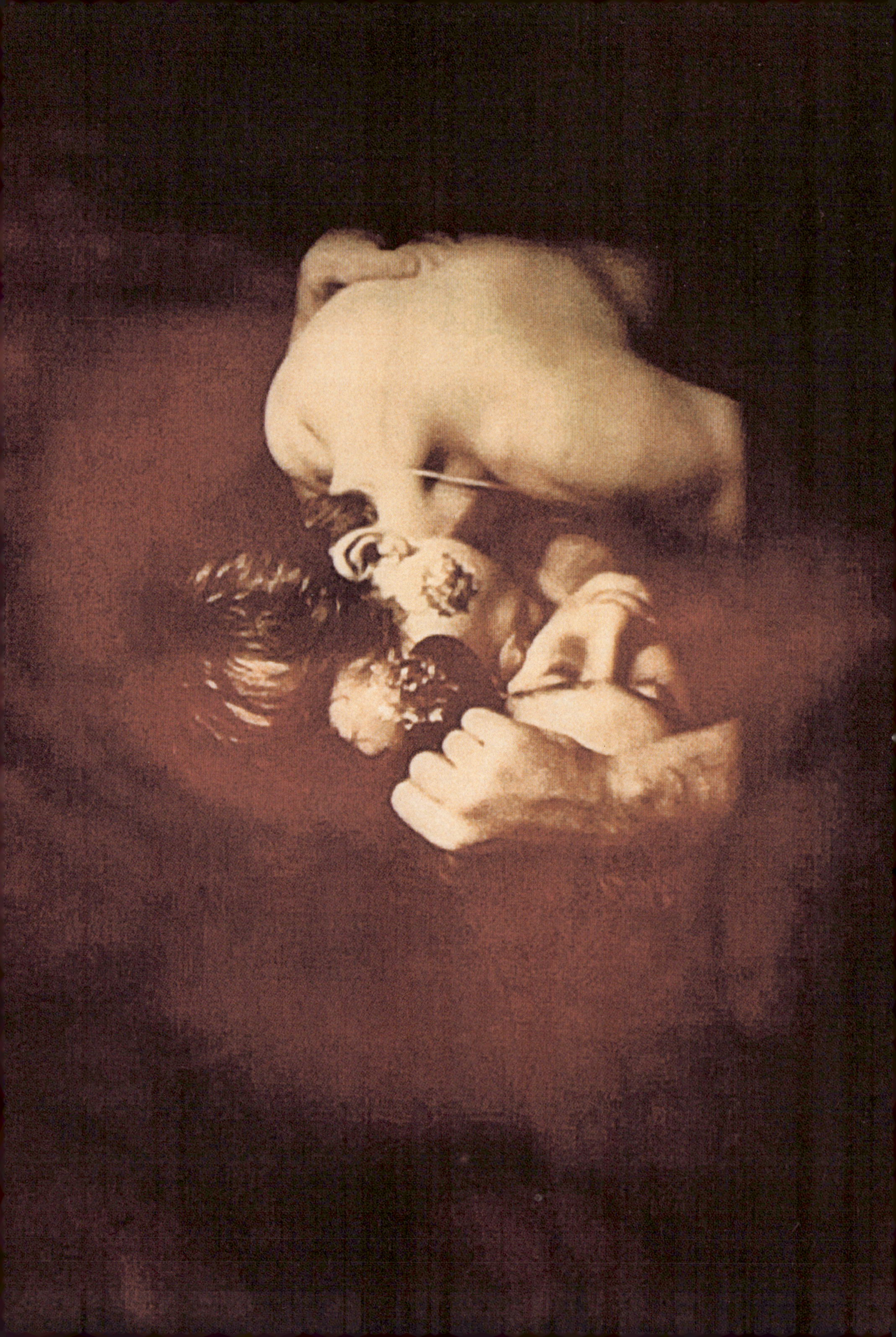

Locusts...

like horses
prepared for battle.
on their heads
were what appeared to be crowns
of gold
their faces were like human faces
and they had long hair like women
their teeth we e like lion's teeth
their breasts were like iron breastplat s
and the noise of their wings
w s like the noise
of a host of chariots
and horses
charging into battle
they have tails that sting like scorpions
and have as their king the angel of th pit

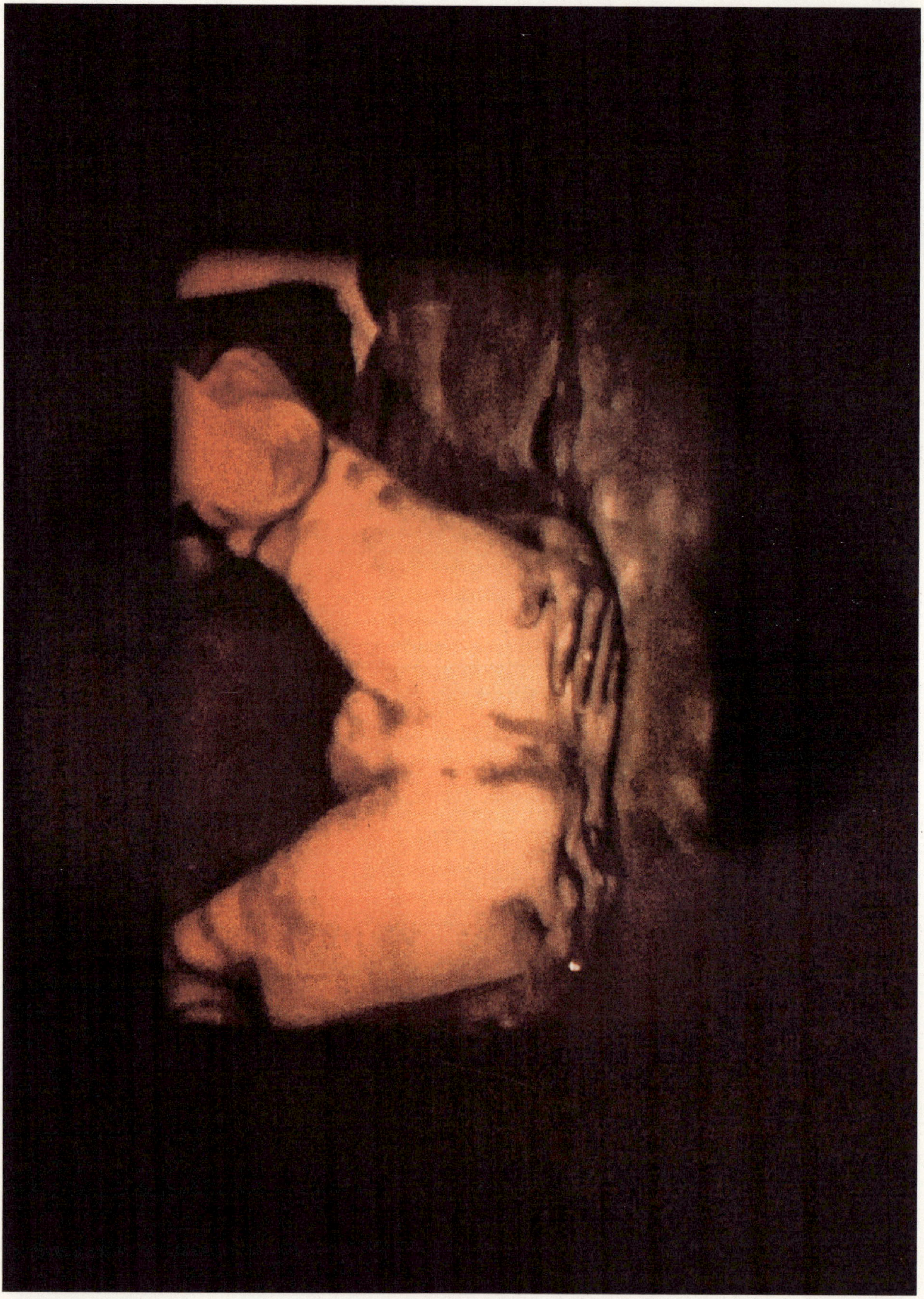

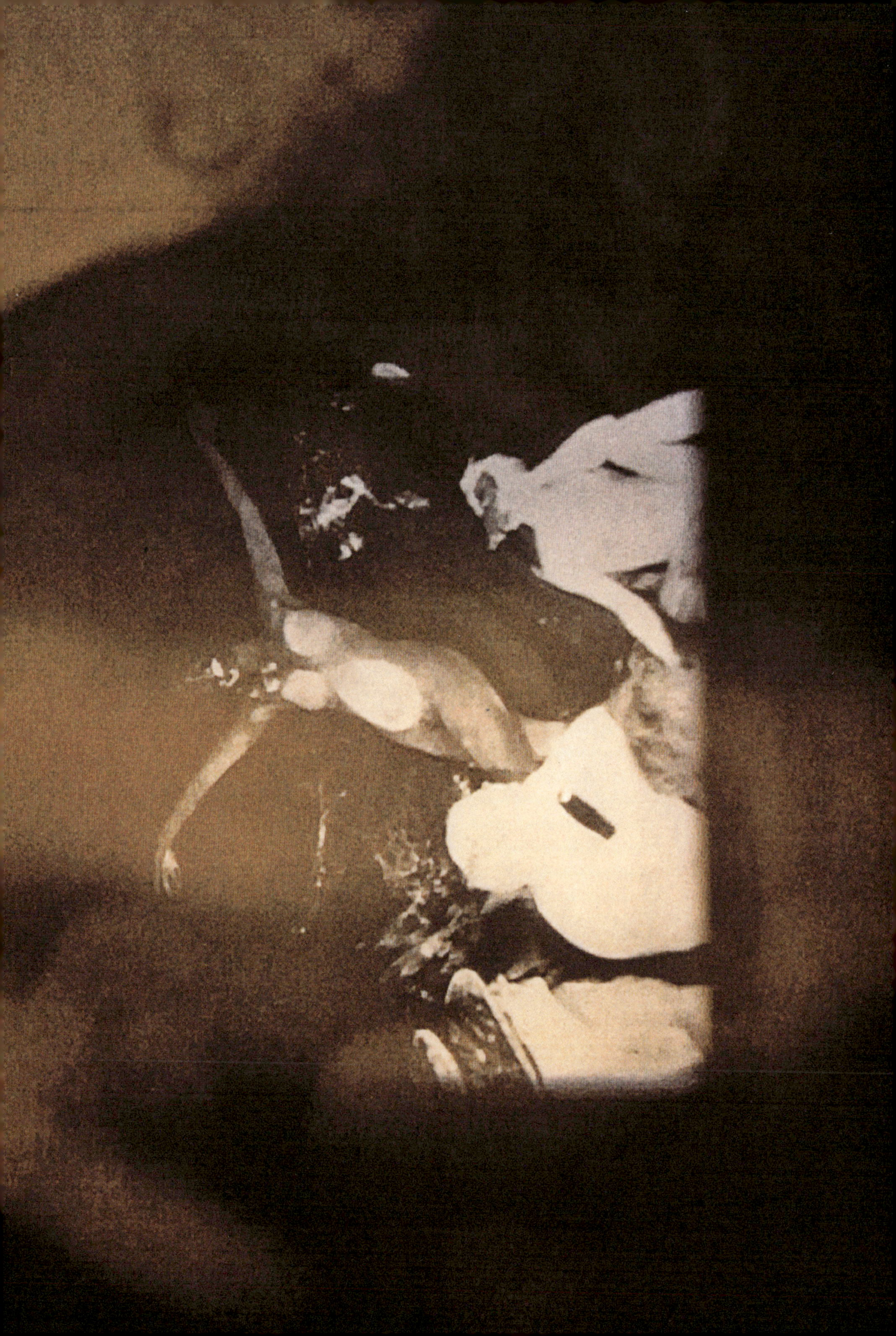

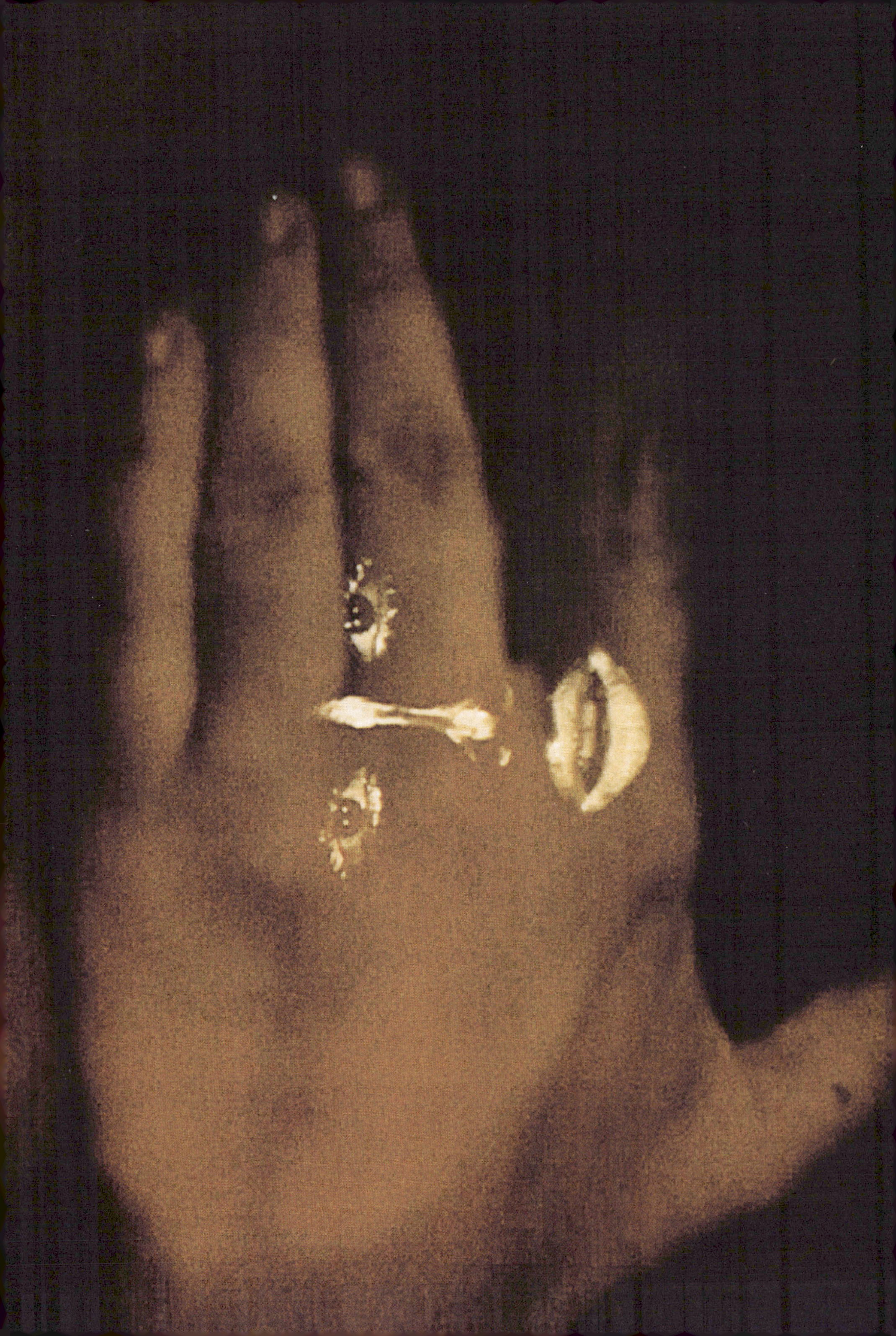

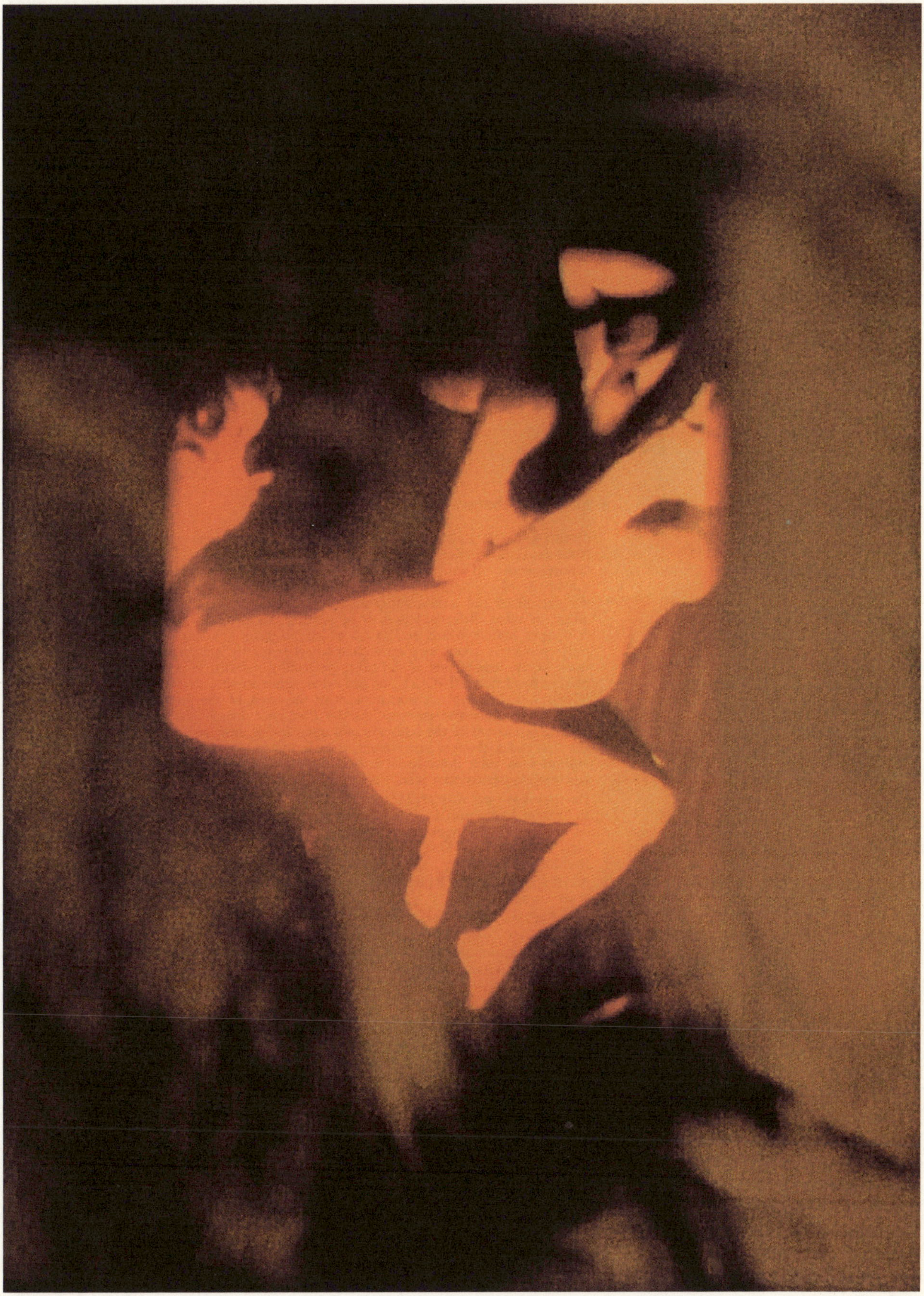

FILM-MAKERS' COOPERATIVE CATALOGUE No. 3

• **RUBIN, Barbara:**

CHRISTMAS ON EARTH **16mm. 40 min.** **Rental: $60.00**
(Projection instructions: The film is on two reels. Both reels must be projected simultaneously. Two projectors are needed. The first projector fills the screen; the image of the second projector is approximately 1/3 smaller and fills only the middle of the screen, superimposing on the first image. This can be done either by using different lenses or by placing one projector closer to the screen. It doesn't matter which reel is on which projector. During the screening, the projectionist is asked to play with color changes by holding colored filters in front of the lens of one or the other projector, or both. Moreover, the film has neither head nor tail – it can be projected either way.)
"*Christmas On Earth*: A woman; a man; the black of the pubic hair; the cunt's moon mountains and canyons. As the film goes, image after image, the most private territories of the body are laid open for us, now an abstracted landscape; the first shock changes into silence, then is transposed into amazement. We have seldom seen such down-to-earth beauty, so real as only a terrible beauty can be: terrible beauty that man, that woman is, are, that Love is.

Do they have no shame? This eighteen year old girl, she must have no shame, to look at and show the body so nakedly. Only angels have no shame. But we do not believe in angels, we do not believe in Paradise any more, nor in Christmas, we have been Out for too long. ('Orpheus has been too long in Hell' – Brakhage).

A syllogism: Barbara Rubin has no shame; angels have no shame; Barbara Rubin is an angel.

Yes, Barbara Rubin has no shame because she has been kissed by the angel of Love.

The motion picture camera has been kissed by the angel of Love. From now on, camera shall know no shame.

Cinema has discovered all of man: as painting and sculpture did from the very beginning. But then: cinema IS in its very beginning." – Jonas Mekas, East Side Review No. 1.

FILM-MAKERS' COOPERATIVE

414 PARK AVENUE SOUTH, NEW YORK 16, NEW YORK • Tel. MU 5-2210

Film-Makers' Cooperative catalogue featuring the screening of *Christmas on Earth*

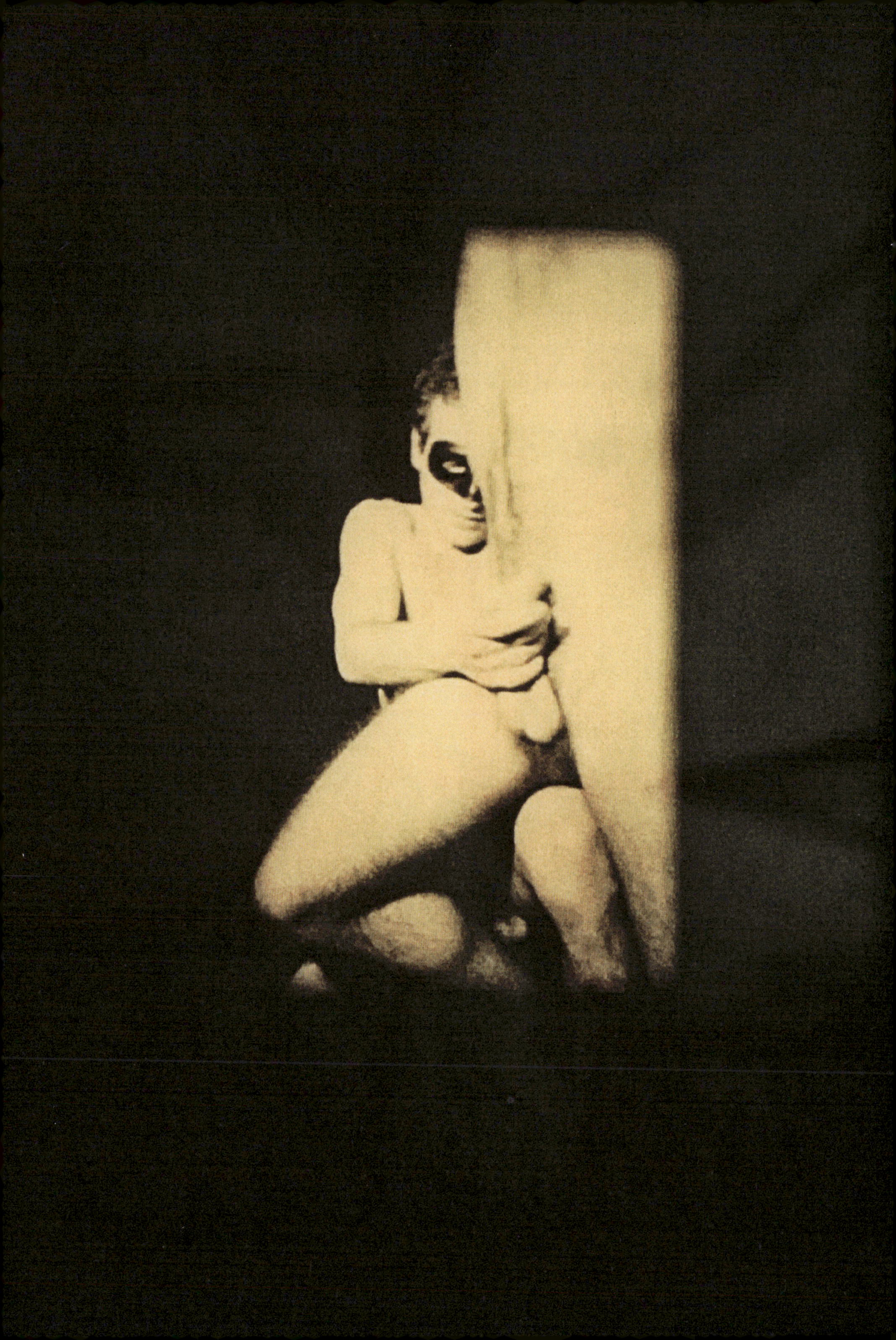

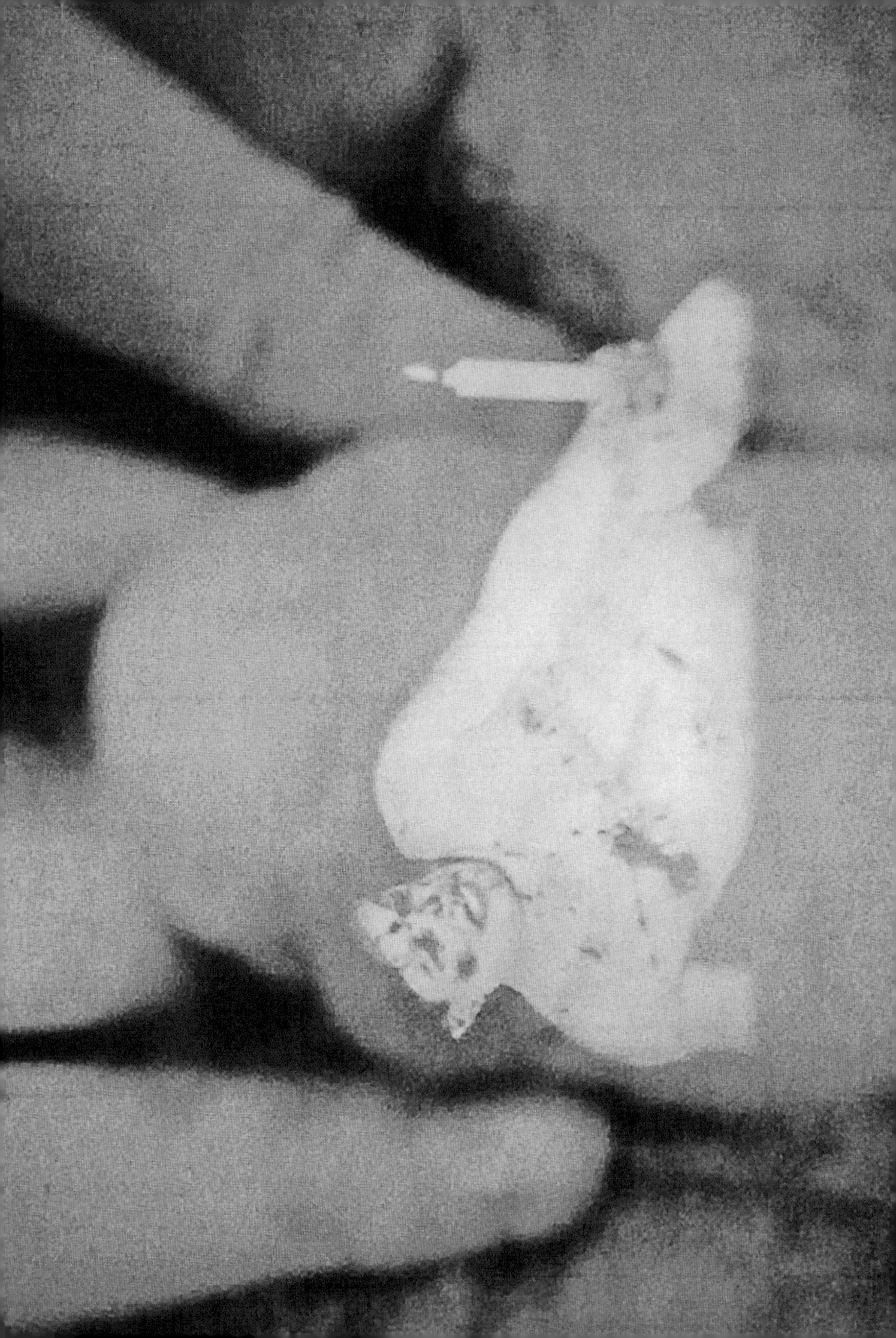

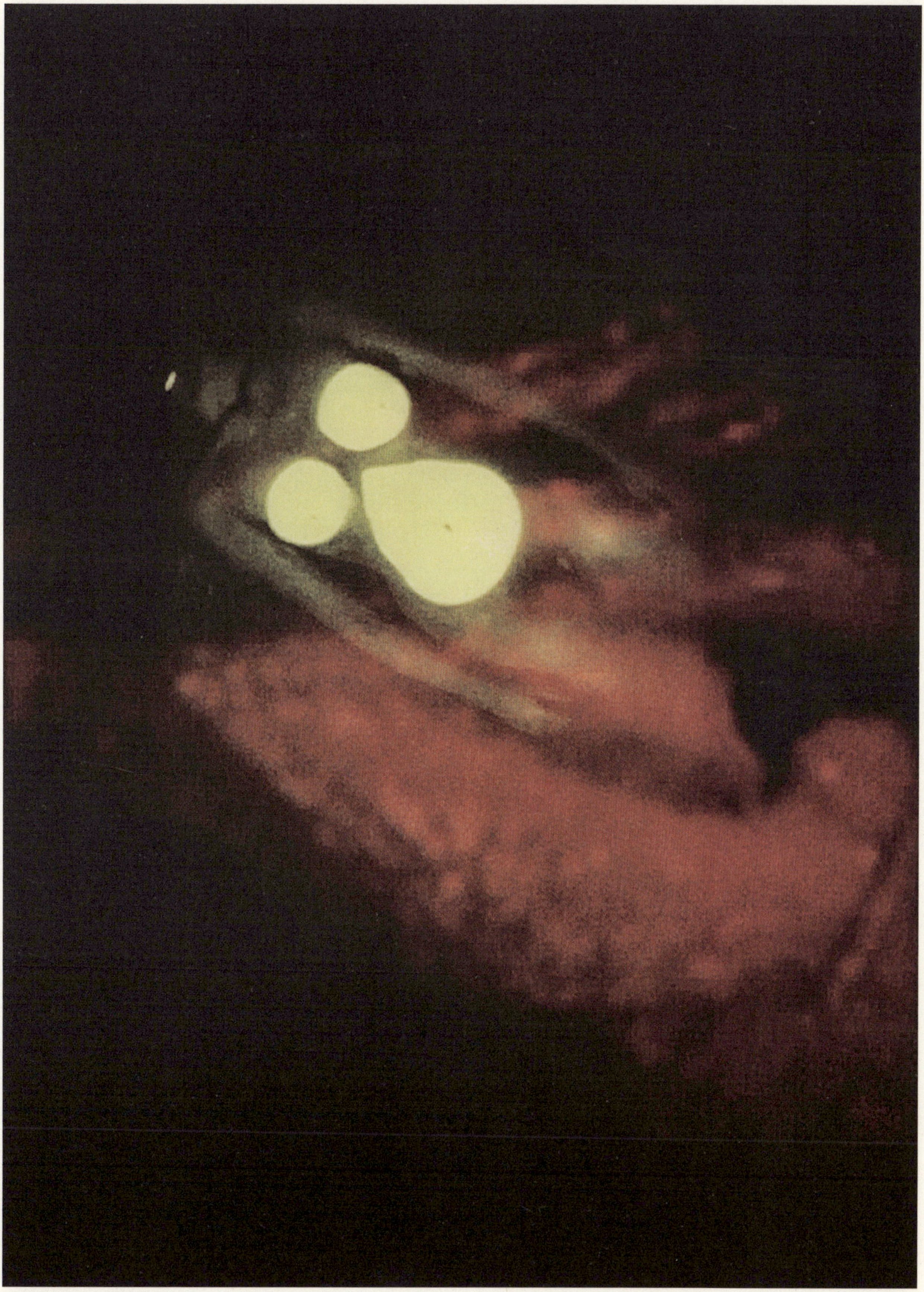

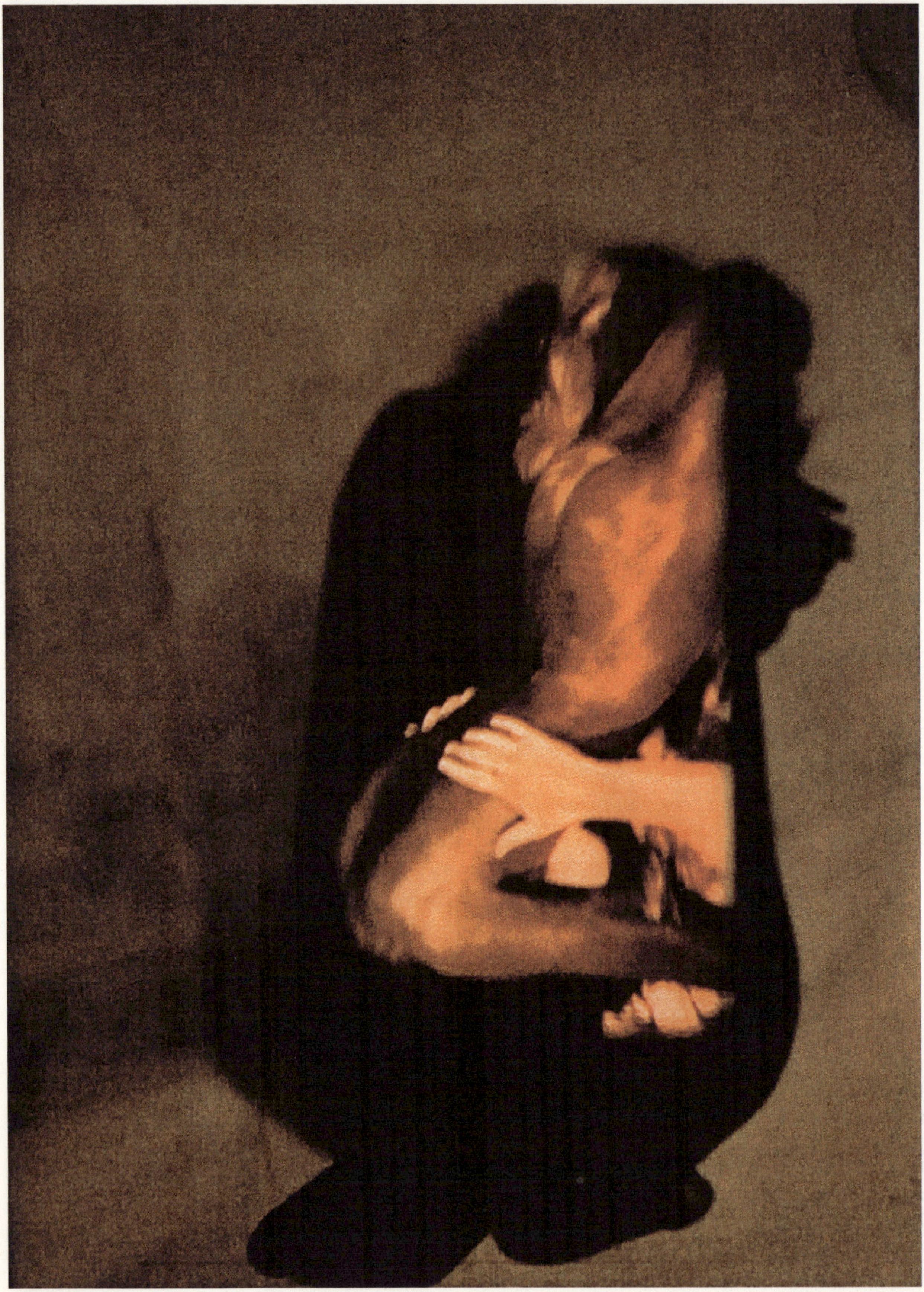

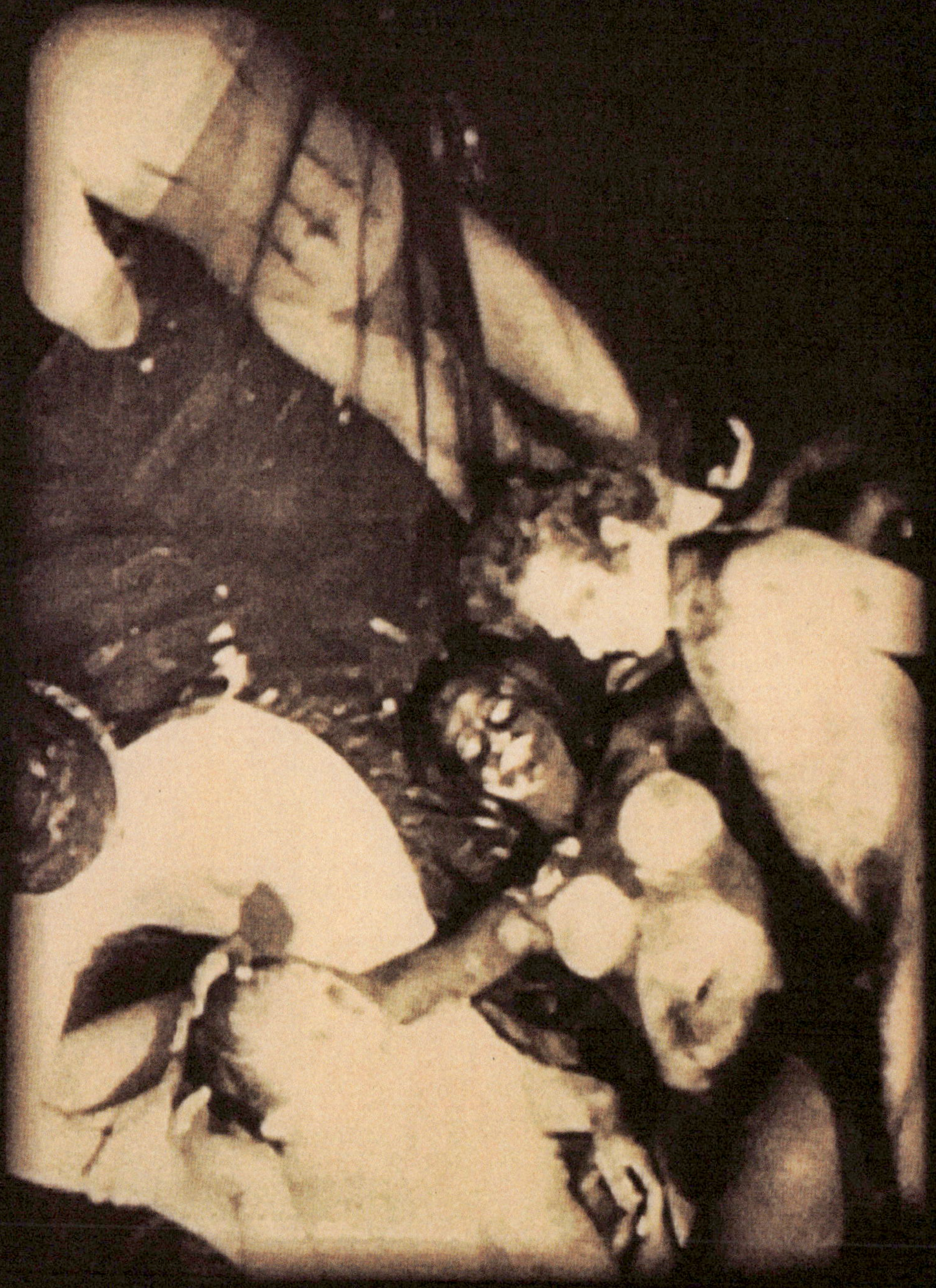

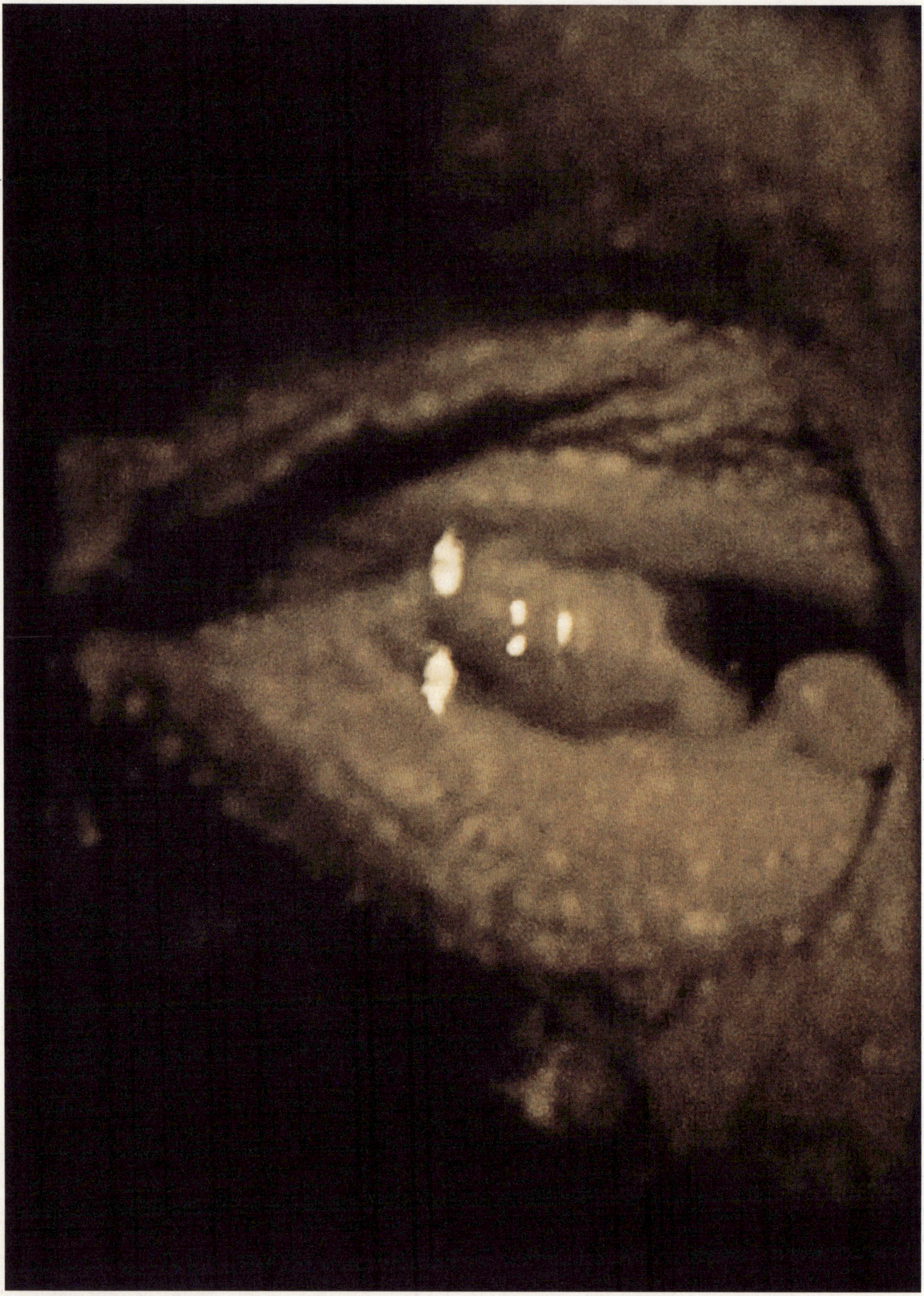

A, P.S. TO CHRISTMAS ON EARTH & ALL THAT FOLLOWS FROM THIS VISION, an example in me

It was one week out of being put away
where coincident held Miss Edie Sedgwick & myself
that was June of 1963 & I'd just turned 18
& i met Jonas & he gives me a camera & film & love & interested trust
so i shoot & shoot & shoot & shreak
up over slow & fast down & often all the way around & rewound many times
the subject, what else could it be, was all about cocks & cunts & fantasies
that freely expressed our sexual needs & dreaming beliefs
painted on their nude bodies
When we did finally film, though quite open & free
it was the beginning for me to see that fantasies repeat
when there's no love there to weep
but that wasn't enough
so i spent 3 months chopping the hours of film up
into a basket
and then toss and toss
flip and toss
and one by one
Absently enchantedly Destined to splice it together
and separate on to two different reels
and then project one reel half the size
inside the other reel full screen size
and then i showed it
and someone tells me, "my what a good editing job that is indeed!"
& God Bless thee
God Bless you

& Swedish Pancakes in 2 days as Bruce De Foreest said to me, "all we wanted to say was the camera was borrowed & the film was free, it's the first movie we ever made & it was pretty good on the bedroom wall."

SOMEHOW THIS EVENING, FRIDAY, DECEMBER 30, 1966, is our
CHRISTMAS of sorts, held together by some SWEDISH PANCAKES
& HARE KRISHNA
somehow this evening naturally happened
somehow we all hope that it's not too much for you

MERRY CHRISTMAS

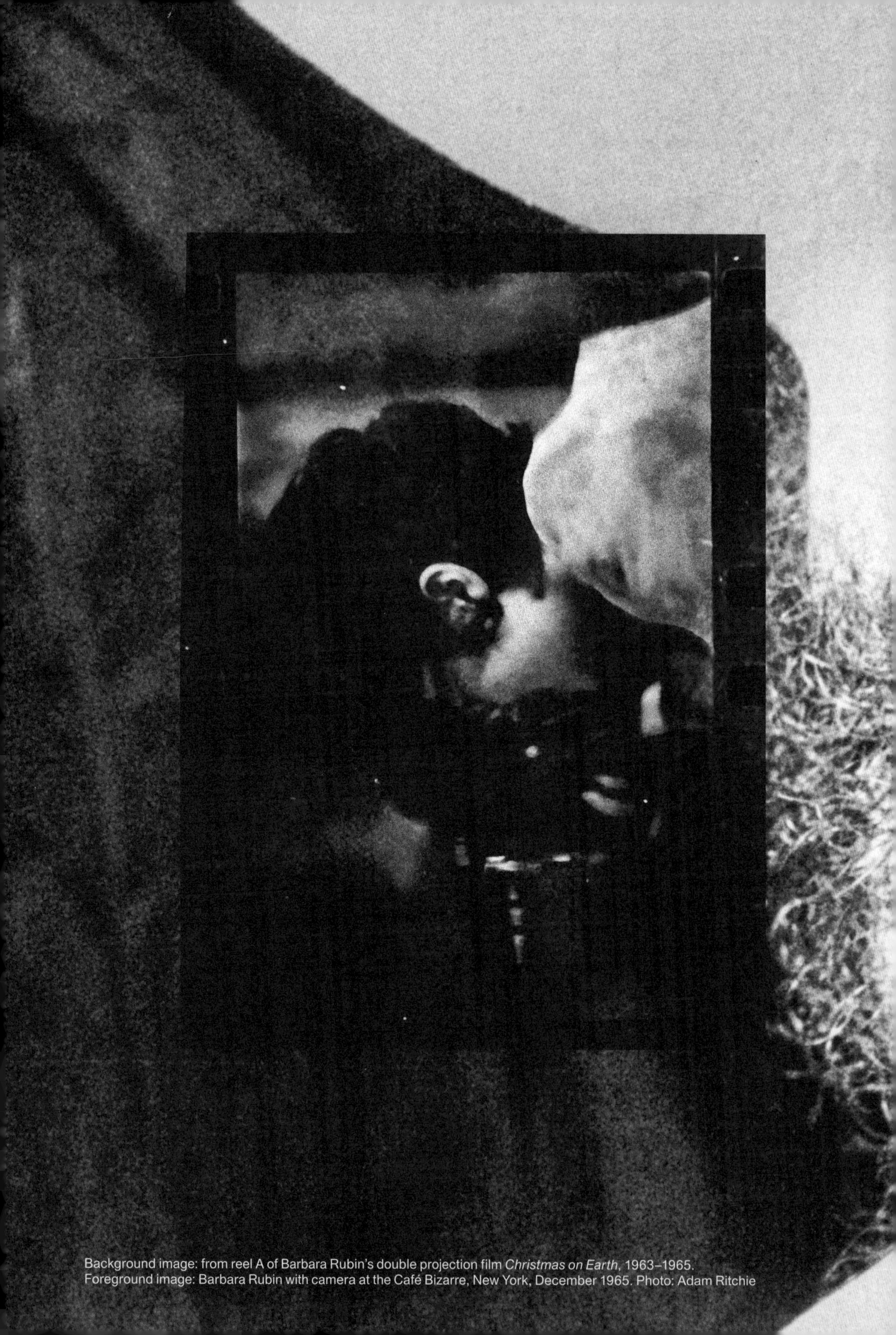

Background image: from reel A of Barbara Rubin's double projection film *Christmas on Earth*, 1963–1965.
Foreground image: Barbara Rubin with camera at the Café Bizarre, New York, December 1965. Photo: Adam Ritchie

Ara Osterweil
Saint Barbara. An Afterword

Barbara Rubin's film *Christmas on Earth* is the most sexually explicit American film of the 1960s. It is also astonishingly beautiful. Shot in 1963 with a 16mm Bolex camera when Rubin was only eighteen years old, the film transforms the sexual orgy it records into a kaleidoscopic, psychedelic, hallucinatory happening. Originally called *Cocks and Cunts* before being re-titled after a phrase from Arthur Rimbaud's epic poem "A Season in Hell," *Christmas on Earth* consists of two black-and-white, twenty-nine minute reels projected simultaneously, one inside the other, in order to mimic the frenetic interpenetration of its onscreen bodies. Add to this the random placement of various color filters on the projector lens, and the addition of an adhoc soundtrack culled from any available radio, and we may have the most limitless, ecstatic representation of sexuality that has ever been recorded—in a medium.

As I have chronicled elsewhere,[1] *Christmas on Earth* depicts at least five nude bodies engaged in a ravishing array of sexual acts including genital penetration, anal sex, fellatio, cunnilingus, and masturbation. Although the differences between Reels A and B are obscured by Rubin's preferred method of double projection, one privileges extreme close-ups of body parts, while the other feature wider shots of the film's performers, whose nude bodies are adorned with lavish amounts of body paint. Through Rubin's evocative use of double projection, extreme close-ups, and wild camera movement, the bodies from the two reels become indistinguishable: faces overlap with genitals, male and female flesh merge, and corporeal appendages from one reel become entangled with, and inserted in, bodies from the other. Watching these fantastically metamorphosed bodies, one becomes immersed in the rhapsodies of the flesh.

Pioneering the use of multi-media projection decades before it became the norm in installation art, *Christmas on Earth* is the quintessence of the "expanded cinema" practice of the 1960s. Often high on amphetamines, Rubin would continually re-edit *Christmas on Earth* before screenings so that each occasion of projection comprised a unique event or performance. Of course, like all artists, Rubin borrowed certain techniques from her friends and fellow travelers: filmmaker Jerry Jofen exposed his film reels multiple times, resulting in dense superimposition; Ken Jacobs pioneered the use of a spontaneous, live radio in *Blonde Cobra* (US, 1963); and Gregory Markopoulos's rapid montage techniques inspired Rubin to slice the long takes of the "first cut" of the film into dynamic fragments. Likewise, although its appearance was novel in cinema, Rubin's use of double projection paid perhaps

1
Large portions of this essay have been previously published in a chapter entitled, "Saint Barbara: The Apocryphal, Ecstatic Cinema of Barbara Rubin," in my book *Flesh Cinema: The Corporeal Turn in American Avant-Garde Film.* (Manchester: Manchester University Press, 2014). For more of my writing on *Christmas on Earth*, see "The Apocryphal, Ecstatic Cinema of Barbara Rubin," *Women's Experimental Cinema*, ed. Robin Blaetz (Durham, NC: Duke University Press, 2007; pp. 127–151). For more about Rubin's relationship with poet Allen Ginsberg, see my essay "Queer Coupling, or the Stain of the Bearded Woman" in *Framework: The Journal of Cinema and Media* 51.1 (2010); pp. 33–60.

unwitting homage to modernist painter Josef Albers's *Homage to the Square* series.[2] Nonetheless, the film's outrageous psychedelic effects of the deconstructed body were all Rubin's own. They were also far more daring than anything made by her male contemporaries.

True to its original title *Cocks and Cunts*, Rubin's film presents a seemingly endless display of cocks, cunts, and assholes, all offered in extreme close-up to the camera as they change shape, are spread open, and penetrated. Although Jack Smith's contemporaneous film *Flaming Creatures* included shots of breasts and limp penises, displayed drag performers in various stages of undress, and featured a highly theatrical group rape scene, Rubin's candor about the corporeal mechanics of sexuality was more direct than Smith's camp approach. Even Andy Warhol's various forays into cinematic pornography in the early to mid-1960s did not focus as explicitly on intercourse and genitalia as *Christmas on Earth*—in spite of his films' provocative (and often misleading) titles.[3] Yet whereas screenings of Underground films by Smith, Warhol, and Kenneth Anger were often met with censorship battles and police seizures,[4] somehow *Christmas on Earth* managed to fly under the censors' radar despite its more lucid images of the flesh. Of course, compared to Warhol's *Blow Job* (1964) or *Blue Movie* (1968), the title of *Christmas on Earth* sounded innocent enough. Although Rubin was known to carry around the only copy of her film while traveling in London to prevent it from being seized, the fact that she was a white, teenaged girl, rather than a flamboyant queer man must have assured her a degree of invisibility—and protection—from the authorities. After all, who in 1963 would have suspected that such a young woman would be capable of making such an outrageous film?

With the exhibition of *Christmas on Earth*, Barbara Rubin quickly became one of the central figures of the emerging artistic vanguard—in spite of the fact that she was a young, untrained woman in a scene dominated by established male artists. Yet had she never picked up a camera, Rubin's contributions to the art, music, and literary countercultures of the time would still be considerable. Rubin's multiple roles as organizer, agitator, and innovator had profound effects on the artistic and musical worlds of the 1960s—and have had a prophetic influence on moving image media and installation practice ever since. Initially through her friendships with Jonas Mekas, Allen Ginsberg, and Bob Dylan, and then through her own determination, Rubin infiltrated the Underground scene, serving as a catalyst for the interaction between individuals whom she regarded as the best minds of her generation. However, while Rubin played an integral role in weaving together the different artistic strands of the 1960s counterculture, she has been virtually omitted from its history.

Like many of the artistic legends from the 1960s, Rubin died young, at age 35. But unlike many of the kindred spirits whose early deaths secured their fame, Rubin's death erased her. Although she created one of the most accomplished and innovative artworks of the period, she did not leave an extensive cinematic oeuvre behind—in spite of the staggeringly ambitious projects the young artist

2
I owe this insight to Daniel Belasco, whose essay "A Vanished Prodigy," (originally published in *Art in America*, December 2005; pp. 61–67) is also an important source of scholarly information on Rubin's life and work.

3
While Warhol's film *Blow Job* (1964) advertises a sexual act in its title, the film actually only shows the face of a male performer who may or may not be receiving oral sex below the frame. Similarly, *My Hustler* (1965) features a lot of characters talking about sex, but none actually having any. With certain important exceptions, including his last film *Blue Movie* (1968), which provoked the censors by showing nudity and heterosexual intercourse, Warhol tended to give his more sexually explicit films innocuous titles such as *Couch* (1964), *Three* (1964), and *Eating Too Fast* (1966). For more information on Warhol's pornographic films, see my chapter "Andy Warhol, Porn Realist," in *Flesh Cinema*, pp. 56–92), as well as my essays: "*Three*'s Company" in *Little Joe*, No. 5, (London; Fall 2015; pp. 132–147), and "Andy Warhol's *Blow Job*: Towards the Recognition of a Pornographic Avant-Garde" in *Porn Studies*, ed. Linda Williams, (Durham, NC: Duke University Press, 2004; pp. 431–460).

4
See Jim Hoberman, "Crimson Creatures: The Case Against *Flaming Creatures*" in *On Jack Smith's Flaming Creatures (and Other Secret Flix of Cinemaroc)*, (New York: Granary Books, 2001); pp. 35–50.

conceived in Christmas's wake. While she was frequently seen wielding a camera at some of the most outrageous media events and happenings of the 1960s, there was often no film in her camera.[5] Like Jack Smith, Rubin was less interested in documenting events in any straightforward fashion, than she was in compelling people to "perform" their personalities. On the occasions when her camera was fully loaded, much of the non-canonical footage that has been attributed to her is fiercely freewheeling. While the absence of critical attention paid to Rubin certainly reveals the extent to which *Christmas on Earth* challenged dominant preconceptions about the limits of representation, her early death—and conversion to Hasidism in the late 1960s—also played significant roles in her disappearance.

Born in 1945 to a middle-class Jewish family in Queens, New York, Barbara Rubin came to the downtown Underground film community as a teenager. Her early experimentation with drugs, sex, and other aberrant behavior had landed her in an institution, where she, like Warhol Superstars Brigid Berlin and Edie Sedgwick, became even more addicted to amphetamines and other drugs. When she was released from a juvenile correction facility, her uncle William Rubin—then manager at the Gramercy Arts Theatre where many avant-garde film screenings were held—introduced her to filmmaker, poet, and critic Jonas Mekas, who was the most important advocate of Underground cinema as well as the founder of New York's Film-Makers' Cooperative and, later, the Anthology Film Archives. Mekas hired Barbara to assist at the Film-Makers' Co-op.

In late 1964, she borrowed Jonas's crank-up 16mm Bell and Howell silent film camera and filmed *Christmas on Earth* in Tony Conrad's Ludlow Street apartment over the course of a few frigid days. Although they can be difficult to recognize because of the copious amounts of body paint that adorn them, the film's players include poet Gerard Malanga, Arnold Rockwood (aka Pasty Arnold of *Flaming Creatures* fame), Johnny "Jackie" Foster, and Underground film star Naomi Levine. The two other women whose solo sexual antics and genitals can be seen in close-up were Barbara's good friend Debbie Feiner and a woman named Adrian.[6]

To say that Barbara Rubin was a mover and a shaker is an understatement. From approximately 1963 to 1968, Rubin facilitated major exchanges and events whose impact extended far beyond their unique nature as happenings. Committed to the spirit of camaraderie and collaboration, Rubin believed that artists were the saints and heroes of her day, and labored, like a modern-day matchmaker, to bring them together. By the time she was in her early twenties, she had traveled extensively around Europe, befriending artistic luminaries such as Polański, Fellini, and Huxley. She had an uncanny way of stumbling onto the defining scenes of her generation.

On a hitchhiking trip across the United States, Rubin managed to show up on California's Berkeley campus just in time for Mario Savio's rousing defense of liberty at one of the Free Speech Movement rallies. A few years later, in October 1967, she was arrested, with Shirley Clarke's daughter Wendy, at the siege of the Pentagon in protest of the Vietnam War.[7] Later, Rubin and Wendy Clarke opened a vintage clothing shop in New York's East Village that functioned more as a gathering place than as a successful commercial venture.

From all accounts, Rubin had notorious powers of persuasion. An intimate friend of Bob Dylan—that's her, sporting shorn hair and a striped shirt on the back of the *Bringing it all*

5
Jonas Mekas, *Movie Journal: The Rise of a New American Cinema, 1959–1971* (New York: Macmillan, 1972). In his journal entry for June 23, 1966 ("On the Tactile Interactions in Cinema, or Creation With Your Total Body"), Mekas writes, "I have seen Barbara Rubin going through entire evenings of shooting with an empty camera" (248).

6
Gerard Malanga helped identify some of the film's players in an email to the author from July 12, 2012. Debbie Feiner (sometimes Debby or Fein or Feinman) was identified by Ken and Flo Jacobs with the help of Jim and Shelley Hoberman.

7
Belasco, Boo Hooray catalogue, from letters to Ginsberg in the Allen Ginsberg file at Stanford University.

Back Home (1965) album cover—Rubin had turned the singer on to Judaism after his 1966 motorcycle accident, and may have served as the inspiration for the tragic zealot Ophelia in his "Desolation Row."[8] She was also a major intellectual influence on Andy Warhol. In addition to bringing musical celebrities like Dylan and Donovan to The Factory—Dylan and Warhol didn't get along, but somehow the folksinger made off with one of Warhol's Double Elvises—she shepherded the Pop artist to Café Bizarre in Greenwich Village in 1965 to meet The Velvet Underground, and then helped to pioneer the multi-media assaults that became known as *The Exploding Plastic Inevitable.* Desperate to dance, Rubin also dragged Warhol to the Dom, an old Ukrainian dance hall in the East Village. Ed Sanders and Tuli Kupferberg (later founders of The Fugs) followed, as did Gerard Malanga, and a host of other poets and artists. As Ginsberg biographer Bill Morgan chronicles, "Just as Barbara hoped, Warhol's Factory people mingled with the poets, and a new movement began in which music, art, and poetry were combined. Out of this union came rock venues like the Balloon Farm, later the Electric Circus, and suddenly the East Village became the New York center of the 1960s psychedelic rock-n-roll scene."[9]

Inflamed by the passions raging in the downtown scene, Rubin led the brigade to bring the raucous gems of the so-called New American Cinema to Europe. On New Year's Eve (1963–1964), Rubin, along with Jonas Mekas and avant-garde film scholar P. Adams Sitney, led the charge to show Jack Smith's *Flaming Creatures* illegally at the Third International Experimental Film Exposition in Knokke-le-Zoute, Belgium. (founded in 1949 by Jacques Ledoux, the film festival hosted five *EXPRMNTL* editions devoted to avant-garde film between 1949 and 1974; it was one of the key venues for experimental film during this period). After smuggling the film into the projection booth, Rubin and her associates tied up the secretly compliant projectionist, locked themselves in the room, seized control of the switchboard, cut the lights, and began to show the film. Even after the authorities arrived and attempted to halt the screening, Rubin remained undeterred. As a riot erupted, Rubin shouted encouragement to the audience while hurling curses at the police. Unrestrained by the probability that she could be prosecuted for showing the film (exhibitors in New York had already endured imprisonment and formidable legal battles), Rubin projected the film on the face of the Belgian Minister of Culture.[10]

As evidenced in many of the letters included in this volume, Rubin's zeal did not diminish as she traveled from Belgium to Cannes, Paris, Munich, Oberhausen, London, Amsterdam, and Italy, meeting countless celebrities, participating in the cultural revolutions *du jour*, and otherwise stirring shit up. Her radical conceptions of the transcendental nature of art often clashed with the conventions of more established tastemakers, exhibitors, and organizers. While her friend and sometimes nemesis P. Adams Sitney struggled to arrange suitable exhibition venues, Rubin followed, canceling screenings that he had organized if they didn't include *Flaming Creatures* and other controversial films. Hoping to start a revolution, Rubin sought to expand the impact of cinema beyond the confines of the screening room; she much preferred to project films on crowded streets and swaths of empty sky. Writing to Mekas from Brussels, Rubin implored him to "show these

8
"Now Ophelia, she's 'neath the window
For her I feel so afraid
On her twenty-second birthday
She already is an old maid
To her, death is quite romantic
She wears an iron vest
Her profession's her religion
Her sin is her lifelessness
And though her eyes are fixed upon
Noah's great rainbow
She spends her time peeking
Into Desolation Row."
Bob Dylan, "Desolation Row," *Highway 61 Revisited*, prod. Bob Johnston (Columbia Records, 1965).

9
Bill Morgan, *I Celebrate Myself: The Somewhat Private Life of Allen Ginsberg*, (London: Penguin, 2006), p. 394.

10
Jonas Mekas, *Movie Journal*, pp. 111–112.

movies as they were made, freer, newer, growing" ↗ letter from January 20, 1964; p. 28 and bemoaned the hypocrisy of *EXPRMNTL*: "It is very sad that this festival, which is supposed to be free and containing the most 'new' and 'different' etc movies lacks depth, feeling and strength and that it has for the most part cockless, bigoted, feminist Hitlers, sell-outs, lonely, unhappy people who make pretentious and outrageous statements like 'I am a Marxist' blah blah blah, 'I believe in censorship, would you like to have films made on racism.'" ↗ letter from January 1, 1964; Knokke-le-Zoute; p. 14 Dismissing any practical concerns for exhibition fees or censorship, Rubin insists: "But you most of all journey beyond fixed patterns, absurd, stupid, ludicrous everything, anything else about censors, society, etc. But do not dwell on that level, transcend to the multitude." ↗ letter from Spring 1964; Paris; p. 61 Although her focus would eventually change from cinema to religion, one gets the impression that Rubin was already a zealot seeking to transcend secular limitations.

Throughout the mid-1960s, however, Rubin remained committed to transforming the multitudes through art. On June 11, 1965, she organized a historic poetry reading at the Royal Albert Hall in London that featured nineteen international poets, including Lawrence Ferlinghetti, Gregory Corso, Ernst Jandl, and Harry Fainlight. The event, which was chronicled by British filmmaker Peter Whitehead in his 1965 documentary *Wholly Communion*, drew a crowd of 7,000 spectators and turned a generation of British youth on to Beat poetry. Soon after, in the early spring of 1967, Rubin organized a two-week long multi-media event, which played at New York's Cinematheque. Dubbed *Caterpillar Changes*, the event included screenings and performances by musicians Gato Barbieri, the ethnomusicologist and film abstractionist Harry Smith, as well as Underground filmmakers Jack Smith, Ken Jacobs, Andy Warhol, Shirley Clarke, Storm De Hirsch, D. A. Pennebaker, Jerry Jofen, Marie Menken, Stan VanDerBeek, Willard Maas, Robert Breer, and Ed Emschwiller, to name just a few.

Like a Mary Poppins of the Underground, Rubin was the social glue that held an unruly community of artists, poets, and dreamers together. But she was not all sweetness and light. Pissing off as many people as she charmed, she frequently used her camera as an *agit-prop* to provoke and disturb her audiences. As one of the primary organizers of the *Andy Warhol Up-Tight* series, Barbara Rubin both appalled and delighted audiences that had gathered for a glimpse of the New York Underground at various colleges and speaking venues. On January 13, 1966, Andy Warhol was invited to be the evening's entertainment at The New York Society for Clinical Psychiatry's 43rd annual dinner, held at Delmonico's Hotel. Bursting into the room with a camera, as The Velvet Underground acoustically tortured the guests and Gerard Malanga and Edie Sedgwick performed the "whip dance" in the background, Rubin shouted obscene questions at the attending psychiatrists, extracting a morsel of delicious revenge from the profession that had once pathologized her. Casting blinding lights in their faces, Rubin hurled derogatory questions, including "What does her vagina feel like? Is his penis big enough? Do you eat her out?"[11] As the horrified guests began to leave, Rubin continued her interrogation: "Why are you getting embarrassed? You're a psychiatrist; you're not supposed to get embarrassed..." The following day, the *New York Herald Tribune* reported on the event; their chosen headline "Shock Treatment for Psychiatrists" reveals the extent to which Rubin's guerrilla tactics had inverted the sanctioned relationship between patient and doctor, expert and amateur. It was not the first time that she made her way into the mainstream press, and it wouldn't be the last.

A fixture of the downtown scene in the 1960s, Barbara Rubin was featured in several American publications of the time, including two *Village Voice* interviews—one of which refers to her as the "Number One Woman" of

11
Steven Watson, *Factory Made: Warhol and the Sixties*, (New York: Pantheon, 2003), p. 259.

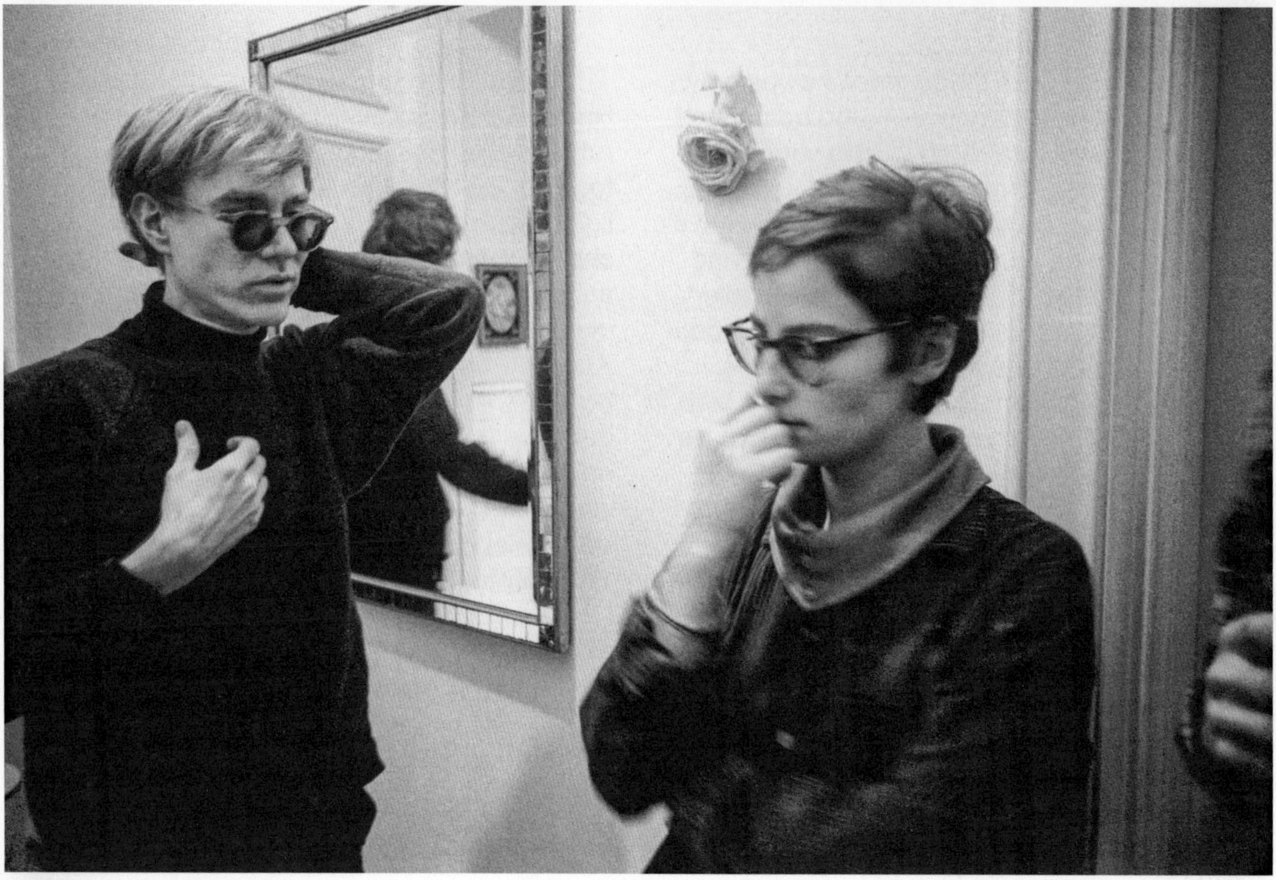

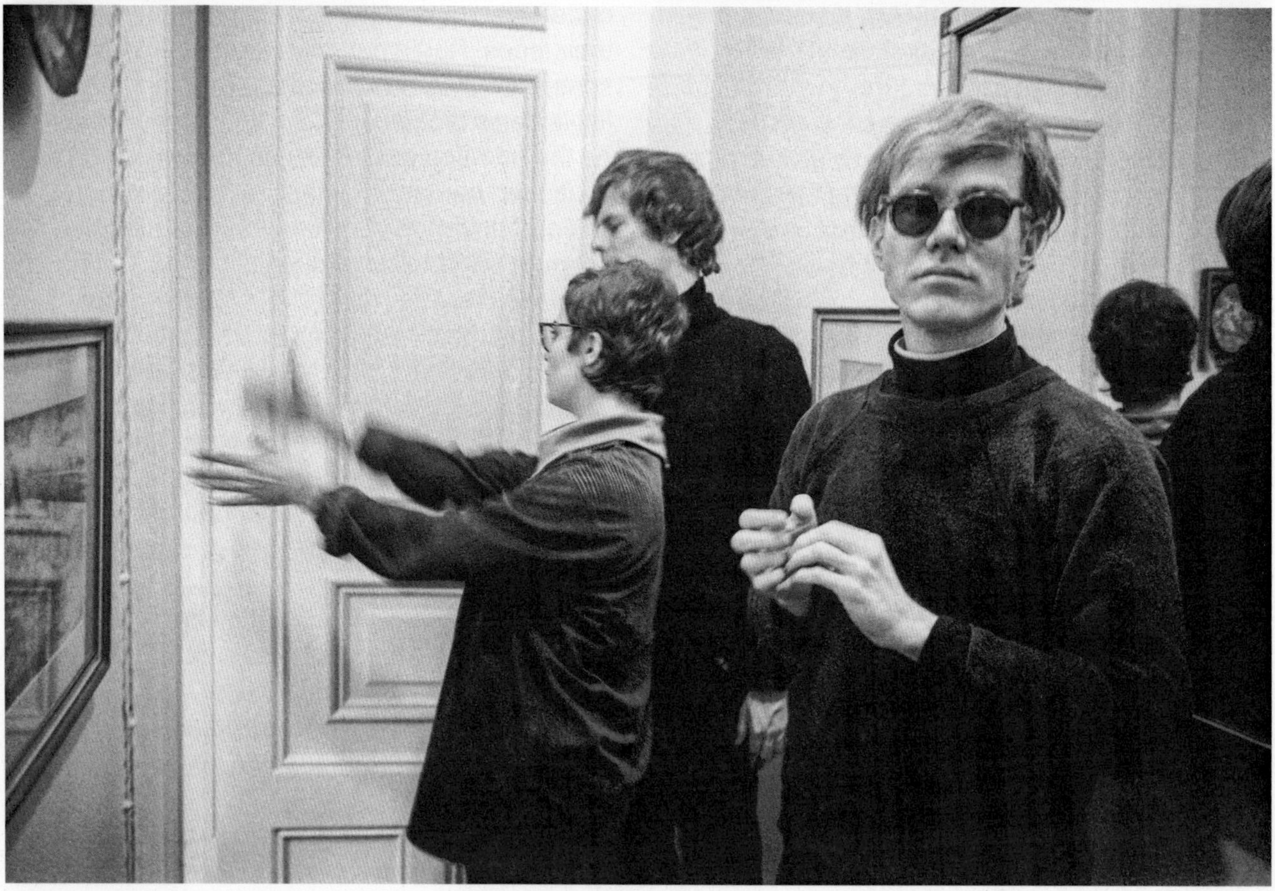

Top image: Andy Warhol and Barbara Rubin, New York, 1966. Photo: Nat Finkelstein
Bottom image: Barbara Rubin, Paul Morrissey, Andy Warhol, New York, 1966. Photo: Nat Finkelstein

the Underground movement[12]—a 1966 feature in *Mademoiselle* magazine,[13] a profile in *Newsweek*, and articles in both *Time* and *Playboy*.[14] More importantly, her presence illumines several experimental films from the period, including one of Andy Warhol's *Screen Tests* (1965), Ron Rice's *Chumlum* (1964), Piero Heliczer's *Venus in Furs*, *Satisfaction*, and *Dirt* (all 1965), and Jonas Mekas's *Walden* (aka *Diaries, Notes, and Sketches*, 1969), where she appears holding court among a group of male artists including Ginsberg, his lover Peter Orlovsky, Ed Sanders, Tuli Kupferberg, and Gerard Malanga.

Rubin's great, unfulfilled desire, however, was to create a "sequel" to her debut film, called *Christmas on Earth Continued*, which she and her close friend Rosebud originally conceived while briefly imprisoned in Kansas City, Missouri on their hitchhiking trip. Planned as a billion-dollar fantasy epic, *Christmas on Earth Continued* required the construction of a massive fairy kingdom in Ireland and the casting of virtually every significant enfant terrible from the music, literary, cinema, and art worlds, including Jean Genet, Lenny Bruce, The Beatles, Bob Dylan, Greta Garbo, the Supremes, and Marlon Brando—to name just a few. Fantasizing that Federico Fellini, Ingmar Bergman, and John Lennon would assist as co-directors, and Walt Disney would design and finance the elaborate set, Rubin distributed hundreds of scripts around Europe and North America in order to generate interest. Penning an "open letter" to Walt Disney, she requested his help in the construction of Fairy City, which she promised would remain a permanent city for children once production had ceased. Perhaps most outrageously, Rubin aimed to cast hundreds of artists, rock stars, and celebrities as the fairies of the day, united in a bizarre quest to "save" Jean Genet—he was cast as a Bowery bum who gets a job playing Santa Claus in a Macy's shop window—and thus usher in a new era of paradise on earth. Perusing the ludicrously ambitious cast list—Rubin promises that The Beatles, Joan Baez, Pier Paolo Pasolini, Federico Fellini, Bob Dylan, Andy Warhol, Pablo Neruda, Salvador Dalí, Charlie Chaplin, and Marianne Faithful had already shown interest—one can only begin to wrap one's head around *Christmas on Earth Continued* as a conceptual art project. While Rubin had actually met and charmed many of the celebrities whose help she enlisted, it is nonetheless hard to imagine that she actually believed such an unfathomable fantasy could come together.

And yet believe she did. Judging from the impassioned, often outraged tone of her letters, Rubin was not kidding. She photocopied hundreds of scripts, and harangued friends, fellow travelers, and world-renowned celebrities alike to help her advance the project. Failing to empathize with other people's worldly limitations, Rubin often became unreasonable about her demands and felt betrayed when they could not be met. As she wrote in one letter to Mekas, "It is life, my life, if you deny it you deny me, and your own experience." ↗ letter from July 1965; London; p. 134 Since Mekas's letters to Rubin have been lost—he kept hers tucked away in his files for decades, while she was constantly on the go—it is not possible to gauge the legitimacy of Rubin's accusations. What is obvious from Rubin's half of the correspondence, however, is that Mekas went out of his way to gratify her innumerable demands, sending money, film prints, and introductions whenever he could. "I want to thank you for the many good things you've been to me, to your many years to be, may G-d watch you in good health and strength in your kindness," Rubin wrote, in a later, more customary display of gratitude.
↗ letter from 1969; p. 173

In the most poignant moments in her letters, Rubin reveals a self-awareness of her

12
"Barbara Rubin Transforms into Bracha Rubin." Interview with Jonas Mekas, *Village Voice*, March 2, 1972, pp. 161–165. Included in this volume.

13
Joan Alleman Rubin, "Staking Out a new World of Film: Young Moviemakers Have Burst the Bounds of Hollywood," *Mademoiselle* 62 no. 5 (March 1966).

14
Jack Kroll, with Frances Heller, "Up From Underground," *Newsweek* 69 no. 7 (February 13, 1967), p. 119.

own tendencies towards excess that retrospectively provide insight into the mystery of her conversion: "My fanaticism, no matter what for, brings not love for which I'm givin' of my being and not forgiveness I'm asking, Jonas. For I am all of these things, they are me, Barbara, but patience and understanding (for that's all we all ask for) because I fluctuate in my journey on." ↗ letter from January 20, 1964; p. 27 Yet in spite of Rubin's characteristically awkward grammar—she complains that she is "still plagued" by "spelling's stupidities" and remains unable "to transcend to communicable vibrations beyond" ↗ letter from Spring 1964; Paris; p. 40—one can nonetheless sense a tension between the loneliness of the spiritual seeker journeying into uncharted lands, and the ecstatic optimism of the collective utopianism she was leaving behind. In one moment, she promises Mekas that, "We are going to turn the world, us, on, a metamorphosis so complete," ↗ letter from Spring 1964; Paris; p. 61. In another, she confesses that in "[l]iving moments I roam outside, apart, one, but not in the trance of fixed patterns." ↗ letter from March 1964; Paris; p. 36

As with many other visionary artists of the period, the tone of Rubin's letters is a mix of utopianism, fanaticism, delusion, ambition, and naivete, all steeped in the drug-addled despair and euphoria of the era. In her rush to describe inner sensations and external phenomena, Rubin rhymes and reasons in equal part all over the page. Careening from absurdist poetry to divine invocation, she can suddenly veer from the wild course of her words to arrive at more canny inquisitions about finances, addresses, agents, and publishers. At her most inspired, she effuses in a rapid flow stream of consciousness that echoes the mystical writing of Carlos Castaneda, as well as other experimental filmmakers of the era. Undoubtedly high on "chemicals," she writes: "Cosmic energy held, forming man, master, disperses at final orgiastic climax eternal. High ecstatic fluid beyond matter do we journey." ↗ letter from Spring 1964; Paris; p. 61

Stuffy grammarian that I am, I am both bewitched and bewildered by Rubin's sustained moments of unruly prose, which she seems to have scribbled across the page in various states of intoxication before signing off with her customary "love love love." Sure, it's crazy talk, but wouldn't the above quotation also serve as an apt description of *Christmas on Earth*? Perhaps if I had read the script for that film—I don't think there was one—I probably would not have believed that it was possible to make it either. With enough money and time, what other miracles could Barbara Rubin have accomplished?

By the mid-1960s, Rubin had begun to channel her spirituality into alternative forms of community and religion. With her friend Rosebud, she moved into Allen Ginsberg's apartment on the Lower East Side; Rubin accompanied Rosebud to a free love commune called Kerista, and together, they explored Eastern philosophy. At Rubin's behest, Ginsberg purchased a farm in upstate New York to house the newly formed Committee on Poetry. Rubin moved there in 1968 in the somewhat misguided hope of marrying the queer poet, bearing his children, and living out some vision of Old World bohemian bliss. "More kibbutz than commune," the farm was designed as a quiet retreat from the city.[15] Judging from its roster of guests, the farm at Cherry Valley was also one of the many sites where the poet outlaws of the Beat Generation interacted with, argued with, and lived with the younger generation of the Underground film, art, and music scenes. Regular inhabitants during this period included Allen and Barbara, Peter Orlovsky and his mostly catatonic brother Julius, filmmaker Gordon Ball and his then-girlfriend Candy O'Brien, and friends Stephen Bornstein and Susan Brustman. Visitors were numerous, and included many of Ginsberg's Beat friends, including Gregory Corso and Herbert Huncke as well as the journalist and brief Velvet Underground manager Al Aronowitz and his children. Although Ginsberg imagined

15
Allen Ginsberg, Letter to Gary Snyder, July 8, 1968. *The Letters of Allen Ginsberg*, ed. Bill Morgan (Philadelphia: Da Capo Press, 2008), p. 343.

1968

Barbara Rubin
R.D.2 Cherry Valley
13320
New York

607-264 7244

Remember
Thanksgiving
Dinner Nov 28.
in Cherry Valley
love Barbara

FILM CULTURE

G.P.O. BOX
NO: 1499
NEWYORK
N.Y., U.S.A.

Love Jonas dear love

love Want to love

Love Get something lo

love love to eat love

love fuck

love MOMENT –

love ALL LY

I hope

the farm commune as a drug-free zone, few observed this policy. Even Ginsberg's lover Peter Orlovsky arrived with his stash in tow.

During her time at the farm, Rubin began regularly visiting a nearby Hasidic community in Sharon Springs, NY. Tensions soared as she began proselytizing the tenets of her new faith to the other bohemian inhabitants of the commune. Disappointed by Allen's romantic rejection of her—in spite of the fact that they had sex at least once, he had no intention of having children with her—and outraged by her friends' unwillingness to share her increasingly fanatical observance, Rubin left the farm. When she returned to New York City, where she lived again with Rosebud, she became involved with a religious community in Brooklyn and started demanding that her roommate light Shabbat candles even in her absence.[16] While she would sometimes reconsider her attempts to convert others to her own obsessions—on one occasion, she confesses, "I was wrong Jonas because I was forcing this on everyone, you can't do it that way, it must come from within" ↗ letter from January 27, 1964; Munich; p. 34—she didn't always operate with such mindfulness.

Like many of her admirers, I've always been troubled by Rubin's attraction to one of the most Orthodox, doctrinaire forms of Hasidism, in which women are not treated as equals and conversation with "outsiders" is of no interest. For a woman who dared to make sexually explicit, formally outrageous films at a time when even the Underground cinema scene was male dominated, it was, at the very least, an unusual choice. And yet there is already in her letters of the mid-1960s, a spiritual yearning for something more. As she writes in one letter to Jonas: "What I feel goes beyond movies." ↗ letter from January 27, 1964; Munich; p. 34 In another, she explains: "I don't know if I'm making myself understood, Jonas, and it's not that I won't always help you and the film-makers but I'm looking deep into doing something else. The dreams I've had I thought they were a part of the Co-op and I discovered it's nothing to do with it as a "co-op" but with me and a way of seeing infinite." ↗ letter from January 27, 1964; Munich; p. 34 Perhaps Rubin does not yet know what she is looking for, but it is clear that she is already searching.

Although its exclusionary practice seemed as far as possible from Rubin's utopian ideal of bringing people of all backgrounds together, the Satmar Hasidic community that she first joined certainly offered the kind of immersion that she had always sought, first in the Film-Makers' Co-op, and then at the farm. In the surviving fragment of a letter to Mekas, Rubin tried to explain the difficulty of finding a form of community commensurate with her longing: "That's why I'm going to try and do it another way, not in an organization and I'm not sure yet how, for I've so much to learn but I will struggle, no matter how often I go off on a tangent... to see me and everyone, freer, loving. I can't accept those things which hurt men and I know that we can live loving together, seeing, feeling, touching to the highest spheres. Please don't feel I'm leaving you," she promises before the letter breaks off, "for I'm closer to you than ever, I'm stronger now and I'm ready to plunge deep into..." ↗ letter from January 27, 1964; Munich; p. 34

Into what depths was Rubin ready to plunge? Unfortunately, we will never know, for the remaining part of the letter has been lost to oblivion. What we do know is that in early 1972, over three years after leaving the Ginsberg farm, Rubin invited everyone to a Hasidic celebration to honor her wedding to Mordecai Levy, whom she had met at Rabbi Freifeld's famed *ba'al t'shuvah* congregation in Far Rockaway. As was customary, the guests were segregated by gender; Hasidic girls were rumored to be seen standing on chairs to get a glimpse of Bob Dylan and Allen Ginsberg dancing on the other side of the wall. Although Rubin's marriage to Levy didn't last very long, her entrenchment in Jewish fundamentalism did. Her second marriage to French Orthodox painter Yitzchak (Isaac) Besançon inspired her move to Europe and provided the children she had long desired. Little is known amongst her secular

16
Rosebud, "Barbara Rubin," published in the catalogue of the show on Barbara Rubin at Boo Hooray Gallery in New York, December 18, 2012–January 15, 2013.

fans about Rubin's life once she severed nearly all of her ties to the New York art world, changed her name to "Bracha," and moved to a religious community in France in the early 1970s. Renouncing her previous work, she wrote to Leslie Trumbull, then director of the Film-Makers' Cooperative, and ordered the destruction of their print of *Christmas on Earth*, a request that was thankfully not fulfilled. In an interview with Jonas Mekas published in *The Village Voice* in 1972, Rubin refers to her former self as a "spoiled American child" and talks about her own journey to renounce American affluence and find truth away from drugs and violence. In spite of acknowledging that there were a lot of male chauvinist pigs who practiced the Torah, Rubin rejected the chaos of her previous life, and embraced the order of religious ritual. In the interview, she speaks reverently about the quiet holiness of housekeeping, and also touches upon her (unfulfilled) plans to make a film about the concentration camps with radical French-German student leader Daniel Cohn-Bendit.

Over the next decade, Rubin gave birth to five children and, as far as anyone knows, never returned to the ethos of drug experimentation and free love that she previously epitomized. In 1980, she died of a post-natal infection, approximately two weeks after giving birth to her fifth child; she was 35 years old. As was customary within her religious community, her husband married one of her closest friends within weeks of her death.

Although she appeared in a handful of films by other experimental filmmakers, Barbara Rubin seems to have only completed two other short films in her lifetime. The first, *Allen for Allen* (1965), was a portrait of Allen Ginsberg. The second, *Emunah* (1972), which she co-directed after her conversion to Hasidism with her friend and Living Theatre denizen, Pamela Badyk Mayo, hints at both the continuities and ruptures that must have characterized her life during her last decade. The film, whose title is the Hebrew word for the "faith" that every Jewish soul is said to inherit, is a mishmosh of diverse footage, all related to her interest in spirituality. Juxtaposing footage of Allen Ginsberg presumably shot for *Allen for Allen* with Hebrew text and photographs of concentration camps, *Emunah* attempts to reconcile Rubin's two seemingly incompatible worlds—the New York Underground art scene and Judaism. Yet rather than illuminating the enigmatic link between the corporeal materialism of *Christmas on Earth* and religious fundamentalism, *Emunah* projects the filmmaker's sentimental longing on to the figure of Ginsberg, who is seen lingering at the gravestone of William Blake. The film is nevertheless a montage of Rubin's 1960s, a poignant collision of past and present. Looking back, it is hard not to see *Emunah* as Rubin's way of saying Kaddish for the life she had left behind.

Twenty years after first seeing *Christmas on Earth* and beginning my investigations into its quixotic author, I am still haunted by the tragedy of Rubin's early death. She packed more in the seventeen years between the making of her first film and her death than most of us can accomplish in a lifetime. Yet while I used to bemoan her lost potential as an artist—*Christmas on Earth* is one of the most precocious debuts in film history—these days, I find her children's early loss of their mother even more devastating. Rubin, by her own admission, was "always falling deep into the abyss recklessly," ↗ letter from January 20, 1964; p. 27 whether she was tumbling headlong into art, spirituality, or, one can only imagine, motherhood. I would wager that her relationship to her young children was characterized by as much "infinite energy" ↗ letter from Spring 1964; Paris; p. 61 and ardent devotion as she had shown to her other creations. Ultimately, I'd rather they grew up with their mother than we had another masterpiece.

Judging from her letters, even Barbara Rubin could not fully comprehend the heights to which she soared. "I'm high up towards bounties flames, rolling on the wind waves," she writes ecstatically, before descending to a lower key: "Let's go on but awakened for I cannot understand." ↗ letter from Spring 1964; Paris; p. 40

What remains of her flights are these fragments, leaking light all over the page.

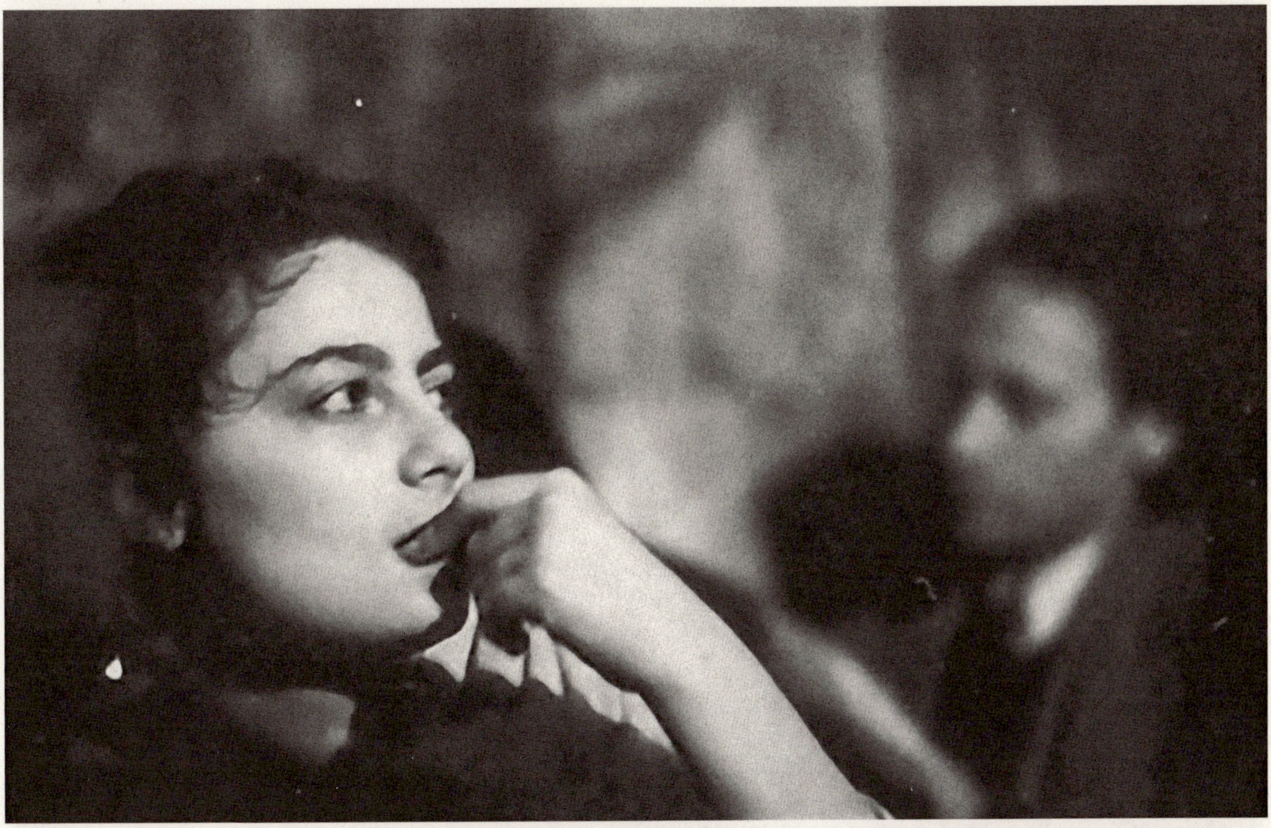

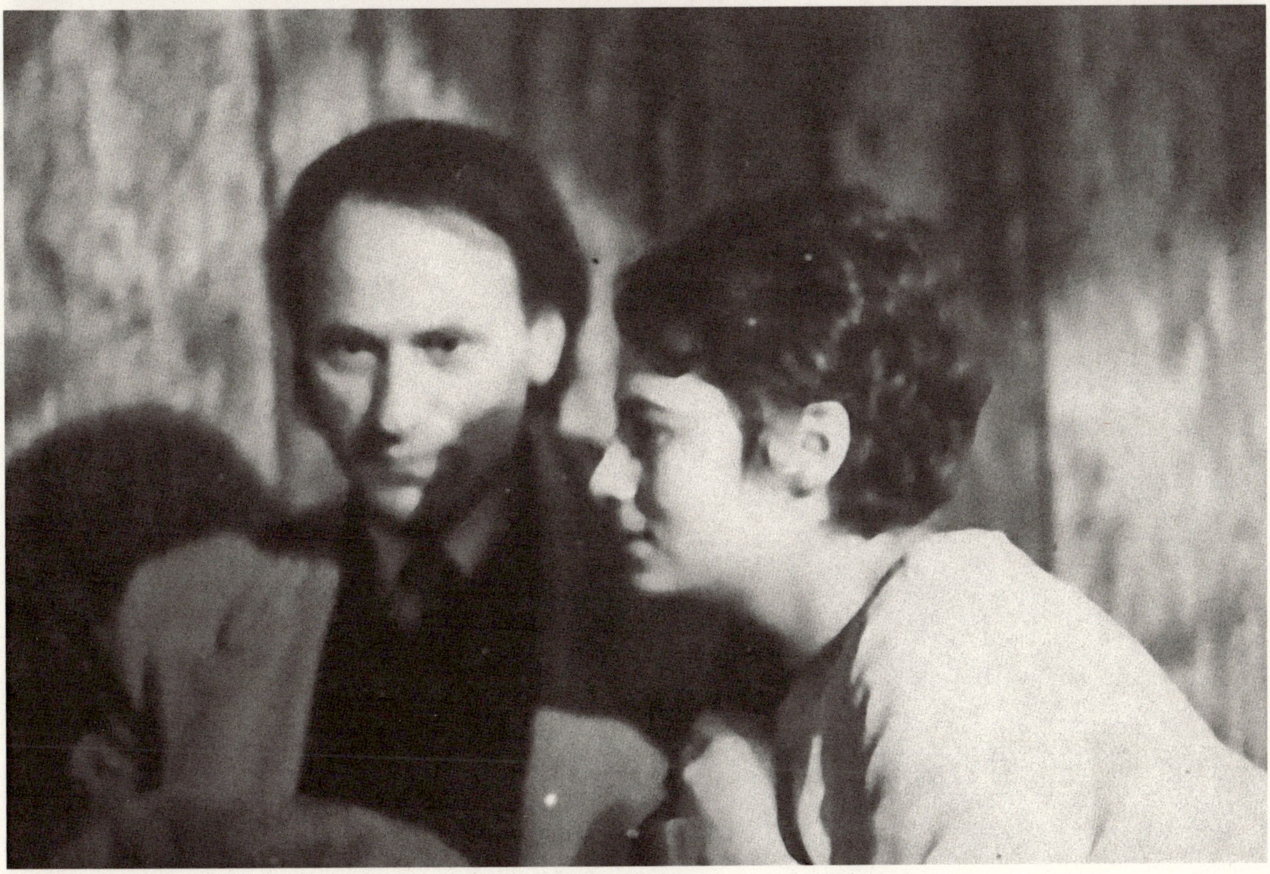

Top and bottom images: Barbara Rubin and Jonas Mekas at the Café Bizarre, New York, December 1965. Photos: Adam Ritchie

Barbara Rubin

Dear Leslie,

I just recieved a letter from Jacques Ledoux. I had whrote him, to turn Christmas, as you suggested. He writes me he will be in town this May 15 to the 25th & wants to discuss this with me, naturally. Could you, or Jonas give him my phone number here 518-284-8361 & if, as it can be, connections fail could you, in the deplomacy you are known for, attempt an explanation. As always my thanks to you dear Leslie and hope well the Spring's with you

love

Bashe Bruche

Christian Hiller and Marc Siegel, for the curatorial team of *Edit Film Culture!*

Film Culture 80: The Legend of Barbara Rubin is published in the context of *Edit Film Culture!*, a project dedicated to *Film Culture* magazine and the role of writing about film in the development of film cultures in various localities today. *Edit Film Culture!*, the festival, took place in July 2018 at silent green in Berlin and featured discussions, presentations, and concerts by a number of international guests, along with a two-week exhibition at Savvy Contemporary and a twenty-program screening series at the Arsenal Institute for Film and Video Art.

A key focus of the larger *Edit Film Culture!* project is to draw attention to the production and design history of the unique magazine founded in New York City in 1954 by the Lithuanian immigrant brothers Adolfas and Jonas Mekas. We are specifically interested in the evolving concept of film culture that was constructed across four decades of the magazine's main period of publication. Between 1955–1996, with very little means, editor-in-chief Jonas Mekas brought out 79 issues of the magazine, a unique periodical that served as a platform for exchanges between filmmakers and audiences, theory and practice, cinema and art. Attending to the European avant-garde, Soviet revolutionary cinema, auteurs in Europe, and Hollywood and personal filmmakers in the United States and beyond, *Film Culture* featured an eclectic mix of interviews, historical articles, manifestos, film analyses, artists' writings, poetry, letters, photographic essays, and documentary reports on the establishment of independent structures for film production, distribution, and exhibition. Contributions to the magazine came from an astounding array of actors, artists, filmmakers, and writers, including Rudolf Arnheim, Peter Bogdanovich, Louise Brooks, Luis Buñuel, John Cage, Lotte Eisner, Hollis Frampton, Jean-Luc Godard, Ken Jacobs, Siegfried Kracauer, Gregory Markopoulos, Taylor Mead,

Anaïs Nin, Yoko Ono, Pier Paolo Pasolini, Leni Riefenstahl, Hans Richter, Andrew Sarris, P. Adams Sitney, Michael Snow, Parker Tyler, and Orson Welles. Beginning with issue number 11 in 1957, Fluxus artist and fellow Lithuanian immigrant, George Maciunas became associated with the magazine, contributing the layout for numerous issues—most spectacularly, the striking special issues dedicated to the expanded arts (No. 44, 1966), the Soviet filmmaker Lew Kuleshov (No. 44, 1966), and the films and Factory of Andy Warhol (No. 45, 1967). Over the course of the 1960s and 1970s, the magazine became firmly associated with the New American Cinema and the broader North American avant-garde film scene. This was partially due to the focus of many of its issues on such filmmakers as Stan Brakhage, Maya Deren, Ron Rice, Paul Sharits, Jack Smith, and Stan VanDerbeek. Moving beyond the written word, however, the magazine also became the energizing center of a constellation of activities in the areas of independent film production, distribution, exhibition, and archival presentation. Without *Film Culture's* advocacy for non-commercial, personal, and artisanal filmmaking, it is difficult to imagine the emergence of such crucial institutions of the avant-garde like the Film-Makers' Cooperative and Anthology Film Archives.

At the very start of our planning for *Edit Film Culture!*, we sought a partnership with Spector Books, the key publisher of numerous works by Jonas Mekas. We toyed around with the idea of jumpstarting the magazine, resuscitating it in Germany over twenty years after its last issue in New York City. What would *Film Culture* look like today? How could we address the complexity of non-commercial and personal filmmaking in a contemporary global context? Should we attempt instead to assemble something like a *Film Culture* reader, with unpublished texts and documentary materials from the history of the magazine's publication? We pondered these questions while we sorted through thousands of documents during a research trip to Jonas Meka's Brooklyn loft in November 2017. When we posed the question of a *Film Culture 80* to Jonas, his answer was clear and immediate: a special issue on Barbara Rubin. He went to a bookshelf and retrieved a ring binder that was filled with his carefully preserved letters from Rubin from her travels in the 1960s and 1970s. Jonas had long planned an issue of *Film Culture* dedicated to the radical film- and scene-maker who entered the New York Underground at the age of 17 in 1963 and died in France at the age of thirty-five in 1980. We were thrilled by the idea and committed ourselves to doing everything within our means to make it a reality. Since *Edit Film Culture!* is guided by a curiosity for those aspects of the magazine's history that have not received adequate attention, such as the contributions of German artist Hans Richter—the premiere of Richter's film *8x8: A Chess Sonata in 8 Movements* in 1957 in New York City, for instance, was a benefit for *Film Culture*—or the essays on silent film by actress Louise Brooks, we were very excited about publishing a volume on the little-known figure of Barbara Rubin.

For those familiar with the bustling New York City avant-garde film and arts scenes of the 1960s, Rubin was not a completely new name. In fact, she surfaced frequently and in a variety of contexts, from the scandals around screenings of Jack Smith's film *Flaming Creatures* to a marathon poetry reading with Allen Ginsberg, Lawrence Ferlinghetti, and others at the Royal Albert Hall in London, from a photograph on the back cover of Bob Dylan's 1965 *Bringing it All Back Home* album to performances of Andy Warhol's Exploding Plastic Inevitable with The Velvet Underground. There was also, of course, her own film, the notorious sexually explicit fantasy *Christmas on Earth*, made in 1963 while she was still a teenager. This double screen epic of two twenty-nine minute 16mm black-and-white films, one projected inside the other, tinted with color filters randomly manipulated by the projectionist and scored to the chance rock tunes of a live radio played during the screening, radically expanded cinema years before the practice took hold of the broader film and arts scene.

Yes, Rubin was certainly a familiar name, but one about which there was nevertheless very little information. Only recently—and thanks to the scholarship of Daniel Belasco and Ara Osterweil—have we come to understand that Rubin did not simply pop up in each of these exciting scenes. She was rather the reason such scenes came together in the first place. It was Rubin who brought Dylan and Donovan to Warhol's Factory; connected Dylan and Ginsberg; organized the historic poetry reading in London that attracted 7,000 spectators; and introduced Warhol to The Velvet Underground. As Osterweil explains in the afterword to this volume, "[c]ommitted to the spirit of camaraderie and collaboration, Rubin believed that artists were the saints and heroes of her day, and labored, like a modern-day matchmaker, to bring them together."

Rubin's commitment is evident in the letters she wrote to Jonas Mekas, many of which document her travels in Europe in the early and mid-1960s. We read about her efforts to arrange screenings of avant-garde films; fight against censorship; meet with key figures in the arts across Europe; foster the founding of film institutions; and secure financing and support for her fantastic film project *Christmas on Earth Continued*. Throughout this passionate correspondence, she gives expression to her belief in the essential role of artistic creation in improving the world around her. The letters also provide some evidence of the transformation of this secular belief in the power of the arts into a religious belief in Hasidic Judaism that came to mark the last decade or so of her life. Rubin eventually turned her back on the lively Underground arts scenes she helped forge and plunged with characteristic energy and commitment into a new life as an Orthodox Jewish woman, a wife, and a mother.

Coincident with our work on this publication, we became aware of Chuck Smith's important documentary, *Barbara Rubin and the Exploding NY Underground* (2018). Chuck also planned a publication with many of the materials he collected through years of research for his film. Jonas suggested we bring everything together in one special issue of *Film Culture*—which is exactly what we did. We're extremely happy about the collaboration with Chuck on this joint project. With his knowledge about Rubin's life and work, he was able to bring order to and provide historical contextualization for the "chaotic pile" of letters that Jonas mentions in his preface.

With its focus on a key figure in the avant-garde film scene in New York City in the 1960s and its mix of letters, interviews, photographs, essays, and film scripts, *Film Culture 80*: *The Legend of Barbara Rubin* retains the subject matter and multi-faceted approach that characterized the magazine during the four decades of its initial period of publication. By zeroing in on a fascinating, young female artist in a scene dominated by men, a woman whose perspectives and experiences have yet to be documented thoroughly, this new issue of *Film Culture* also exemplifies the goals of the *Edit Film Culture!* project.

I can feel the time soon
when man
confronted with love
through the History
passed in song
words
thoughts
will be confounded
incomprehensibly
unable to experience
then soon
conceive
the idea
let alone the soul
of LOVE

and memory pass
will slide
and you and I
will be blurred
in the sense of conscious
time

will be the only evidence
when
held
suddenly
to take back time
spirals a vacumn
of what
once existed
as the soul of love

and you and I
too
will pass slowly
into SUCK

But What Will Come
MY SOUL
What Will Be Man
When Love
HIS SOUL FORCE
THAT CHANGED
ROCKED
MADE MAN
is nonexistent
even to comprehension

yes I
Who Slips Time
Felt The Tide
and I grasp
hold hard
stand time still
FOR IT SLOWLY
WILL LEAVE
MY AWARENESS TOO

LOVE JONAS
BARBARA

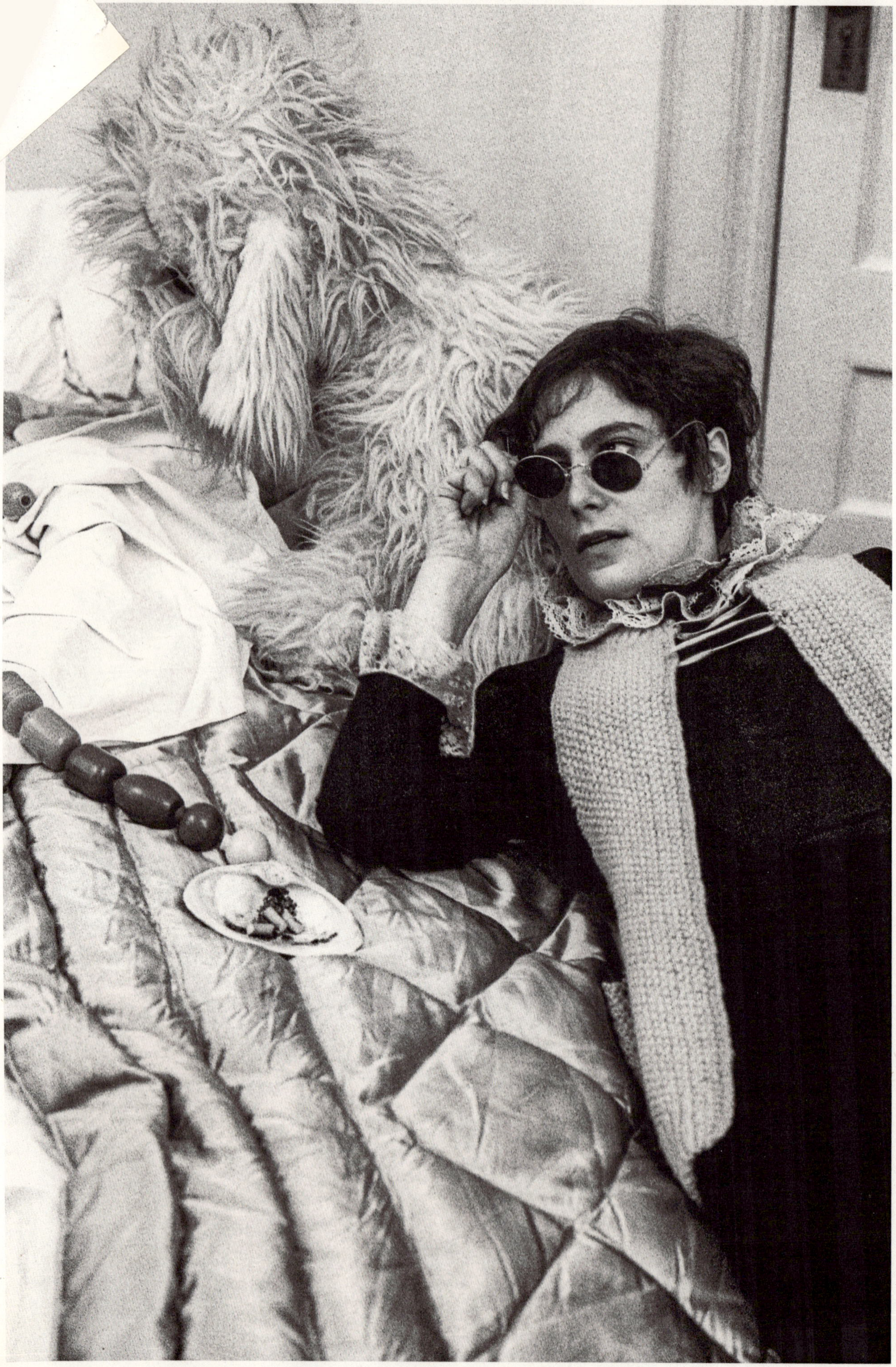

Barbara Rubin, 1966. Photo: Nat Finkelstein